HOOSIERS
Through and Through

Terry Hutchens

Blue River Press
Indianapolis

www.brpressbooks.com

Hoosiers Through and Through © 2014 Terry Hutchens
ISBN: 9781935628385
Library of Congress Control Number: 2014949108

Cover designed by Phil Velikan
Cover photo from iStock000003460553/eyerush
Packaged by Wish Publishing

Printed in the United States of America
10 9 8 7 6 5 4 3 2 1

Published by Blue River Press
Indianapolis, Indiana
(800) 296-0481
A Tom Doherty Company, Inc., Imprint

Distributed in the United States by
Cardinal Publishers Group
www.cardinalpub.com

This book is dedicated to my two wonderful sons,
Bryan and Kevin.

They both make us proud every day, and unlike my wife,
Susan, and I, they have something in common with the title
of this book. Born and raised in Indiana, Bryan and Kevin
are both *Hoosiers Through and Through*.

Preface &
Acknowledgements

In the summer of 2012, while then writing for the *Indianapolis Star*, we came up with the idea of a summer blog series to try to increase our readership through the summer months. In past summers, my blog had dipped to something like 50,000 page views for the entire summer.

So in an effort to attract more page views in 2012, we came up with the idea of a daily blog that would count down the top 50 Indiana University basketball players of all time. More than 750,000 page views later, the series was a smashing success.

I always wanted to do something similar in book form but slightly different. I didn't want it in any way to copy what I had done in 2012. So I came up with the idea of looking at the top 50 IU basketball players of all time that hail from the state of Indiana. As I looked into it, I found there were 587 of them in history.

In Chapter 1 I explain how I decided on the order of the players. In this space I want to thank all of the people who made this book possible.

I want to begin with my colleague at AllHoosiers.com, Justin Albers, who interviewed four of the subjects of this book for me. Justin talked to Bobby 'Slick' Leonard, Ted Kitchel, Greg Graham and Quinn Buckner. Justin is a terrific young writer who I have known since he was in middle school and hopefully there will be a book in the future that we can co-author or something like that.

Bill Murphy was another one who helped out with a couple of interviews. Bill has written two books. One is *The Cardiac Kids: A Season to Remember*, published in 2007, which looks back at IU's 1967 Rose Bowl season. The other, published in

2013, was called *Branch*, which is the story of legendary IU coach Branch McCracken. If you're interested in IU basketball and one of the greatest coaches ever, this is a must read. I turned to Bill to help make Don Schlundt come alive to a generation that knows very little about him. Schlundt is the only member of my top 10 who is deceased so that made it more difficult to completely tell his story. Bill agreed to interview Marvin Christie and Jim Schooley, contemporaries of Schlundt, as well as Tom Van Arsdale. In addition, I was able to interview Bill, who is a historian of IU basketball himself and was able to provide some great insights.

The other interviews in the book were all conducted by me. With one of them, I was able to drive to Kokomo, Indiana one day and sit down with Jimmy Rayl and his wife Nancy. That was a treat. For another, I drove to Bloomington and visited Archie Dees, another old-time IU alumni who had stories to share as well. I also had phone interviews with (in alphabetical order) Steve Alford, Tom Bolyard, Danny Bridges, Calbert Cheaney, Chronic Hoosier, Dan Dakich, Clarence Doninger, Steve Downing, Brian Evans, Don Fischer, Fred Glass, Pat Graham, Bob Hammel, Joe Hillman, Jordan Hulls, Kit Klingelhoffer, Todd Leary, George McGinnis, Bill Murphy, Jake Query, Jim Schooley, Randy Wittman and Mike Woodson. My only regrets were that I was unable to reach Alan Henderson and Kent Benson, but fortunately I found plenty of people to talk about them.

What those interviews allowed me to do was to tell story after story about players in the top 10. I'm confident that some of these are stories you'll be reading for the first time. In each of the chapters featuring the top 10 I was able to use a minimum of nine voices per subject. Hopefully that gives a well rounded depiction of that player.

I also want to thank Jason Hiner for the *IU Basketball Encyclopedia* which I leaned on often for some of the seasonal information in this book. In 2013, I was lucky enough to be asked to write the second edition of that book and add the nine seasons that had followed since Jason originally wrote it in 2004. If you ever want the most complete and detailed account of Indiana basketball from the very first season, the *IU Basketball Encyclopedia* is a must have in your library.

I want to thank the IU Archives for giving me permission to use the photographs in this book. Brad Cook was extremely helpful in getting me the images we were able to use for this project.

I want to thank the IU athletics department for its support, specifically Scott Dolson and Laura McCrea for helping me locate some people. Mike Dickbernd helped me find a Cody Zeller photo at the last minute and assisted with a shot of Eric Gordon that was taken by IU athletics. I want to thank Jay Torrell of Scout.com and his staff for putting together the AllHoosiers.com ad that is at the end of this book. I also want to thank several others for their support in this project. There's a good chance I'm missing someone (which is my disclaimer) but that list would include Chris Smith, Kirk Jenkins, Steve Sears, Mark Ping, Kevin Hunt, Jeff Kellerman, Dave Murphy, Jay Roudebush, Kevin Mulholland, Tom Bertelotti, Dale Armbruster, Steve Demas, Chris Barnes, Al Purdom, Mark Vershaw, Dave Lubovich, Joe Chiapetta, Bob Boynton, Knute Lentz, Kevin Wyatt, Dave Frey, Matt Watson and Jeff Smith. I would also like to lift up the memory of Michael Peed, a huge IU fan who died way too young in the fall of 2013.

I want to thank everyone at Cardinal Publishing and especially publisher Tom Doherty for taking on my second IU basketball project. The first one, *Rising from the Ashes* that was published in 2012 was very successful. This is my fifth book and I've worked with Tom on each one.

I want to thank Jordan Hulls for agreeing to write the foreword. When I was thinking of people who were quintessential Hoosiers, Jordan was right there in a very select group of people. When he not only agreed to do it but was honored to be a part of the project, I couldn't have been happier.

I want to thank my Hilton Head proofreaders (my mother Dena Hutchens and my wife Susan) as well as my three AllHoosiers.com interns Ben Faunce, Stuart Jackson and Sam Rumpza for assisting with compiling the Roll Call chapter.

I want to thank my family. My wife Susan, my bride of 28 years, is always my biggest supporter. I feel the same way about my sons, Bryan (23) and Kevin (21). Thanks to all of you for enduring my divided attention when writing this book.

Finally I want to thank the 587 basketball players to date who have chosen to play high school basketball in the state of Indiana and then move on to play at IU. You were my inspiration for writing this book. I hope I was able to do it justice.

— Terry Hutchens

Table of Contents

Jordan Hulls (Photo by Mike Dickbernd/IU Athletics)

Foreword

As a young boy growing up in Bloomington, Indiana, I used to dream about one day playing big-time college basketball at a place like Indiana University.

In our family, basketball was in our blood. My grandpa, John Hulls, coached with Coach Knight at West Point and then came with him to help him at IU as the shooting coach. They had known each other a long time. My dad's mom, Connie Sawyer, grew up in Ohio around the game of basketball as well. So basketball for me was more of a foregone conclusion.

I started playing at a very young age, and honestly, there wasn't much choice. I was told that I always had a basketball in my hands while at my brothers' games when I was two years old, and I've been the same ever since. Growing up in Indiana kind of makes it easy for you to have a passion for basketball, but I also had a little help from my family considering almost everyone played the game. So, it was only natural for me to start young and instantly have a passion for it while dreaming to play basketball for a living one day.

My earliest memories of playing basketball were when I was about four or five years old and doing ballhandling cone drills with my mom in our driveway. She was a stay-at-home mom throughout all of our childhood, so she was always there for us, even for basketball drills. We would set up five or six of the orange cones up in zig-zag fashion and just get to work. At that age I would just do simple crossovers and work on both hands. I still do these drills to this day, with some tweaks of course, but I'll never forget those days out in the driveway with my mom during the day and then at night with my dad.

As I got older, I would imagine myself hitting buzzer beaters to win the game for my team, the Hoosiers or Phoenix Suns. I'm not quite sure why I was a Suns fan other than I had a Suns trashcan, and I wore Charles Barkley shoes, but I've always been a fan. Whether the buzzer beater was a clutch three pointer or a crazy lay-up, I always wanted to make the big shot and help my team win, even if it was just in my driveway.

Honestly, growing up I don't remember attending too many IU games in Assembly Hall. We would always go to my grandparents house to watch the games when I was younger because it was a way for us as a family to enjoy the Hoosiers together, as opposed to spending a lot of money for our big family to go to the game in Assembly Hall. If I did go to games, I would go with my friends most of the time, but again that wasn't like an every week type of thing. Despite the fact that I didn't attend many games in person, it didn't keep me from dreaming of one day playing at a big time school like IU.

Aside from watching IU games, there were two movies that I watched constantly that also helped me dream big and want to play at a school like IU, *Hoosiers* and *The Pistol: The Birth of a Legend*. *Hoosiers* is obviously one of my favorite movies because it's about Indiana basketball and how even when people doubt the underdog, they can still come out on top. *The Pistol* was about "Pistol" Pete Maravich and about his journey through his eighth grade year and how he overcame adversity and helped carry his team to be one of the best teams in the state and prove the doubters wrong. "Pistol" Pete Maravich was my favorite player growing up, and I used to watch all of his "Homework Basketball" tapes because I wanted to do all the drills that made him become one of the greatest players to ever play the game. These movies had me daydreaming all the time and helped me imagine what it would be like if I put in all the hard work and achieved all the goals I set out for myself, despite all the people who would doubt me.

I wasn't heavily recruited until late in my junior year of high school at Bloomington South and that all changed after I had a great weekend in Pittsburgh at an AAU tournament. From that point forward, my life changed because all I had ever dreamed about growing up was to be able to play at a big time college and become the best player I could be. So, when all this interest finally started following me, I knew all the hard work had paid off. I was a gym rat and knew I had to be in order to prove the doubters wrong and achieve my goals, and that's exactly what I was able to do.

As for IU, I wasn't really recruited much by the Hoosiers during my early high school years, and really only Coach Dan Dakich showed interest in me in his short stint as head coach, which was awesome. However, as much as I loved Bloomington, Coach Knight and the Hoosiers, I honestly didn't think I would be able to play there since there hadn't been much interest early on. Fortunately, all of that changed when Coach Crean and his staff got to IU. After that weekend in Pittsburgh, I was receiving interest from schools such as Purdue, Stanford, Wake Forest and Duke, to name a few, as well as IU. Some of my AAU teammates had already committed to some of these schools, which was pretty cool to know that maybe I had a chance to play with one of them in college: DJ Byrd went to Purdue, Mason Plumlee went to Duke and Bobby Capobianco had committed to IU. I had scheduled visits with these three schools for certain and had some others I was planning as well, but it didn't go quite according to plan.

Purdue had asked me to come up and take a visit of the campus and everything one week and apparently planned to offer me a scholarship while I was on my visit with them. Somehow, some way, Coach Crean heard about them wanting to offer me a scholarship, and he thought there's no way he was letting them be the first to offer this Bloomington kid a scholarship. I had already met Coach Crean and the staff but nothing had been said about an offer, and I was planning on going to Purdue for a visit anyway. That didn't stop Coach Crean.

I'm pretty sure it was the night before I was going to visit Purdue that I got a call from Coach Crean. Mind you it was 10 o'clock at night when I got the call, and I ran down to my parents saying, with a confused looked on my face, "Umm, Coach Crean just called and asked me to come to Assembly Hall to talk with him." My parents were just as confused but we were obviously going to check out what he wanted to talk about. So, my dad and I jumped in his truck and drove over to Assembly Hall. When we walked in there was a scene right out of a movie in front of us. As we walked in the arena, there was nothing but spotlights on the banners and dim lights on the court, just enough to make the spotlights really stand out. We gathered and talked down at center court on the state of Indiana logo, and we just admired the banners. We talked about the opportunities that I could have if I came to IU to play for him and be a part of something special: bringing back Indiana University Basketball. Right then and there Coach Crean offered me a scholarship to play basketball for my home-town school at IU. I was ecstatic. This was my first big time offer and not to mention for my hometown school, so it was appealing right away. Fortunately I had my dad there with me and he was able to talk me into taking it all in and not just commit based purely on emotion. Coach didn't expect me to commit right then and there I don't think, but he sure sold the possibility of me helping to bring back the rich IU basketball tradition, and the rest is history.

I still went on to visit Purdue and they were great with me. They helped me throughout all of high school even if they hadn't offered me a scholarship early on. They always told me what I needed to work on to become a Division 1/Big Ten player, and I was always thankful for that. They did offer me a place the day of my visit, which was a huge deal to me as well, but it was going to be awfully hard to get a kid from Bloomington to go to Purdue, despite their success at that time.

Two weeks had gone by after the night with Coach Crean, and I was ready to commit. This was especially hard because we were trying to set up a visit with Duke, but our schedules never matched up and I was going to have to wait a little longer to go on the visit. I sat down and thought long and hard those two weeks, weighing the pros and cons of commit-ting to IU then or just waiting and making more visits to see what else was out there. Duke had been another team that I loved watching because I was a fan of Coach K and how he ran his teams. He also played for Coach Knight and my grandpa at West Point, so I was always connected that way and thought it was cool.

I was ready to commit to IU. My neighbors, friends, and family were all very supportive but a little biased at times

(HaHa!). My neighbors actually wrote on my car with paint saying "Commit to IU! Go to IU!", which was pretty neat to see that even locals wanted to be able to see me play college ball in Bloomington. As hard as it was to not even go on a visit to Duke or any other schools, I still felt like IU was the place for me, and I have never regretted it since. The thought that I could be a part of something special, help bring back Indiana basketball, be in my hometown and be able to be a key contributor early on were all huge things for me. The first two years were very hard but the last two made it all worth it. I hope that I left a legacy at IU and that people will always remember me for the guy who was a great teammate, role model and did whatever was going to help IU win.

After I committed and later graduated from high school, it was time to begin the next chapter in my life: Playing basketball for the Hoosiers. I think the first time I realized that I wasn't in high school anymore was at the first weight/conditioning workout and then a basketball individual workout because it's just a completely different level of work. I loved to push myself but it still took some getting used to!

I can still remember the first time I put on an IU basketball uniform. It was at my first Hoosier Hysteria when it really hit me that I was playing for Indiana University. At that point, there was no other feeling like it. I had never been in front of that many people before and to actually be a part of the Hysteria instead of just watching from the crowd was a surreal experience. And you feel it well before your name even gets called out onto the floor. As you get to the gym and go to the locker room with warm-ups laid out on your chair, it sinks in that you're a part of something bigger than yourself. The first time your name gets called and you run out onto the floor, throw a shirt into the crowd... it's a feeling that you never forget. I would always try to explain to the freshmen what it was like but ended up telling them that it's something you just have to go through to really understand.

I had a great run in my four years playing at Indiana. I met some great people, made lifetime friends and had the chance every night to play in front of the best fans in college basketball. How could you ask for too much more? Sometimes people ask me what my favorite memory was playing at IU. Several things stand out. Of course beating Kentucky on Christian's buzzer beater is right there. Another one would be beating North Carolina State at their place for our first big road win while playing for IU. As far as Big Ten games, when we beat Michigan State at their place for first time in 20 years that was a big one as well. They were all great memories for me. However, the most lasting memory will be winning a Big Ten Championship. We had just lost to Ohio State on Senior Night at home with a chance to clinch the Big Ten Championship outright, so we had to go play Michigan at their place with it all on the line. If we lost, then we had to share the Big Ten title but if we won, we'd have it all to ourselves. Winning on the road for the Big Ten Championship was a bittersweet moment because we would have loved to have won it at home with our fans behind us, but we wanted to make things interesting I guess.

It kind of was a cool ending to what we had started. We had been pretty bad the first two years. The third year we started bringing it back, and the fourth year we accomplished one of our main goals in winning a Big Ten title. It was fitting that we had to fight and claw our way to win on the road in dramatic fashion since it's all we had known the previous three years. Being down five with 55 seconds to play, there was a slim chance that we could win, but we all had faith and kept our cool. We were able to execute exactly the way we wanted and things fell into place for us. It was a moment that I'll never forget. Right after Trey Burke missed the layup and it got tipped out, I remember getting the ball with maybe a fourth of a second, or maybe the clock had already gone off. I just threw the ball to the other end of the court and was so overjoyed that I didn't know what else to do. All our hard work had paid off, and we will forever be etched in IU History because of it.

When Terry Hutchens approached me to write the foreword for his book, *Hoosiers Through and Through*, I was so honored because Indiana basketball is all I've ever known. I care deeply about the program and am humbled by all of the opportunities that IU gave me, even when others wouldn't. I love my hometown, my university and will forever bleed the Cream and Crimson as I will always be a *Hoosier Through and Through*.

Terry asked me a simple question to help me think about what I should write. It was: What does it mean to be a Hoosier? Here is the best way I know how to answer that question.

A Hoosier is someone who...

- Puts his teammates before himself.

- Holds his teammates and himself accountable for doing things the right way, no matter what.

- Understands that you're a role model for some kid out there and that you never know who's watching you, on or off the court.

- Understands to treat people with respect and to always take time out to sign an autograph or take a picture because it's the right thing to do and you should be humbled that people know who you are.

- Understands the importance of getting a good education because you can't play basketball forever.

- Understands it's an honor to run out onto Assembly Hall with those Candy Striped Pants and that it should never be taken for granted.

- Understands why there isn't a name on the back of the jersey and the rich traditions at IU.

- Understands that it takes team work, hard work, sacrifice, and dedication to get to where you want to be; individually and as a team.

- Understands that WINNING MATTERS.

I will always be thankful that I was born a Hoosier and later was able to play basketball for the Indiana Hoosiers. It doesn't get any better than that.

— Jordan Hulls

1

Introduction

In the summer of 2012, I did a daily blog series for my former employer where I counted down the top 50 players in Indiana University basketball history.

For a span of about 53 days, I revealed one player every day. We even had a contest for people to guess the top 10 in order, and we had more than 2,000 people enter it.

In terms of traffic, that blog series attracted more than 750,000 page views in that two-month span. To say it was wildly popular would be an understatement.

One former IU All-American, Brian Evans, told me in September of that year that every day when the next player would be revealed he would get on a conference call of sorts with several former IU players, and they would talk about that day's selection and if they thought that was accurate or perhaps the player should have been ranked either higher or lower.

He said they did that for the most part, but the consensus of the players was that I had it pretty close to correct. There were going to be a lot of subjective claims on any kind of a list like that but for the most part, they thought my list was a pretty good one.

And if the people I was writing about in the countdown thought the list was pretty accurate then that was good enough for me.

Now of course, there were a few players who were left off the top 50 that many people believed should have been included. I would say there were probably up to 10 names that you could have made a strong argument for in terms of inclusion.

In at least one case, the player that was not included has pretty much stopped talking to me. I won't name any names. There's no point in that. But I do hope that over time we can put this perceived slight behind us.

There were other players, one in particular, that actually started calling me as that series was revealed day by day to lobby for where they thought they should rank on my list.

Fast forward to the 2014 season, and I always wanted to do a variation of that project in book form. But I wanted it to be a little more indepth than what I wrote in the blog series and try to flush out some stories and memories about the players, especially the top 10 players on the list.

I didn't want the book to be in any way confused with what I did for my previous employer because I didn't want there to be any claims that I had used material that technically belonged to them. And so I changed the format from the top 50 IU players of all time to the top 50 Indiana University basketball players of all time who hailed from the state of Indiana.

These guys would truly be Hoosiers Through and Through.

Another thing I promised myself was that I wouldn't go back and take any copy from any of those blogs from 2012. Everything I wrote for this book was new material. We interviewed more than 30 former Indiana basketball players and other experts in putting this book together.

The first thing that surprised me when I started getting into this project was the number of players that had actually played at IU from the state of Indiana. I thought 587 was a staggering number. That just seemed like a lot.

The great thing about the number was that it gave me a good enough pool of players to choose from.

So how did I go about narrowing down the list and selecting both the top 50 and eventually the very best players, in my opinion, from the state of Indiana.

First of all, let me say that the final list is my list. I solicited input from a great number of people I believe to be very close to the Indiana program. I asked several people to give me a list and then I put them all on a spread sheet and from that I put together my own list.

I received lists from 10 people. A few people I asked said they could help but then for one reason or another I never received the list back. But that's OK, I feel like getting 10 opinions from people I trust was a good representation.

There were a lot of varied opinions. Of my top 10 players of all time for example, there were more than 20 players that different people had that were nominated in a top 10 slot at least once.

The top 10 I settled on though were guys that were named consistently on every list. The player I chose as number 1 (who you will read about later) was picked as the top player overall on five of the 10 lists and in the top three of four others. One person said that since he was too far before his time he couldn't rank him higher than seventh.

When I approached my panel and asked for their input, this is what I told them I was looking for.

I had a very specific criteria in mind when I looked to rank the best players of all time. In fact, I came up with 70 names that I passed on to the panel in no particular order as players that fit the criteria. At the same time, I made it clear that just because a player wasn't on that list of 70 didn't mean they couldn't add other Indiana players that they believed to be worthy.

Here is the criteria I used and asked the panel to take into account when ranking the best players of all time that hailed from the state of Indiana.

The first criteria was individual accomplishments. I said that a player had to qualify in at least one of the following categories but that the more places they showed up obviously would give strong consideration to them being ranked higher.

- An Indiana Mr. Basketball
- An All-American at IU
- Scored at least 750 points in his career
- Big Ten MVP
- Played in the NBA
- Inducted into the IU Athletics Hall of Fame

- Appears on a top 10 career list in either scoring, rebounds, assists or blocked shots.

- Led IU in scoring in at least one season.

The next criteria had to do with the players' playing career. This has always been the most difficult intangible when putting these lists together. How do you compare a player that played just one season at IU with the four-year players that claimed numerous accolades? I tried to spell out my thoughts there as best as I could.

The best way I could narrow this category down was to say that the player had to have completed his college eligibility at Indiana. So for example whether a player played one season (such as George McGinnis or Eric Gordon) or two seasons (in the case of someone like Cody Zeller) it doesn't matter because they concluded their career at IU. But a player like Luke Recker or Delray Brooks, for example, would not be eligible.

With those being considered for the top 10, I added another criteria. I said the player needed to have played on at least one good team. It didn't have to be a national championship team but a good team.

Finally, I said that the player had to have grown up in the state of Indiana. He didn't have to be born there, but on the IU roster, his hometown had to be listed somewhere in the state of Indiana. Alan Henderson is a good example of this. He was actually born in Morgantown, West Virginia, but he grew up in Indiana from the time he was a young boy. No one is going to think that Henderson was not a Hoosier Through and Through.

My final instructions were to really focus on the top 25 but to feel free to give me a complete top 50 if possible. A few guys just listed a whole bunch of players that they believed should be considered for the number 26 spot and beyond.

And to be honest, after I took all of these lists and I started trying to determine whether players belonged in the top 50 or not, I was reminded again of what had happened with my 2012 blog list when people really wanted to argue if so and so should really be No. 47 and not No. 39. There was a lot of that.

And so I decided that in order to take that piece out of the puzzle with the players ranked No. 26 to 50 I would just list them in alphabetical order along with their accomplishments. I'll leave those names for you to decide where in the top 26-50 you think they belong.

The following people submitted lists that I included in my overall selection process.

- Don Fischer, Radio Voice of the Hoosiers for more than 40 years.

- Kit Klingelhoffer, Long time Sports Information Director at IU and later an Associate Athletic Director.

- Jeremy Gray, Associate Athletic Director at IU.

- Scott Dolson, Deputy Athletic Director at IU, and former IU basketball manager from 1984-87.

- Brian Evans, Indiana basketball All-American.

- Bill Murphy, IU basketball historian and author of the books *Branch* and *The Cardiac Kids*.

- Jake Query, Indianapolis radio sports talk show host on WNDE 1260-AM.

- Danny Bridges, IU fan and major George McGinnis supporter.

- Chronic Hoosier (I promised not to use his real name), Big IU fan.

- Mike Pegram, Publisher of Peegs.com.

After I received all of the lists, I put together my own selections and began the interview process.

My cohort at AllHoosiers.com, Justin Albers, assisted in several interviews as did Bill Murphy. Bill was able to help with some of the old-time guys, which was a huge help especially when it came to learning about Don Schlundt, the only player in my top that is deceased.

On the following pages you'll find what I consider to be the best Indiana University basketball players of all-time who hail from the state of Indiana.

I'm reminded of a line I used to use back when I worked at the *Indianapolis Star*. When I would meet someone and we would talk about IU basketball or debate a topic, sometimes at the end of that conversation they would say, "What's your name again?"

I would say, well, if you agree with me my name is Terry Hutchens. If you don't, my name is Bob Kravitz.

Hopefully after reading these pages, you'll think of me by my real name.

2

What it Means to Be a Hoosier

The idea in writing this book was to celebrate Indiana basketball players. Not just Indiana University basketball players but IU players that had hailed from the state of Indiana. As I dug a little deeper in my initial research, I found that there were 587 players that were from the state of Indiana that had gone on to play basketball at IU.

These players were truly Hoosiers Through and Through.

As I spoke to dozens of former Indiana basketball players who had grown up in the Hoosier State while researching this project, I heard over and over the pride that so many of them felt to be able to take the step being an Indiana prep player to be a true Indiana Hoosier. I thought Jordan Hulls, in the foreword for this book, did a tremendous job articulating what it meant to him to be a Hoosier. If somehow you skimmed over that, go back and read it. To hear those words from a young man who I've always looked at in terms of being the quintessential Hoosier just seemed to really hit the mark.

So let's start at the beginning. What is a Hoosier? There are seven or eight variations that are out there that attempt to provide an explanation for what has been an age-old question.

If you go to the Indiana Historical Society website there's a story with several of the possibilities. One of them talks about a woman named Sarah Harvey, identified as a Quaker from Richmond, who explained in an 1835 letter to her relatives that "old settlers in Indiana are called 'Hooshers' and the cabins they live in are 'Hoosher nests.'"

In 1848, also according to the Indiana Historical Society website, Bartlett's Dictionary of Americanisms defined "Hoosier" as 'A nickname gave at the west, to natives of Indiana."

The same source also talks about some of the theories and stories about the origin of the word "Hoosier" that are 'known to be false.'

Included in that list is the following: 'Hoosier's Men was a term used for Indiana employees of a canal contractor named Hoosier.'

Myself, I found that note to be disappointing because that was always the one that clearly made the most sense to me when I moved to Indiana from Southern California in 1986. The story as I had heard it was that there was a landowner in Ohio near the Indiana/Ohio border named Samuel Hoosier. He needed a lot of workers in his fields and found that there were a group of men across the border in Indiana that were particularly hard workers. He would hire them every season and over time they became known as 'Hoosier's Men' or eventually simply, 'Hoosiers.'

When I interviewed Indiana athletic director Fred Glass for the book, he had a similar story that he had heard about Samuel Hoosier too. He also said an IU athlete had written a paper on the topic and had shared it with him.

"He wrote that being a Hoosier wasn't a person, place or thing, it was a state of mind," Glass said. "I think that's pretty close. For me it's about certain characteristics. It's people who are down-to-earth, hard working, humble, tolerant, kind of mind their own business. Those are the characteristics that I like to connect with being a Hoosier.

"Add in the fact that basketball runs through everything we do here and I think it's cool that it was that way all those years ago and it's still that way now."

So the debate wages on but what we can agree is on is that for those young men and women who have played athletics over the years at Indiana University it is something that brings with it a great sense of pride.

••••

Randy Wittman, an All-American at IU in 1983, grew up in Indiana and played his high school basketball at Ben Davis High School in Indianapolis. He said one thing he knows is that once you're a Hoosier you're always a Hoosier.

At the time of the writing of this book, Wittman hadn't lived in Indiana for the past 24 years. He currently is the head coach of the Washington Wizards in the NBA.

"I might not ever live (in Indiana) again for the rest of my life," Wittman said. "But whenever we come back there to play the Pacers, that's the biggest game of the year for me. Whether the Pacers are good as they are now or if they're bad it doesn't matter.

"Coming back to that state just brings chills to me. As we land at the airport and get off I feel it. All of my family lives there and that makes it special from that standpoint."

Wittman said Indiana will always remain a special place for him.

"That's always home," Wittman said. "It's home for me now, and I haven't lived there since 1990. I have so many guys that I played with or I knew growing up that still live there that you always feel comfortable whenever you go back."

Wittman said a testament from his own family is the fact that his daughter, Lauren, made the decision that she wanted to attend Indiana University. She graduated in 2013.

"That was her decision, her choice and it really didn't have a lot to do with me," Wittman said. "She grew up in Minnesota. She went down there and visited and said that was where she wanted to go. It's a special place. It always will be. And it will always be home."

Clarence Doninger played at IU for a short time as a sophomore in 1955 and then appeared in five games his senior year in 1957. His sophomore season turned out to be a disappointment because he was cut halfway through the season because of circumstances out of his control. Two scholarship athletes had returned from the war, and Branch McCracken needed a pair of roster spots.

"One of the biggest disappointments in my life was being cut," Doninger said in a 2014 interview, "because I really wanted to play there. But from the first time I ever saw an Indiana basketball game in person as a senior in high school I knew that Indiana basketball was something I wanted to be a part of."

Despite that disappointment, Doninger is clearly a Hoosier Through and Through. He has been attending Indiana basketball games for more than 50 years as a fan and spent 10 years as IU's athletic director retiring early in 2001. In 1990, Doninger won the prestigious Clevenger Award, given to IU lettermen "who, as graduates, have made significant contributions to IU athletics and best perpetuated the ideals that Zora Clevenger personified as an IU student, athlete, coach and administrator."

Doninger, in his short stint in the one full season in '57, was part of a team that tied for a Big Ten title with Michigan State. Having had a very brief IU basketball career, though, was all that Doninger needed to remain a lifetime supporter.

"I will always believe that it is truly a matter of great pride to put on that IU uniform," Doninger said. "It just makes you proud of a tradition that includes not only the national championships and the Big Ten championships but one that has had so many terrific players over the years."

• • • •

That tradition comes through on so many fronts. Whether it's not having names on the back of jerseys, the candy-striped pants, Hoosier Hysteria or the mop lady to name a few, IU basketball is filled with tradition.

Jordan Hulls, the former Indiana Mr. Basketball from Bloomington South, said that is clearly one of the things that sets the IU program apart from others.

"One of the things I loved most about IU was that rich tradition," Hulls said. "If I had to pick one favorite it would have to be the candy-striped pants because it's unique. I love the no names on the jerseys because it's about playing for the name on the front and not on the back, and Hoosier Hysteria because of the experience for the players and the fans, but the candy striped pants are just awesome and uniquely IU.

"I love seeing people out in public with their candy stripes on. It's one way to know an IU fan right away. Hoosier Nation is everywhere!"

Greg Graham was a first-team all-Big Ten selection in 1993 who hailed from Warren Central High School in Indianapolis. He talked about the pride that exists to be able to one day wear the Indiana University basketball uniform.

"I feel honored, I feel blessed and I'm humbled that I even had a chance to go there and put on an Indiana jersey," Graham said. "Because growing up in Indiana, that's what you grow up dreaming about. And then to not only have it come true but to have some success down there playing with some pretty good individuals, that's always going to be a lifetime memory for me."

Mike Woodson said it's all about the culture, the system and the belief when you go to Indiana.

"I can say this without hesitation and that's that I never stepped on the floor once in my career at Indiana not thinking that I was going to win that game," Woodson said.

• • • •

Growing up and playing basketball in the state of Indiana brings with it its own sense of pride.

This is especially true in the smaller communities where having success on the basketball floor was something that was an ongoing topic of discussion at the grocery store, the barber shop or anywhere you would go in town.

Ted Kitchel had that kind of experience. Kitchel was born in Howard County, Indiana, and grew up in a rural area of Cass County. As a high school senior in 1978, Kitchel led Lewis Cass High School to a 20-0 regular season record and its first sectional basketball title in history.

Kitchel averaged 26.2 points and 13 rebounds per game.

Looking back on his basketball career, Kitchel was a part of several championship teams at every level. But he fondly looks back on that high school run.

"It was very special to play basketball in the state of Indiana," Kitchel said. "The most important victory of my life was winning the sectional title at Lewis Cass High School. That was much more important to me than winning the national title and three Big Ten championships."

And Kitchel wasn't being facetious. It really was *that* important for his community.

"That was much more important to me because that was a community that had kind of been starved for a sectional championship," Kitchel said. "To win a sectional championship was such a big deal. Lewis Cass is a small school."

To then go from that experience to a storied career at Indiana was the icing on the cake.

"To have a chance to play in your state and play for Indiana, it was unbelievable," Kitchel said. "While it was great there was a tremendous amount of pressure to succeed. You didn't go to Indiana to just put on the candy stripes and run out on the court and play. You were there to win, and you were there to prepare and work harder than anybody else.

"You were there to do whatever it took to prepare yourself mentally and physically to win basketball games, to win championships. You just didn't show up and play on Thursday and Saturday. It was much more than that."

• • • •

Legendary Indiana University basketball coach Branch McCracken was a strong believer in what you could accomplish with a roster full of Indiana players. He believed in Hoosiers. He was born to Charles and Ida McCracken on June 9, 1908 in the tiny community of Monrovia, Indiana. McCracken was an All-American himself at IU in 1930. Later, he came back to coach IU for 24 seasons, leading the Hoosiers to two national championships and four Big Ten crowns. His overall record was 364-174 including 210-116 in conference play.

But if you talk to McCracken's former players, like we did in doing research for this book, one theme you heard over and over was how much McCracken believed in players from the state of Indiana.

Dr. Marvin Christie, who played at IU as a sophomore in 1950, said knowing the way McCracken felt made it easy for IU players to harbor the same level of pride.

"Mac took great pride in recruiting Indiana boys," Christie said. "He could get boys from all over the state, from way up north to the bottom of the state down south. Every one of us wanted to play for Mac at Indiana because it was our home state school. We were proud to play for a coach that felt that way. We all talked about how much pride you took in wearing that 'Indiana' across your chest. It put pride in your britches.

"We just played harder because we were from Indiana playing for Indiana."

In the book, *Branch,* by Bill Murphy, Christie recalled McCracken saying that if you gave him players from the state of Indiana that he could beat anybody. According to Christie, McCracken said, "I can win a national championship with kids from Indiana."

And he did – twice. Indiana's first two national championship banners that hang in Assembly Hall came with McCracken at the helm in 1940 and again in '53.

Many former Hoosiers, when told of what McCracken had said, absolutely agreed with him.

Randy Wittman heard those words and quickly agreed. There were nine Indiana kids on the '81 national championship team.

"I still think it can happen that way," Wittman said. "Coach Knight won a lot of games without the best athletic talent. What he was really good at was that he knew when he recruited somebody whether that kid could really play for him or not. And the best Indiana kids more often than not wanted to play at IU.

"We didn't lose many of those battles in the 70s, 80s and 90s. If there was a talented kid in Indianapolis or Fort Wayne or wherever in the state and you wanted him, then he was going to come."

Steve Alford said he always thought the level of play in Indiana was very high at the high school level but since he became a college coach he has realized it even more.

"I have the utmost respect for the high school coaching and the level of high school coaching in basketball in the state of Indiana," Alford said. "I kind of learned that through my dad.

I got a front row seat of just how good coaches are in that state and how hard they work at it."

Alford said as he has progressed in his coaching career, he has always been on the lookout to have an Indiana player on his roster. He has done that at every step along the way in his coaching career with the exception of his current school, UCLA. But technically he has Hoosier players there, too. His two sons, Kory and Bryce, list Albuquerque, N.M. as their hometowns but both were born in Indiana.

"When you get an Indiana kid you get somebody who has been well coached, and he's played against very good competition in big buildings with very good crowds," Alford said. "It's not near the transition that a lot of players have to transition into in the collegiate level. That's probably why I've worked so hard in the different stops where I've been from Manchester to Missouri State to Iowa to New Mexico, I've always had an Indiana player.

"UCLA is the exception except for my sons, but I'm always trying to get one here, too."

When Randy Wittman heard Alford's comments, he shook his head in agreement.

"That's a great point. There's no question about it," Wittman said. "In Indiana, you grow up playing basketball. It's still that way today. If it wasn't that way you'd have great football teams. But there's a lot of truth to that. Kids are schooled in playing basketball and taught and usually have the work ethic and determination to be the best they can be."

••••

Calbert Cheaney said you know when you're around Hoosiers simply because of their love for the game of basketball.

"If you're not in tune with what basketball means to the state of Indiana, then you're not a Hoosier," Cheaney said.

Cheaney, now a Division I assistant college basketball coach at Saint Louis University, said he believes more talent comes out of the state of Indiana for college basketball than anywhere else.

And he always believed (before he was recruiting for an out-of-state school that is) that Indiana kids should stay in-state when possible.

"I always thought it was really important to keep the great talent from the state in the state of Indiana," Cheaney said. "It might be Purdue and Notre Dame or Butler, too, but the quality of talent is just so good in Indiana. Everybody talks about the level of talent on the East Coast or the West Coast and maybe down South, but I believe that basketball in the state of Indiana is always going to be right there at the top."

Bobby 'Slick' Leonard, a two-time IU All-American, said playing at Indiana after growing up in the state was "a dream come true."

He said the first dream for kids in junior high or high school was to get to Butler and play in the Fieldhouse for the Final Four of the state tournament. Leonard never achieved that goal.

"That was a big dream of high school kids all over the state," Leonard said. "Of course there wasn't any class basketball back then. When I was in high school, there were 714 teams in the state tournament. Every little town had a high school team. And Friday nights, they packed those gyms. It was just a terrific thing."

To go from that experience to playing at IU, Leonard recalled, was simply the icing on the cake.

"You know, we were known at Indiana as the Hurryin' Hoosiers," Leonard said. "If you look back and check the records, we still have the record against Purdue. We scored more points against Purdue than anyone else. We beat Purdue 113-78 in Bloomington."

Leonard recalled that Ray Eddy was the coach of that team and a Purdue graduate.

"When they were coming into Bloomington, Ray let the newspapers know that he was going to play a zone against us because he said, 'We can't handle those guys man to man'," Leonard said. "We started out the ball game and had this zone on us. And in the first four and a half minutes, we were up 21-0.

"He called a timeout, called them all over, and I got this story from a guy from Bedford, Indiana that was on that bench. Ray told them, 'We're gonna have to get out of that zone. They're killin that zone.' And the kid from Bedford, Indiana spoke up and said, 'Hey coach, does anybody ever get skunked in this game?"

••••

Todd Leary accomplished what he considers the perfect trifecta at the end of his senior year at Lawrence North High School in Indianapolis.

His high school team proved some doubters wrong by winning the state championship. Individually, he was named to the Indiana All Star team, something he called "a nice pat on the back."

But the crown jewel for Leary was when he was an eleventh hour addition to Indiana's vaunted recruiting class of 1989.

"You can call it a dream come true or however you want to phrase it but I couldn't have drawn that scenario up any better," Leary said.

All three happened at about the same time, but the scholarship offer almost never came. In fact, late in Leary's senior year, that was the one piece of the puzzle that didn't look like it had much of a chance.

Leary was barely a blip on IU's radar. Indiana had six scholarships to give in the class of 1989 and when Calbert Cheaney signed on the dotted line as the sixth and final member, the class was wrapped up.

Leary was focusing on other options. The weekend after he had helped lead his team to the Indiana High School basketball championship, he and future Purdue head coach Matt Painter were on a recruiting visit the same weekend to Minnesota.

It was spring break and lots of high school recruits were taking advantage of the time off to make visits. The next weekend both Leary and Painter were scheduled to visit Purdue.

But when Leary's mom picked her son up at the airport coming home from Minnesota that Tuesday, she had some interesting news.

"I got off the airplane and my mom met me at the airport and the first thing she said was that Coach Knight had called the house that morning," Leary said. "She said that Knight had told her that he was going to call back that night. He had said that Jay Edwards had declared for the NBA Draft and there was a scholarship open.

"Coach Knight called me that night and offered me a scholarship."

Leary said he probably should have thought about it and weighed his options and looked at how he would fit in, etcetera. But this was Indiana. Leary was the biggest IU fan ever and the coach of the one school he wanted to play for more than any other had just offered a scholarship.

"I committed on the spot," Leary said. "There was no other place that I wanted to play than Indiana. I wasn't going to let that scholarship offer slip by. I wanted to be an Indiana Hoosier."

Pat Graham was Indiana's Mr. Basketball in 1989 out of Floyd Central High School in Floyds Knobs, Indiana. He was an Indiana All-Star who would go on to play at IU. He said he hates to sound selfish but looking back he wishes he could have had one more jewel in the crown.

"Selfishly if I could get Leary's state championship you probably could have laid my head down in the casket and I could have ended it there because that would have been the pinnacle," Graham said.

Graham said growing up in Southern Indiana he was in basketball heaven. He was 10 minutes from the University of Louisville, 90 minutes from Lexington, Kentucky. and about the same distance to Bloomington.

"Growing up in Southern Indiana and winning Mr. Basketball, and frankly that doesn't happen because quote/unquote kids in Southern Indiana aren't seen, was huge," Graham said. "So winning Mr. Basketball and being able to wear that jersey, and going to the state school, to say that wasn't beyond special I would be lying."

Brian Evans, like Leary, said he grew up dreaming that one day he would play basketball at Indiana but as his high school

17

career played out he became more and more convinced that it wouldn't happen.

"You're either being recruited by IU or you're not," Evans said, "and I wasn't. I didn't spend a ton of time dreaming about it after I got to about my junior year but that was because it just became clear they weren't going to recruit me."

Evans said he knew that it was time to snap into reality and really focus on where he would ultimately play.

Evans said he was being recruited by Evansville, Ball State, Butler, Western Illinois and Indiana State.

"I couldn't spend my time thinking about Indiana because I was being recruited by those other schools," Evans said. "I think quietly I had this confidence that the big schools were missing out but at the same time I figured they all knew what they were doing and I just needed to put my focus somewhere else."

But like with Leary, things happened very quickly for Evans.

"Coach Felling decided to come over and watch an open gym, Coach Knight and Felling came back the next day, and the following day another one of the assistants was there," Evans said. "In a span of a week, I went down to a football game with my dad and gave my commitment while I was there.

"Coach asked for a commitment and I gave him one."

Mike Woodson summed it up this way.

"To me, being a Hoosier and being able to play basketball at Indiana University, it really just doesn't get much better than that."

• • • •

And then there are the transplanted Hoosiers, too. These are the ones who are adopted into the Indiana family. There may be 587 players in history who were from the state and then played for IU, but there are hundreds more who still think of themselves that way.

Archie Dees came to Indiana in the fall of 1954 from Mt. Carmel, Illinois. He admitted that he didn't know much at the time about what it meant to be a Hoosier.

He found out pretty quickly. Some of that was because his coach was Branch McCracken, clearly a Hoosier Through and

Through. But he said he just felt a sense of community in Indiana like he hadn't experienced before.

Sixty years later, Dees still lives in Indiana. He came in '54 and hasn't left.

"I definitely consider myself a Hoosier," Dees said. "I can't remember being anything else. It's something that brings with it a great deal of pride. I still wear my Indiana gear all the time because I want people to know where I'm from."

Myself, I never played basketball in Indiana, but moved to the state after growing up in Southern California. Now, 28 years after I decided to make Indiana home, I completely get what Dees had to say about being a Hoosier. It gets in your blood. It's a matter of pride.

I still remember the first few times I returned to California after moving to Indiana and if I would meet someone new they would ask where I lived. I remember one woman when hearing that I was from Indiana saying, "And you like it there?"

That's the thing. Sometimes I think Indiana is a pretty well kept secret from those who aren't from the Hoosier State.

• • • •

Talk to Indiana basketball players and you constantly hear the term 'family.'

It doesn't matter that Jordan Hulls never played with Steve Alford, Quinn Buckner or Jimmy Rayl. There's still a connection there. Archie Dees didn't even grow up a Hoosier but became an adopted one when he joined the 'family' as an IU freshman in 1954. Many of these guys didn't meet until they got to the NBA but then they were fast friends because of their IU experiences and connections.

When Tom Crean was hired at Indiana in 2008 one of the first things he did was to try and bridge the gap with former players and make them feel welcome to be around the program again. He felt like there was a disconnect there somewhere and he wanted to facilitate a change there.

One of the things he did was hosting a two-day basketball reunion in West Baden, Indiana, that first August. More than 180 former players and managers attended with every decade represented back to the 1940s. On the second day there was a dinner and golf outing that more than 250 players, managers and guests attended.

The majority of those who attended said that feeling of an Indiana family was strong throughout the weekend.

Brian Evans said that's what makes being a Hoosier that much more special.

"I know I still pinch myself today because I know how close I was to not having been a part of that," Evans said. "I've often wondered if things had gone differently if I'd even still live in Indiana. I think so many things would have changed if I had not gone to Indiana."

Evans looks at it like being a huge fraternity with some great guys.

"To think I'm in a fraternity with guys like Randy and Ted and Steve and Calbert and Alan and some of these guys like Steve Green that are older than me is amazing," Evans said. "I know these guys. Quinn Buckner is a friend of mine. I mean, seriously? Those guys are considered friends. It's not like we hang out all the time or get together every year and talk about our playing days but it's more of a mutual respect especially with the guys who played for Coach (Knight).

"We have a bond because of that. We wore that uniform and we know what that means and with how much pride we wore it. It's super special."

Evans said he is reminded of his IU basketball heritage all the time because he still lives in Indiana.

"I get asked about the team today, teams I played on, teammates I had, pretty much every day of my life," Evans said. "It's pretty awesome."

Randy Wittman said when Bob Knight first started recruiting him it was the family atmosphere that really came through. All of a sudden he was getting to meet Quinn Buckner, Scott May, Kent Benson and all of the mainstays from the 1976 national championship team.

"I think it has been that way all the way through," Wittman said. "Take Steve Alford for example. I never played with Steve, I was older than Steve, but they had a correlation with us because of that family atmosphere.

"Any kid that came up before or after there was great camaraderie between guys that had played there. I mean I'm close with guys that I never played with like Steve Green, Tom Abernethy and Jim Crews to name a few."

Wittman said the common bond of being Hoosiers is what brings everyone together.

"They went through it and you go through it and it becomes a situation where it feels like we all played together," Wittman said. "And each team passes that down. They took care of us when we got there and we did the same for the people that were coming in after we left."

3

The Countdown Begins

With Players 26-50 (in Alphabetical Order)

When I tried to narrow the list of the top Indiana basketball players of all time from the state of Indiana from 50 to 25, I found that once again this may be the most difficult exercise of the project.

How do you compare an All-American in 1937 that averaged 8.6 points per game to players of today? Because of that, I decided that it would be easier, and less stressful after the fact, to list the players from 26-50 in alphabetical order.

The following players comprise that list.

Now, not surprisingly, a few names will jump off this list and many will question how this player could not have made a list of the top 25 Indiana basketball players of all time from the state of Indiana.

And it will always be that way. But if I had chosen to make this a top 30 list then the same problem would have happened with guys in the 30-35 range. There would always be an argument and a debate that certain players deserve to be ranked higher or some should be dropped in the list.

But that's what makes this project fun. It opens things up for a lot of discussion.

Here are the top 26-50 players all-time in Indiana University basketball history from the state of Indiana listed alphabetically.

Ernie Andres

Andres, from Jeffersonville, Indiana, was named an All-American in his junior season in 1938, which was also Everett Dean's final season after 14 years as the IU head coach. Andres had a big junior season, scoring 250 points for a 12.5 average. He scored a school-record 162 points in Big Ten play. In the season finale of his junior year, Andres set a school and conference single game record by scoring 30 points in a 45-35 victory over Illinois. Andres finished his IU career with 511 points and a career average of 8.7 per game.

Andres had an impressive basketball career where he twice won the Balfour Award as IU's top athlete and was named both All-American and All-Big Ten. He played professional basketball with the Indianapolis Kautskys of the NBL, winning the 1947 World Tournament in Chicago. He was inducted into the Indiana Basketball Hall of Fame in 1975.

But basketball wasn't even Andres' best sport. He also played professional baseball with the Boston Red Sox. Nicknamed 'Junie,' Andres batted and threw right-handed. His professional baseball career included stops from 1939-41 and again from 1946-47. The time in between, Andres served in the United States Navy in the Pacific Theater of Operations during World War II.

After he left professional baseball, Andres returned to IU where he was the Indiana baseball coach from 1948-73. He also spent 11 seasons during that time as an assistant basketball coach at IU under Branch McCracken.

Andres was inducted into the Indiana University Hall of Fame in 1983.

Andres died Sept. 19, 2008 at the age of 90 in Bradenton, Florida.

••••

Hallie Bryant

Hallie Bryant was Indiana's Mr. Basketball in 1953 at Crispus Attucks High School in Indianapolis.

As a junior at Indiana University, Bryant was the third leading scorer on a team that also featured Wally Choice and Archie Dees. Bryant averaged 14.4 points per game. His senior season he averaged 12.5 points per game.

He was a member of IU's 1957 Big Ten co-championship team coached by Branch McCracken.

After two years as a commissioned officer in the United States Army, Bryant embarked on a career where he would gain his most individual fame.

Over the next 13 seasons, Bryant played for the Harlem Globetrotters. He visited 87 countries in those 13 seasons playing for the Globetrotters. When he retired as a player he spent the next 14 years with the Globetrotters as an official spokesperson and director of team personnel.

Bryant is a lifelong resident of the state of Indiana.

He was inducted into the Indiana High School Hall of Fame in 1983 and into the Indiana University Athletics Hall of Fame in 1998.

••••

Tom Coverdale

Coverdale came to Indiana from Noblesville (Indiana) High School where he was named the state's Mr. Basketball in 1998. He also played one season at New Hampton Prep before attending IU.

At Indiana, Coverdale accomplished a feat that no other IU player has ever achieved. Coverdale is the only player in IU history to score more than 1,000 points, make more than 200 3-pointers and dish out more than 500 assists. He ranks third all-time in assists with exactly 500. He played in 125 games in his IU career, scoring 1,217 points. He was considered the heart and soul of the 2002 IU team that advanced to the national championship game before losing to Maryland. Coverdale, who was a junior that season, was second on the team in scoring behind Jared Jeffries. Coverdale averaged 11.9 points per game. He averaged in double figures in each of his final three seasons at IU.

After college, Coverdale played one season in the CBA and one season in Europe before taking a job as a coaching intern at Louisiana-Monroe. He did that for two seasons before being hired at the school as a full time assistant. As of 2014, he was working in the insurance business in Carmel, Indiana.

••••

Bob Dro

A 6-foot guard from Berne High School in Berne, Indiana, Dro was a four-year athlete in high school and led his team to the state tournament in 1935. The next season, Berne was undefeated in regular season play. He played on three sectional championship teams. At Indiana, Dro played for coach Branch McCracken from 1938-41. His teams only lost nine games in three seasons at IU. He was a three-year starter for the Hoosiers and was a member of IU's first national championship team in 1940. He was a second team all-Big Ten selection as a junior and first team as a senior.

He also played baseball for three seasons with the Hoosiers and played every position except pitcher. After leaving IU, Dro played one season with the Indianapolis Kautskys of the NBL. He also played minor league baseball for the Grand Rapids Colts in the Brooklyn Dodgers organization. Dro then served in the United States Navy during World War II. After returning from the war, Dro went on to coach high school basketball in Pendleton and Bluffton, Indiana. From 1957-84, Dro worked in the IU athletic department, first as an assistant athletic director and then as an associate A.D. beginning in 1973. After that, he was IU's director of community relations.

Dro was inducted into the Indiana Basketball Hall of Fame in 1978 and into the Indiana University Athletics Hall of Fame in 1985. He died at age 87 on May 4, 2006.

●●●●

Dick Farley

A 6-4 shooting guard/small forward from Winslow High School in Winslow, Indiana, Farley is best known in IU circles as being a member of the 1953 Indiana national championship team. There, he was teammates with players such Don Schlundt and Bobby 'Slick'Leonard. Farley played at IU from 1952-54 where he played in 50 games and averaged 10.3 points per game.

In the first game of his college career against Valparaiso in 1952, Farley led all IU scorers with 19 points in a 68-59 victory. He wound up averaging 8.9 points per game.

In the *Indiana Basketball Encyclopedia* account of the 1953 national championship team, Jason Hiner had this to say about Farley. "The 6-3 Farley would have been probably been a top scorer on almost any other team in the Big Ten. As a sophomore he was Indiana's third leading scorer at 8.9 per game and he upped that to 10.1 in the 1952-53 season, when his field goal percentage of .443 led the conference. He was also a strong ball handler and passer, but above all, he served as Indiana's defensive stopper. He almost always guarded the opposing team's top scorer."

When IU clinched the Big Ten title in '53 against No. 10 Illinois in Champaign, Farley had 19 points.

As a senior against Purdue, Farley had a 22-point game. He also had 18 in an early season game against Montana.

After IU, Farley was a second round draft pick of the Syracuse Nationals in the 1954 NBA Draft, the 15th selection overall. He played with the Nationals from 1954-56 and then with the Detroit Pistons from 1958-59.

Farley died at the age of 37 on Oct. 1, 1969 in Fort Wayne, Indiana.

●●●●

Kevin 'Yogi' Ferrell

At the time of this printing, Kevin 'Yogi' Ferrell was entering his junior season at Indiana. Ferrell played for head coach Ed Schilling at Park Tudor High School in Indianapolis where he was ranked as the 19th player overall in his class in high school and the second-best point guard. He was the 17th IU recruit all-time to have played in the McDonald's All-American game.

Ferrell had an impressive high school career as he led Park Tudor to the state championship in both his junior and senior seasons. He just missed a triple-double in his senior season in the state championship game when he had 17 points, 12 assists and nine rebounds. He was an Indiana All-Star and helped lead his team to a two-game sweep of Kentucky. As a sophomore his team played in the state championship game but got beat.

In his first two seasons at Indiana, Ferrell started all 68 games. His freshman season he averaged 7.6 points on a team that was a No. 1 seed in the NCAA Tournament and made it to the Sweet Sixteen for the second season in a row. As a sophomore, he led IU in scoring with a 17.3 points per game average. In his first two seasons, he had scored 824 points.

He made the all-Big Ten freshman team his first season and was an honorable mention all-Big Ten selection. As a sophomore, Ferrell was a second team all-Big Ten selection.

••••

Greg Graham

Greg Graham had a solid Indiana University basketball career and still ranks No. 13 all-time in scoring with 1,590 points and a 12.1 career average. It's safe to say he was right there on the fringe in terms of being ranked in the top 25 all time.

Graham played his high school basketball at Warren Central in Indianapolis and then returned there later and is currently the head varsity basketball coach.

Greg was part of an impressive 1989 recruiting class that also included McDonald's All Americans Pat Graham and Lawrence Funderburke, high school state champion Todd Leary, Chris Lawson and Chris Reynolds. Perhaps the least heralded recruit that year went on to become IU's all-time leading scorer – Calbert Cheaney.

Graham was IU's third leading scorer as a freshman at 9.7 points. His sophomore season he averaged 8.7 points per game. As a junior on the IU team that lost to Duke the in Final Four, Graham was IU's second leading scorer 12.8 points per game.

His senior season, he was again the second leading scorer (behind Cheaney) at 16.5 points per game.

Graham was a first round draft pick of Charlotte, the 17th selection overall, in the 1993 NBA Draft. He played five seasons in the NBA from 1993-97 and also played with Philadelphia, New Jersey, Seattle and Cleveland.

••••

Pat Graham

Graham came to Indiana from Floyd Central High School in Floyds Knobs, Indiana, where he won the coveted Mr. Basketball honor in 1989, and led Floyd Central to the state's Final Four. He was also a McDonald's All-American. Graham is one of 26 IU players all-time that came to Indiana after winning the state's Mr. Basketball award.

28

Graham was part of a Dream Team recruiting class at IU that also included Calbert Cheaney, Greg Graham, Lawrence Funderburke, Chris Lawson, Todd Leary and Chris Reynolds.

Bob Knight once described Graham as being one of the best shooters the state had turned out for a long while. At Indiana, Graham played in 102 career games and had a career average of 8.7 points. Injuries cost him one season and several games in another.

He averaged 7.7 points his freshman season in 1990 and 7.4 points as a sophomore in 1991. After redshirting in '92, Graham averaged 6.5 points in 1993 and 11.8 points as a senior in '94.

He had a big game against Ohio State his senior year when he rallied Indiana to an 87-83 overtime win over the Buckeyes. Graham scored a career-high 29 points and hit 6-of-7 3-pointers.

Graham still resides in Southern Indiana.

••••

Ken Gunning

Gunning was an All-American at Indiana in 1937, where he played for coach Everett Dean.

Gunning led the Hoosiers in scoring in all three seasons and 512 points for his career. As a senior, his All-American year he averaged 8.6 points per game. He was a co-captain on that team along with fellow top 50 player Vern Huffman.

Twice in his career, both times in his junior season, Gunning had high games of 19 points. The first time was against Chicago and the second, Northwestern.

Indiana went 45-15 in Gunning's three seasons in Bloomington.

Gunning came to IU from Shelbyville (Indiana) High School. He later went into coaching and was at Connersville for a number of years. He was also the head coach at Wichita State University.

••••

Ralph Hamilton

A 6-1 forward from Fort Wayne, Indiana, Hamilton gradu-ated from Fort Wayne South in 1940. He was an all-state player that season for South and broke the tournament scoring record en route to a Final Four appearance. He was named all-city and to every all-tournament team that season.

Hamilton played three seasons at Indiana in a career inter-rupted by military service in World War II. Hamilton's first two seasons at Indiana were the 1941-42 and 1942-43 cam-paigns. In '43, he scored 247 points, averaging 13 points per game. From 1944-46 Hamilton served in the United States Army. He returned to IU as a 25-year-old senior for the 1946-47 IU basketball season. That year, he scored 261 points and averaged 13.7 points per game earning consensus first team All-American honors. The other consensus first team All-Americans that year were Ralph Beard, Alex Groza, Sid Tanenbaum and Gerry Tucker.

His 632 career points and 10.9 career average was an IU school record when he graduated. It was bested a few years later by Lou Watson, who was his teammate in the 1946-47 season.

Hamilton played in the NBA with the Detroit Pistons in 1947-48 before being traded to the Indianapolis Jets for the 1948-49 season. He was inducted into the Indiana Basketball Hall of Fame in 1991, and into the Indiana University Athletics Hall of Fame in 2007. He died in 1983.

••••

Marv Huffman

Marv Huffman was one of two Indiana brothers from New Castle that made the top 50 list. His brother, Vern, an IU All-American in 1936 is listed in detail below.

He may be best remembered as one of the integral players on IU's 1940 national championship team. He wasn't known for his scoring (he only averaged 3.7 points per game) but Ja-son Hiner in the *IU Basketball Encyclopedia* said Huffman was an excellent passer, defender and rebounder. He did lead In-diana in scoring with 12 points in the national championship game against Kansas, a 60-42 victory.

In Huffman's final two seasons at Indiana he played for IU's new coach at the time, Branch McCracken.

Huffman came to IU from New Castle where he started every game in his four-year high school career and was the team's leading scorer twice. He was a three time all-North Central Conference team selection, three times all-sectional and all-regional and he was all-state as a senior in 1936.

He was inducted into the Indiana High School Basketball Hall of Fame in 1981 and the Indiana University Athletics Hall of Fame in 1989.

••••

Vern Huffman

Huffman is the only Indiana player in IU history to be named to major All-American teams in both football and basketball. He is from Mooreland, Indiana, a town of 375 people as of the 2010 census, located in Blue River Township in Henry County. According to the Wikipedia page on Mooreland, it has three famous former residents. One is author, novelist and poet, Haven Kimmel. A second is aviation giant Wilbur Wright, who was raised three miles from Mooreland. The third is Vern Huffman.

Huffman's high school basketball team at New Castle, won the 1932 Indiana state basketball championship. He was inducted into the Indiana Basketball Hall of Fame in 1968. He was inducted into the Indiana University Athletics Hall of Fame as part of the very first class in 1982.

Huffman went on to IU where he was an All-American in football and basketball in 1936. He led the Hoosiers to an 18-2 record and the conference championship. His point total for the 1935-36 season was 95. His senior season he scored 100 points total. In football, Huffman was the Big Ten's Most Valuable Player and IU's Big Ten Medal winner. He would go on to play two seasons of professional football in the National Football League for the Detroit Lions in 1937 and 1938. He graduated from IU with a law degree.

Later in life, Huffman managed a dairy and also held a job with the Federal Bureau of Investigation. He died March 18, 1995 in Bloomington at the age of 81.

••••

Jordan Hulls

Hulls, who was named Indiana's Mr. Basketball at Bloomington South in 2009, comes from a basketball family. His grandfather, John Hulls, came to Indiana from Army with Bob Knight in 1971 and served as IU's shooting coach. His sister, Kaila, plays on the women's team at Indiana and his dad is a coach as well.

Hulls played three years on varsity at Bloomington South and had a record of 66-7. His senior season, along with being named Mr. Basketball, Hulls' team won the state championship in the 4A class with a perfect 26-0 record. He averaged 15.8 points, 5.2 assists and 2.6 steals as a high school senior.

Hulls had a solid four-year career at Indiana, scoring 1,318 points and helping lead his team to back-to-back Sweet Sixteen performances. He was a career 44.1 percent 3-point shooter, hitting 254-of-576 3-pointers. He ranks second all-time in Indiana history with the 254 which is 54 ahead of third place Tom Coverdale as of 2014. A.J. Guyton is the all-time leader with 283. His career percentage for 3-pointers ranks fourth all time. Hulls also holds the IU record for most consecutive free throws made in a season at 41 in the 2010-11 campaign.

Along with his on the court excellence, Hulls came up big off of it as well. He was named a 2012-13 Academic All-American selection.

••••

Butch Joyner

Harry 'Butch' Joyner was a 1963 graduate of New Castle who was the leading scorer and rebounder his senior year and earned all-conference an all-state recognition. He was selected as a member of the Indiana All-Star team. He was inducted into the Indiana Basketball Hall of Fame in 2000.

Joyner then attended IU where he played for both Branch McCracken and Lou Watson. With the Hoosiers, he scored 1,030 points and is one of IU's 47 all-time 1,000-point scorers.

His career scoring average was 15.1 points. He led the Hoosiers in scoring in 1967 with a 18.5 points per game average. He led the Hoosiers in rebounds in 1966 and 1967. In '67, he averaged 10.5 rebounds per game. He won the Balfour Athletic Award while at IU, given to IU's best athlete.

Joyner was drafted by the Cincinnati Royals and the Indiana Pacers out of college. He played for the Pacers in 1969. Joyner currently resides in Payson, Ariz. where he works as a real estate agent.

••••

John Laskowski

Laskowski played at South Bend (Indiana) St. Josephs where he played for future Bob Knight assistant Bob Donewald. As a senior in the 1970-71 season, Laskowski averaged 28.9 points per game with a high game of 49. He was inducted into the Indiana Basketball Hall of Fame in 1999.

At Indiana, Laz rarely started but averaged 10.8 points and 3.8 rebounds per game as IU's sixth man. He came off the bench to score 20 points or more six times and in double figures a total of 40 times. He was called the 'Super Sub'. In the 1973-74 season he scored 350 of his career total 903 points.

Laskowski was a second round pick of the Chicago Bulls in the 1975 NBA Draft and played two professional seasons. As a rookie he averaged 9.2 points per game and made the NBA's All-Rookie second team.

In recent years, Laskowski has remained involved at IU both with the IU Alumni Association as well as working as a color commentator and play by play analyst for Indiana basketball games, most recently on the Big Ten Network. He also authored a 2003 book on IU basketball entitled *Tales from the Hoosier Locker Room*.

••••

Michael Lewis

When Lewis arrived at Indiana University in 1996, he was one of the most prolific high school scorers in the history of the state of Indiana. Lewis, who hailed from Jasper (Indiana) High School, came to IU tied for 12th in state history in scoring. He

33

scored 2,138 points in high school. That's more than players like Steve Alford or Calbert Cheaney accomplished during their high school careers. Lewis was named to the Indiana All Star team in '96.

At Indiana, Lewis played in 127 games and averaged 7.0 points per game. But Lewis will be better known for his ability to distribute the ball in college. He holds the Indiana school records for career assists (545) from 1997-2000. He also holds school records for career assists in Big Ten play (325) and is tied with Keith Smart for the IU school record for assists in a game. Lewis had 15 at Iowa in 1998.

Since leaving IU, Lewis has become known for his coaching abilities, too. He spent two seasons as a graduate assistant for Bob Knight at Texas Tech, one year at Stephen F. Austin, six seasons as an assistant at Eastern Illinois, and as of 2014, he was on the staff at Butler as an assistant.

• • • •

Jon McGlocklin

McGlocklin came to Indiana after a solid career at Franklin (Indiana) High School where he won the scoring championship of the South Central Conference his senior season and was an all-state selection. He was inducted into the Indiana Basketball Hall of Fame in 1990.

At IU, McGlocklin played from 1963-65 where he was overshadowed a bit by some pretty good players in his day. His first season he played with Jimmy Rayl, Tom Bolyard and the Van Arsdale twins. His final two seasons he continued to play with Tom and Dick Van Arsdale. His junior season he averaged 15.7 points per game and was third on the team in scoring. His average was 17.2 as a senior but he was still third in scoring behind the two Van Arsdales.

He played three seasons at IU for Branch McCracken and was IU's captain in 1965. He also won the Balfour Award at IU, given to the best athlete. While he did score 873 points at IU, his bigger accomplishments came at the next level where he was initially a third round pick of the Cincinnati Royals in 1965, the 24th player selected overall.

McGlocklin played two years with Cincinnati, one with the San Diego Rockets and eight seasons with the Milwaukee Bucks. With the Bucks, he was a starting guard along with Oscar Robertson on the '71 Bucks team that won the NBA championship. McGlocklin scored 9,169 points in his NBA career and his No. 14 jersey was retired by the Milwaukee franchise.

After ending his playing career, McGlocklin became a member of the Milwaukee Bucks television broadcasting team. He has done that alongside Jim Paschke for more than 25 years.

McGlocklin was inducted into the Indiana University Athletics Hall of Fame in 2006.

••••

Bill Menke

A 6-3 center, Menke was the leading scorer as both a junior and a senior at Huntingburg (Indiana) High School. He earned all-sectional honors both years. As a junior his team beat rival Jasper for the sectional championship and as a senior his squad was 20-4 before losing to Jasper in the sectional final. He was named to the Indiana Basketball Hall of Fame in 1988.

He spent one season after high school at Kemper Military Institute in Missouri. He then moved on to IU where he was a three-year player and named to the NCAA's All-Tournament team in 1940 when the Hoosiers won their first national championship. He was an All-American that season averaging 7.9 points. He played for Branch McCracken and one of his teammates that year, Marv Huffman, was also selected to the All-America team. His younger brother, Bob, was also his teammate at IU. Menke finished his IU career as the all-time Indiana leading scorer at the time with 530 points. Following college, he played in the Amateur Athletic Association with the Great Lakes Naval Training Station team.

He was inducted into the Indiana University Athletics Hall of Fame in 2011.

••••

Wayne Radford

Radford arrived at Indiana at a magical time in its history.

His first season was 1974-75 when IU went 31-1. The next season, the Hoosiers went a perfect 32-0 and captured the national championship.

Radford played in 26 games in '75 and averaged 3.1 points. On the national championship team, he was also a role player who played in 30 games and averaged 4.7 points per game.

His junior and senior seasons were very productive. In '77 he averaged 9.2 points per game and then in '78, he was IU's second leading scorer behind Mike Woodson with a 15.6 points per game average.

He scored a total of 922 points in his IU career.

He came to Indiana from Arlington High School where he was a three-year letterman. He scored 1,307 career points in high school and was an Indiana All-Star in 1974.

He was later the 27th player selected in the 1978 NBA Draft by the Indiana Pacers.

He was inducted into the Indiana High School Basketball Hall of Fame in 2009.

••••

Frank Radovich

A 1956 graduate of Hammond (Indiana) High School, Radovich made all-sectional and all-regional teams his last three years of high school and was an NEA All-American in 1956. As a high school senior at Hammond, Radovich scored 656 points.

Radovich went on to IU where he played three years and won the Balfour Award in both 1959 and 1960. In 69 career games at Indiana, Radovich averaged 11.3 points and 9.6 rebounds. As a junior, he averaged 12.5 points and as a senior he averaged 14.8. He was on teams that had their share of good players, too. In '58, he was a teammate of IU legend Archie Dees and in '59 and '60 he played with Walt Bellamy.

Radovich was selected in the second round of the 1960 NBA Draft by the St. Louis Hawks. He played for the Philadelphia Warriors in the 1961-62 season. He later coached at Georgia

Southern University from 1967-70 and compiled a 48-24 record in three seasons. He spent one season as a graduate assistant at IU in the 1971-72 season when he was earning his Masters degree. If that year sounds familiar, that would have been Bob Knight's first season as the IU head coach.

Radovich was inducted into the Indiana Basketball Hall of Fame in 1993.

• • • •

Don Ritter

A 5-10 guard from Aurora, Indiana, Don Ritter was a standout basketball and baseball player at Indiana. In basketball, he won letters in 1947, 1948 and 1949. He was a two-year starter in basketball and led the Hoosiers in scoring in '48 with a 13.8 points per game average. He was also IU's basketball captain as a senior in '49.

He played in 61 career games and averaged 9.2 points per game.

Ritter was a clearly a two-sport athlete though at Indiana. In baseball, he was a first team All-American selection in 1949. He still ranks in the top 10 in IU baseball history in hitting with a career .382 batting average. He won the Balfour award in 1949 as well as the IU Gimbel Award.

In 2011, he was inducted into the IU Athletics Hall of Fame.

• • • •

Ray Tolbert

Tolbert came to Indiana from Anderson (Indiana) Madison Heights where he won the Indiana Mr. Basketball Award in 1977. His senior season at Madison Heights he averaged 25.1 points per game, 13 rebounds and six blocks per game. He played high school basketball for legendary Indiana high school coach Phil Buck. He was elected to the Indiana Basketball Hall of Fame in 2005.

Tolbert then had a solid career at Indiana where he played on a pair of Big Ten championship teams in 1980 and '81, starred on the '81 national championship team and also played on an NIT championship team in 1979. In '81, the year that IU won the title, Tolbert was named the Big Ten's most valuable player and a second-team All-American. That season he had shooting percentage of 62.6 percent. In the national championship game against North Carolina, Tolbert had 11 rebounds in helping lead his team to a 63-50 victory.

Tolbert scored 428 points as a senior at IU in '81 and finished his career with 1,427 points. He played in 127 games at IU and started 123.

Tolbert was selected by the New Jersey Nets in the first round of the 1981 NBA Draft. He was the 18th player selected overall. He played five years in the NBA for six teams including New Jersey, Seattle, Detroit, the New York Knicks, Los Angeles Lakers and Atlanta. His NBA career spanned 261 games and he scored 928 points.

He was elected into the Indiana University Athletics Hall of Fame in 2011.

•••

Landon Turner

Like Tolbert, Landon Turner was an instrumental player on the 1981 Indiana national championship team. He averaged 9.5 points in 33 games and was the team's fourth leading scorer.

His senior year at IU was expected to be his breakout season as he would have joined Randy Wittman and Ted Kitchel as being two of the more experienced players on that team.

But Turner was involved in a tragic car accident in July of 1981 that left him paralyzed from the waist down. He was injured when the car he was driving went out of control on a two-lane highway about 50 miles southeast of Indianapolis.

As a high school player at Indianapolis Tech, Turner was a member of the '77 City Championship team. He took home all-city, sectional, regional and semi-state awards in 1978. He was a McDonald's All American and a 1978 Indiana All Star.

He was honored as a Sagamore of the Wabash in 1989, the highest civilian honor by which the governor of the state of Indiana could bestow.

Turner was inducted into the Indiana High School Basketball Hall of Fame in 2007. He was also inducted into the Indiana University Athletics Hall of Fame in 2012.

••••

Lou Watson

A 6-5 guard/forward from Jeffersonville, Indiana, Watson was a four-year starter at Jeffersonville High School. He was a three-time all-sectional and three-time all-regional selection there. He left with all of the school's scoring records at that time. He graduated from high school in 1943.

Over the next seven years, Watson had a four-year basketball career at IU but also served a stint in the military. At IU, Watson had an impressive career for head coach Branch McCracken. He played in 76 games in four years and was a starter the last 68 of them. He was IU's most valuable player his final two seasons in both 1949 and 1950. He was a team captain and was both an All-American and All-Big Ten in 1950. His 757 career points, at the time, was an Indiana school record. Ralph Hamilton had held the record before. He was a two-time winner of the Balfour Award, given to IU's top athlete.

After leaving IU, Watson took a job first as an assistant and then as the head coach at Huntington (Indiana) High School. Beginning in the 1954-55 season, Watson returned to Indiana as an assistant basketball coach on McCracken's staff. He would hold that spot for 11 seasons until McCracken moved on. When his coach and mentor left, Watson became Indiana's head basketball coach for the next six seasons. He will always be known as the coach who gave way to the hiring of Bob Knight at IU in the 1971-72 season.

In his six seasons as head coach, Watson coached the Hoosiers to a 62-60 overall record including a 31-39 mark in Big Ten play. In 1970, Watson coached IU legend George McGinnis, who would average 29.9 points and 14.5 rebounds per game that season for the Hoosiers before leaving for professional basketball. Watson led IU to a Big Ten co-championship in 1967.

When he stepped down as IU's head basketball coach, he took a position in the IU athletic department as a special assistant to the athletic director. He retired from that job in 1987. Watson died on May 25, 2012 at the age of 88 in Fairfax, Virginia.

He was inducted into the Indiana University Athletics Hall of Fame in 1990.

• • • •

Bobby Wilkerson

Bobby Wilkerson is best remembered at Indiana as being a starter on the 1976 unbeaten national championship team. He played in 32 games that season and averaged 7.8 points.

IU's starting backcourt of Wilkerson and Quinn Buckner weren't big scorers though they could score in bunches if needed.

Wilkerson may also be remembered as the player in the national championship game in '76 who started but did not score and only had one field goal attempt. That's because less than 3 minutes into the game Wilkerson got hit by an inadvertent elbow by Michigan's Wayman Britt. Wilkerson was knocked out cold and had to be taken to the hospital. He never did return to the game.

Wilkerson averaged 7.2 points per game as a junior and 3.6 points as a sophomore.

Wilkerson hailed from Madison Heights High School in Anderson, Indiana.

He was a first round pick, the 11th selection overall by the Seattle Supersonics in the 1976 NBA Draft.

He played for four NBA teams (Seattle, Denver, Chicago and Cleveland). He scored 5,424 points in his NBA career, a 10.1 average.

4

The Countdown Continues
With Players 11-25

25. Tom Bolyard

Tom Bolyard never led the Indiana Hoosiers in scoring in his three seasons at IU.

But that's because a couple of other legendary names took care of that for him.

As a sophomore at IU in 1961, Bolyard averaged 15.5 points per game which was second on the team behind Walt Bellamy.

Bolyard's junior and senior seasons he was second in scoring behind Jimmy Rayl. Bolyard averaged 18.6 points per game as a junior and 20.0 points per game as a senior.

Tom Bolyard (Indiana University Archives — P0020611)

His career scoring total of 1,299 points ranks 28th all-time in Indiana University history. Only nine players in IU history had a higher career average than Bolyard's 18.0 points per game.

Bolyard ranks as the 10th fastest player in Indiana history to score 1,000 points. He did it in 60 games.

Bolyard came to IU after leading Fort Wayne South to the 1958 state championship. He graduated as the school's all-time leading scorer and was a two-time all-state selection.

He was inducted into the Indiana Basketball Hall of Fame in 1963.

He was inducted into the Indiana University Athletics Hall of Fame in 1998.

Out of college he was drafted and signed with the Baltimore Bullets. He later went on to serve as an assistant basketball coach on Lou Watson's staff at IU from 1965-71. He was the lead recruiter for a pretty good prospect named George McGinnis.

24. Steve Green

Steve Green played during one of the most storied times in Indiana basketball history.

He was a senior in 1975, when the Hoosiers won their first 31 games before falling to Kentucky in the NCAA Tournament. Many consider that Indiana's best team ever. Unfortunately a broken arm suffered by Scott May late in the season likely prevented IU from securing back-to-back national championships.

The year after Green left, IU went a perfect 32-0 and captured the 1976 NCAA title.

Steve Green (Indiana University Archives — P0021058)

Green was an All-American at Indiana in both 1974 and '75.

His junior year, in 1974, Green was IU's leading scorer with a 16.7 points per game average and shot 54.5 percent from the field. He was IU's most valuable player that season and a first team All-Big Ten selection.

And let's not forget that he was the leading scorer on a team that also featured Scott May, Kent Benson, Quinn Buckner, Tom Abernethy, Bobby Wilkerson and John Laskowski.

It's clearly an impressive feat. He scored in double figures in 24 of 28 games that season.

His senior year, he averaged 16.6 points per game and helped his team to a perfect 18-0 Big Ten season. IU's average margin of victory in conference play that year was 22.8 points per game.

For his Indiana career, Green scored 1,265 points, a 14.5 points per game average. He had a career field goal percentage of 53.8 percent.

Green was also a two-time Academic All-American at Indiana in both 1974 and '75.

Green attended Silver Creek High School in Sellersburg, Indiana where he played for his father, Ray. He scored 1,404 points in his high school career and played on teams that finished 58-14. His IU teams went 76-12.

After college, he was drafted by both the Chicago Bulls in the NBA and the Utah Stars in the ABA. He played with both Utah and St. Louis in the ABA his first season and then three years with the Indiana Pacers. He also played one season overseas in Italy.

After playing professional basketball, Green returned to IU to enter dental school and has been practicing dentistry in Central Indiana since 1984.

Green was inducted into the Indiana Basketball Hall of Fame in 1999 and into the Indiana University Athletics Hall of Fame in 2010.

23. Eric Gordon

Eric Gordon is one of two Indiana players to make the top 25 list that did so having only played one season of college basketball.

To say he left his mark in IU history would be a huge understatement.

He came to IU from North Central High School in Indianapolis where he was the state's Mr. Basketball and led his team to the state championship game. He was a McDonald's All-American and the No. 2 rated high school prospect his senior year behind Michael Beasley.

Eric Gordon (Photo courtesy of IU Athletics)

Gordon's freshman numbers at Indiana were staggering. He scored 669 points for a 20.9 scoring average. That was good enough to set both an Indiana and Big Ten scoring record for points by a freshman.

He was a first-team All-American by more than one publication and a third team Associated Press All-American.

With his 20.9 scoring average, Gordon became the first freshman in IU history to average more than 20 points. He led the Big Ten in scoring and was both a first team All-Big Ten selection and the Big Ten freshman of the year.

He hit 231 free throws in 32 games, the third highest total of made free throws in school history.

In his first college game against Chattanooga, he scored 33 points which was the highest scoring debut of any player in Indiana history.

He made himself available immediately after his freshman year for the NBA Draft and was the seventh player selected overall by the Los Angeles Clippers. To date, he has played three seasons with the Clippers and the last three seasons with the New Orleans Pelicans.

His brother Evan Gordon, played in the 2013-14 season for Indiana as a fifth year senior transfer from Arizona State.

22. Branch McCracken

Branch McCracken
(Indiana University
Archives — P0021435)

Most people remember Branch McCracken for his accomplishments as Indiana's coach.

In 24 seasons as the IU coach, McCracken had a 364-174 record including 210-116 in conference. Two of the five national championship banners that hang in Assembly Hall belong to McCracken. He also won four Big Ten titles.

But McCracken was a pretty fair player, too.

McCracken came to IU from Monrovia (Indiana) High School.

A 6-foot-4 center, McCracken wasted little time making an impact at IU.

His first season, in the 1927-28 campaign, McCracken scored 24 points in the first game of his career. That was the most points ever scored by an Indiana player in a game and would not be broken for 10 seasons. In fact, McCracken outscored his opponent, Chicago, that day by himself, 24-13. IU won the game, 32-13.

McCracken averaged 10.1 points in 17 games that season and helped lead IU to a share of the Big Ten title.

As a sophomore he averaged 8.9 points. His junior season, he averaged 12.1 points per game and scored 146 points in conference play which was a Big Ten record.

McCracken earned All-American honors in 1930.

He finished his IU career as both the leading career scorer in Indiana and Big Ten history.

After college, McCracken had a short stint as a professional player but then coached eight seasons at Ball State before succeeding Everett Dean as IU's coach.

He was inducted into the Indiana Basketball Hall of Fame in 1963 and was part of the first six-man class enshrined into the Indiana University Athletics Hall of Fame in 1982.

21. Brian Evans

Brian Evans had a solid Indiana University career that culminated his senior season when he was selected as a third team All-American and the Big Ten's most valuable player.

Evans came to IU from Terre Haute South where he helped lead his team to the 1991 high school Final Four in the Hoosier Dome in Indianapolis. He was an Indiana All-Star following his senior year in both basketball and baseball. He was 7-0 as a pitcher for his high school baseball team his senior year.

Brian Evans (Indiana University Archives – P0020217)

At Indiana, his statistics simply got a little bit better every season. As a freshman, he started four of 35 games on a star-studded team that included Calbert Cheaney, Greg Graham, Alan Henderson and Damon Bailey. He still averaged 5.3 points per game on a team that went 17-1 in Big Ten play.

His sophomore season Evans started 24 of 27 games and averaged in double figures with 11.9 points per game. He also averaged 6.8 rebounds. In the NCAA Tournament that year, he averaged 14 points and nine rebounds per game.

As a junior, Evans started 30 games and averaged 17.4 points and 6.7 rebounds. He was a third-team All-Big Ten selection that season.

His senior season was his best. He averaged 21.2 points per game and 7.1 rebounds in 31 starts. He was first team all-Big Ten, third team All-American and won the Big Ten MVP award.

He became the first Indiana player to win the Big Ten's scoring title under Bob Knight and the first Hoosier to win it since George McGinnis in 1971.

His Big Ten scoring average that season was 22.2 points.

His career totals rank him in the top all-time in scoring with 1,701 points, a 13.7 career scoring average. He also averaged 5.9 rebounds per game for his career.

His high scoring game of his career was 37 points against Chaminade his junior season.

Evans was selected by Orlando in the first round of the 1996 NBA Draft. He played sparingly in his rookie season because of a shoulder injury and later played briefly with both New Jersey and Minnesota. He scored 375 career points. He also played professionally in Italy and Japan from 1999-2005.

20. Everett Dean

Everett Dean (Indiana University Archives — P0044208)

A 6-foot center from Salem, Indiana, Dean will forever hold the distinction of being Indiana's first All-American.

He accomplished the feat in 1921 when he averaged 10.7 points per game in helping lead his team to a 15-6 record. He scored 21 points against Ohio State that season, become the first IU player in 10 years to eclipse the 20-point barrier in the one game. In his three-year Indiana career the Hoosiers had a record of 38-21.

Seven times in Dean's Indiana career he scored more points than the opposing team combined.

The first time came in the season opener his junior season when Dean scored 16 points to lead the Hoosiers to a 32-10 victory over the North American Gymnastics Union (a team from Indianapolis). Two games later, he scored 18 points in a 24-15 victory over Valparaiso.

In the Big Ten opener that season, Dean scored 12 points in a 22-11 victory over Ohio State. Dean accomplished the feat again against Northwestern when he scored 14 points in a 32-11 victory.

Academics were also big for Dean. As a senior, he won the Big Ten medal of honor for academic and athletic excellence.

But Dean was more than just an excellent Indiana player. He also spent 14 seasons as IU's head basketball coach beginning with the 1924-25 season. His coaching record was 162-93 including a share of three Big Ten championships. His conference mark was 96-72. He coached future IU All-Americans Jim Strickland, Branch McCracken, Vern Huffman, Ken Gunning, Ernie Andres and Marv Huffman. And his former player, McCracken, turned out to be the man who would replace him as IU's head coach.

Along with coaching basketball at IU, Dean also coached baseball. Along with winning three Big Ten basketball titles in his career, he also guided the Hoosiers to three Big Ten baseball championships, too.

After leaving IU in 1938, Dean moved on to Stanford where he coached basketball from 1938-55. While at Stanford, his 1942 team won the national championship in basketball.

19. Jared Jeffries

The majority of the top 25 players in Indiana basketball history from the state of Indiana are from the Branch McCracken or Bob Knight eras of IU hoops.

There are three players on the list from 2000 and beyond. Eric Gordon and Cody Zeller were two of them.

One of the most decorated though, was Bloomington's own Jared Jeffries.

Jeffries, the Indiana Mr. Basketball from Bloomington North, played in the first two seasons after Bob Knight left the Indiana program. He made a quick impact on the program and then de-

Jared Jeffries (Photo by Michael Dickbernd/IU Athletics)

parted for the NBA Draft where he was the 11th player selected overall by the Washington Wizards.

As an Indiana freshman in the 2000-01 season, Mike Davis's interim season as the IU coach, Jeffries averaged 13.9 points and 6.9 rebounds. He was named the Big Ten freshman of the year.

His sophomore season, when he was a consensus second team All-American, Jeffries averaged 15.0 points and 7.6 rebounds and helped lead the Hoosiers to the 2002 national championship game against Maryland. Jeffries did score a bucket early in the second half that gave IU a 44-42 lead over the Terrapins but Maryland took control from there and won the title, 64-52.

As a sophomore, Jeffries was a finalist for the 2002 Naismith Award and the United States Basketball Writers Association's player of the year award. He was the only player in the Big Ten to rank among the top 10 in six different statistical categories: scoring, rebounding, steals, blocked shots, offensive rebounds and defensive rebounds.

He became the first Indiana player since A.J. Guyton to win the Big Ten player of the year honor.

Despite only playing two years in Bloomington, Jeffries is a member of the 1,000-point scoring club. He finished with 1,008 points and a career average of 14.4 points. He also averaged 6.7 rebounds for his career.

After Indiana, Jeffries played 11 seasons in the NBA with four teams. He played four seasons in Washington, parts of six seasons in New York with the Knicks, parts of two seasons with Houston and one season in Portland. He finished his career with 3,003 career points and 2,563 rebounds.

In the fall of 2013, Jeffries was hired by the Denver Nuggets for a front office position in scouting.

18. Cody Zeller

Cody Zeller was a program changing recruit when he decided to play his college basketball at Indiana. He chose Tom Crean's program over North Carolina and Butler.

Zeller earned All-American honors in both of his seasons at Indiana. Despite playing just two years, Zeller scored 1,157 points for a 16.1 career scoring average. He also averaged 7.3 rebounds for his career. He holds IU's record for career field goal percentage at 59.1 percent.

Cody Zeller (Photo by Michael Dickbernd/IU Athletics)

Zeller came to Indiana from Washington High School where he helped lead the Hatchets to three Indiana state basketball titles. He was a key contributor in both his junior and senior seasons in particular. As a junior he averaged 20.5 points and 11.4 rebounds. His senior season he earned Indiana Mr. Basketball honors when he averaged 24.6 points and 13.1 rebounds per game.

He is one of three brothers (Luke and Tyler were the others) to capture the Mr. Basketball honor in high school. Luke went on to play at Notre Dame and Tyler at North Carolina.

He was a 2011 McDonald's All-American.

As a freshman at Indiana, Zeller averaged 15.6 points and 6.6 rebounds. He was the 2012 Big Ten freshman of the year and a consensus freshman All-American. He shot 62.3 percent from the field.

His sophomore season, Zeller averaged 16.5 points and 8.1 rebounds and won the Big Ten title outright. IU was a No. 1 seed in the NCAA Tournament. The Hoosiers advanced to the Sweet Sixteen in both of Zeller's seasons at IU but never got beyond that point.

Zeller was also an Academic All-American at Indiana.

In Zeller's sophomore season, Indiana closed the regular season with a game at No. 7 Michigan, needing a win to capture the Big Ten title outright. Michigan led by five with under a minute to play but IU scored the final six points to win. Zeller had a layup with 13 seconds remaining to put IU ahead 72-71. On the other end, he altered a shot by Trey Burke in the final seconds. Zeller finished with 25 points.

After his Indiana career came to an end, Zeller was the fourth player selected in the 2013 NBA Draft by the Charlotte Bobcats.

17. Bill Garrett

Bill Garrett (Indiana University Archives – P0023606)

Bill Garrett has the distinction of being the first African-American player to ever play at Indiana.

But by the time he left IU, he was known for so much more. Garrett came to the Hoosiers after capturing Mr. Basketball honors in 1947 and leading Shelbyville High School to the state championship his senior season.

At Indiana, he led the Hoosiers in scoring and rebounding all three of his years of college basketball. Not only was he the first African-American to play basketball at IU but he was the first one to start regularly on a Big Ten team.

When he graduated in 1951, his 792 career points were No. 1 in IU history. He had a career average of 12 points per game and in the 1950-51 season, Garrett averaged 13.1 points and was tabbed an All-American.

The 6-foot-3 center was drafted by the Boston Celtics in the second round of the NBA Draft becoming just the third black player to drafted in the NBA.

He spent two years in the military before returning to play basketball. He played with the Harlem Globetrotters and later was a high school head basketball coach at Crispus Attucks High School.

He was assistant dean for student services at IUPUI in Indianapolis when he died of a heart attack at age 45 in 1974.

That same year he was inducted into the Indiana Basketball Hall of Fame. He was inducted into the Indiana University Athletics Hall of Fame in 1984.

15 (tie). Tom Van Arsdale

Tom and Dick Van Arsdale can never be separated when doing all-time lists of Indiana basketball players. Besides being twins, the two players' statistics at Indiana over three seasons were so close it is difficult to tell them apart.

They played 72 career games at Indiana and yet finished up 12 points apart in scoring and four rebounds apart.

Branch McCracken once said that getting the Van Arsdale's to come to Indiana was "my greatest recruiting achievement."

Like his brother Dick, Tom Van Arsdale was an All-American as a senior in 1965.

Tom Van Arsdale (Indiana University Archives – P0020312)

As a freshman in 1963, Tom Van Arsdale averaged 12.5 points and 9.3 rebounds per game. His junior year was his highest scoring campaign when he averaged 21.3 points and 12.3 rebounds. As a senior, the averages were 18.4 points and 8.5 rebounds.

His career totals were 1,252 points, a 17.4 points per game average. He also averaged 10.0 rebounds for his career. That was 12 points and four rebounds more than his brother.

He scored his career-high of 34 points including 20 in the second half in a 108-102 victory over Notre Dame as a junior. Interestingly, his brother Dick also had a career high for scoring in that game. Dick Van Arsdale had 42 points including 25 in the second half.

Against Missouri his junior season, Tom Van Arsdale had 26 points and 17 rebounds. He had a 21-point and 15-rebound game against DePaul that season. In a Big Ten win against Illinois, he had 27 points and 13 rebounds.

Tom was a co-Indiana Mr. Basketball with his brother Dick at Emmerich Manual High School in Indianapolis in 1961. The pair won two sectional titles along with a regional and a semistate in

1961. He was inducted into the Indiana Basketball Hall of Fame in 1988.

Tom played 12 seasons in the NBA with Detroit, Cincinnati, Kansas City, Philadelphia, Atlanta and Phoenix. He retired in 1977 after scoring 14,232 career points and pulling down 3,942 rebounds.

15 (tie). Dick Van Arsdale

Dick Van Arsdale (Indiana University Archives – P0021963)

Dick Van Arsdale's Indiana career mirrored that of his brother in most every way.

They were co-Indiana Mr. Basketball's in 1961, had nearly identical IU basketball careers and were both All-Americans as seniors in 1965.

As was mentioned in the segment on brother Tom, they both even had their career scoring highs in the same game against Notre Dame their junior seasons. Dick had 42 points and Tom had 34 in a 108-102 victory.

They both had the distinction of also playing on Branch McCracken's final three teams at Indiana.

When they were eligible to play on the varsity as 6-5 sophomores in 1963, the Van Arsdales were on a team with a pair of highly-touted seniors in Tom Bolyard and Jimmy Rayl. While Rayl and Bolyard were the stars and both averaged better than 20 points per game, both Dick and Tom Van Arsdale each averaged better than 12 points per game and were solid contributors.

In a January win over Purdue in West Lafayette, Dick Van Arsdale scored 10 points and pulled down 20 rebounds. His career high for rebounds was 26 against Missouri in 1964.

As a freshman, Dick averaged 12.2 points and 8.9 rebounds. His sophomore season, like his brother, was his best when he averaged 22.3 points and 12.4 rebounds. As a senior, he averaged 17.2 points and 8.7 rebounds.

His career totals were 1,240 points, a 17.2 average. He also, like his brother, averaged 10.0 rebounds for his career.

Dick's high school accomplishments were the same as his brother coming out of Emmerich Manual High School in Indianapolis. Both players shared Mr. Basketball and the Trester Award their senior seasons.

Both players were inducted into the Indiana High School Basketball Hall of Fame as well as the Indiana University Athletics Hall of Fame. Dick was also a two-time Academic All-American, while Tom earned the same distinction as a senior.

Like his brother Tom, Dick played 12 NBA seasons and also like his brother was a three-time NBA All-Star.

Dick was drafted by the New York Knicks in the second round of the NBA Draft and played in New York from 1965-68. He finished his career in Phoenix from 1968-77. His No. 5 jersey was retired by the Phoenix Suns.

He scored 15,079 points for a career average of 16.4 points per game. He also had 3,807 rebounds and 3,057 assists.

14. Ted Kitchel

Think of Ted Kitchel and you think of a winner.

In his Indiana basketball career, the Hoosiers went 90-33, won an NCAA championship and three Big Ten titles. If you add in his redshirt year of 1978-79, Kitchel also has an NIT title to his credit.

Kitchel started 27 games as a sophomore on the 1981 national championship team and was the team's fifth leading scorer with a 9.2 average.

His junior season, Kitchel led the Hoosiers in scoring with a 19.6 points per game average and he was the second leading scorer in '83 at 17.3 points per game before suffer-

Ted Kitchel (Indiana University Archives – P0021297)

ing a late season back injury that cost him the season.

He earned All-American honors twice at Indiana in both '82 and '83. He finished his career with 1,336 points while shooting 49.6 percent from the field. As a junior, he made 53 percent of his shots and as a senior hit 51.1 percent.

In the '81 national championship season, Kitchel had a memorable game against Illinois in the second game of the Big Ten season. Kitchel scored a career-best 40 points and nearly did so without missing a shot from the field or the free throw line. Kitchel hit 11-of-13 shots from the field and set a school record when he hit all 18 of his free throws. The 40-point performance is one of 20 40-point efforts all time in Indiana basketball history.

In high school, Kitchel was a three-year starter at Lewis Cass High School in Walton, Ind. He was a three-time all-conference selection, two-time All-State and a 1978 Indiana All-Star. As a senior his team went 20-0 in the regular season and won the first sectional title in the school's history.

He was inducted into the Indiana Basketball Hall of Fame in 2009 and into the Indiana University Athletics Hall of Fame in 1996.

He was a second round pick of the Milwaukee Bucks and later played professionally in Italy.

13. Damon Bailey

Damon Bailey (Indiana University Archives – P0020611)

There are few players any more synonymous with a program than Damon Bailey is with Indiana University basketball.

Does he belong in the top 10? You could make that argument. In the 10 lists received to narrow the top 10 of all time, Bailey was a top 10 player twice. Most of the experts had him in the 11-15 range.

Bailey became a cult figure in Indiana basketball lore when Bob Knight recruited him as an eighth grader. He was featured in *Sports Illustrated* before he entered high school as the top ninth grader in the country. He led teams to three national AAU championships and led his high school team, Bedford North Lawrence, to the state's Final Four in three out of four seasons.

As a senior, a national record crowd of 41,046 at the Hoosier Dome watched Bailey and his Bedford North Lawrence teammates beat Concord for the state title.

He was named *USA Today*'s High School player of the decade.

At Indiana, Bailey had a solid career that wrapped up with an All-American season in 1994. For his four-year career, Bailey averaged 13.2 points per game. As a senior, he averaged 19.6 points.

His yearly averages were 11.4 as a freshman, 12.4 as a sophomore, 10.1 as a junior and 19.6 as a senior.

He played in 132 games with 95 starts and amassed 1,741 career points. That ranks seventh all-time in IU history, one point ahead of Kent Benson.

He had a high-scoring game of 36 points at Kansas in December of 1993.

He was a second round pick of the Indiana Pacers in the 1994 NBA Draft.

Heading into the 2014-15 season, Bailey is an assistant women's basketball coach at Butler.

12. Jay Edwards

Jay Edwards scored 1,038 points in his Indiana career.

With 46 players in school history over 1,000 points, why is that particularly significant? Edwards accomplished the feat in two seasons.

He averaged 15.6 points, scoring 358 points as a freshman and then averaged an even 20 points per game with 680 points as a sophomore. He eventually gave up his final two years of eligibility to enter the NBA Draft. He was a second-round pick of the Los Angeles Clippers.

Jay Edwards (Indiana University Archives – P0020200)

As a freshman, Edwards was the Big Ten Freshman of the Year. He shot 53.6 percent from beyond the 3-point line that season on 59-of-110 attempts. That percentage is still the third highest in IU history. He made 57.1 percent from beyond the arc in Big Ten games his freshman year which still ranks second in IU history in that department.

His career 3-point field goal percentage is 48.1 percent which is second all time behind Steve Alford at 53.0. But Alford's total was just in one season.

He made eight 3-pointers against Minnesota on Feb. 4, 1988. In doing so, he hit 8-of-9 from beyond the arc for the game. Five times in his career, he made six 3-point field goals.

In his sophomore season he had 20 games in a row with at least one 3-point field goal. That ranks second in IU history behind A.J. Guyton (33).

As a sophomore, he was an All-American, all-Big Ten first team and the Big Ten player of the year as voted on by the media. He helped lead the Hoosiers to a 15-3 record and a Big Ten championship.

Edwards had his share of famous last second shots in IU lore.

He had three last second shots his sophomore season alone, two that won games for the Hoosiers. The other was followed by a heart-breaking moment from Illinois.

In the first one, with the score tied at 62 against Purdue and the clock winding down, Edwards drove the ball to the left side, stepped back and hit a game-winning 16-foot jumper to give the Hoosiers a 64-62 win.

But that was just the set up for what would be his most memorable game-winner. The next game, with No. 13 Michigan in Assembly Hall, Edwards and the Hoosiers trailed 75-73 with 8 seconds to play when Glen Rice missed a bank shot from the wing. Eric Anderson grabbed the rebound, got it to Lyndon Jones who tossed the ball to Edwards at the top of the key. He let it fly and the buzzer sounded with the ball in the air. It hit nothing but net to give IU a 76-75 victory.

Edwards had another miraculous shot his sophomore season, this one against Illinois. IU trailed 67-65 when Edwards faked a drive to the basket and then falling out of bounds hit a shot that just cleared the corner of the backboard and went through the net to tie it at 67. Illinois called a timeout and 2 seconds were put back on the clock. Nick Anderson then caught a length of the court baseball pass and turned to put up a 35-foot shot at the buzzer that went in and gave the Illini a 70-67 win.

11. Steve Downing

Entering the 2014-15 season, Steve Downing still held a special place in Indiana basketball history.

As difficult as it may be to believe, Downing was the only player in IU history to ever record a triple-double. Twenty-two All-Americans have come and gone since Downing accomplished the feat on Feb. 23, 1971 in a home game against Michigan.

Downing had 28 points, 17 rebounds and 10 blocked shots. And he didn't even lead IU in scoring in the game. George McGinnis held high-point honors with 33.

Steve Downing (Indiana University Archives – P0020193)

As a senior, Downing became the first All-American under Bob Knight when he averaged 20.1 points and 10.6 rebounds per game, leading IU to a Big Ten championship.

He averaged 24 points per game in IU's final eight conference games. He led the Hoosiers to the Final Four where they dropped a 70-59 loss to UCLA. Downing was named all-Final Four, Big Ten MVP and All-American.

He was later selected in the first round by the Boston Celtics and would win an NBA championship with the Celtics in 1974.

While the triple double is memorable because it's the only one in IU history, Downing had another game that really stood out in his career.

In a game against Kentucky on December 11, 1971, Downing poured in 47 points and pulled down 25 rebounds. The 47 points is tied for the fourth highest individual game scoring total in IU history and the 25 rebounds in one game is tied for the seventh highest single game total.

In February of his senior season, Downing also scored 41 in a game against Illinois. He is one of only four players in Indiana history to have two games where he scored 40 points or more in a game. The other three are Don Schlundt, George McGinnis and Jimmy Rayl.

As for rebounds, along with his 25 against Kentucky, Downing also had 26 rebounds against Ball State in 1971. He had six games in his career where he had 20 rebounds or more. That's more than any other player in IU history.

Downing was a three-year starter at Washington High School in Indianapolis and along with teammate George McGinnis played on the 1969 undefeated Washington team coached by Bill Green that won the state championship. He averaged 20 points per game his senior season.

Downing was an Indiana All-Star and was inducted into the Indiana Basketball Hall of Fame in 1996. In 2009, he was inducted along with coach Bob Knight into the Indiana University Athletics Hall of Fame.

Downing worked as an associate athletic director in the IU athletic department and later had a similar role at Texas Tech while Bob Knight was the head coach of the Red Raiders. As of the publishing of this book, Downing is the athletic director at Marian University in Indianapolis.

5

Number 10
Bobby Leonard

Bobby 'Slick' Leonard is a living legend in the state of Indiana.

He played high school basketball in Terre Haute at Gerstmeyer High School, graduating in 1950. He was an alternate on the Indiana All-Star team.

He played college basketball at Indiana University where he was a starter on the 1953 national championship team. He was a two-time All-American for the Hoosiers.

After playing seven years in professional basketball, he became the head coach of the Indiana Pacers. He was the

Bobby Leonard (Indiana University Archives – P0021348)

Pacers head coach for 12 seasons and helped lead Indiana to three ABA Championships. He then coached the team for four years in the NBA.

He returned to the Pacers in 1985 as a television commentator and later became the radio color man for Mark Boyle on Pacers radio broadcasts, a position he still holds.

Slick is best known as the man who coined the phrase "Boom Baby!" for a successful 3-point shot and got used to saying it

59

regularly when Reggie Miller was hitting long range shots for Indiana.

He was inducted into the Indiana Athletics Hall of Fame in the first class in 1982 along with Walt Bellamy, Everett Dean, Vern Huffman, his coach Branch McCracken and teammate, Don Schlundt.

That same year, he was inducted into the Indiana High School Basketball Hall of Fame.

He was also named to Indiana's All-Century team in 2000.

In 2014, he was inducted into the Naismith Memorial Basketball Hall of Fame.

The Naismith award was the crown jewel. He said in the interview for this book that it was hard to put into words what it means.

"At this stage in my life, I've had tons of honors but this one kind of caps it off," Leonard said. "It is a special thing for our family. It is a legacy to Nancy and the kids, the grandkids, the great grandchildren. That's what it is. I can't say any more than that really."

● ● ● ●

When many people think of Leonard, they think of the colorful coach of the Pacers who roamed the sidelines and was well known for his in-game antics.

Another generation of Pacers fans know him more as a broadcaster.

But Bobby Leonard was a terrific player in his own right.

IU historian Bill Murphy, who wrote the book *Branch* about Leonard's college coach, Branch McCracken, said Leonard was clearly a leader when he played for the Hoosiers.

"He was the conductor to the symphony of IU basketball in the '53 and '54 seasons," Murphy said. "He ran the show. He really did. He was an extremely good ball handler as good as anybody I've ever seen. It seemed like he made the right judgment on passing the ball and passing it to the right person on every time down the court. It just seemed like he knew who to get the ball to and where to deliver the ball to them every time."

Murphy said the other thing that stands out about Leonard as a player was his clutch abilities.

"When you needed a basket, when you needed a shot under extreme pressure situations, Bob Leonard was the guy you wanted to take that shot," Murphy said.

Dr. Marvin Christie, who played for Indiana in 1950 and had a chance to watch Leonard play when he was at IU, remembered Leonard for his clutch abilities, too.

"He was the best player on the team when there was pressure," Christie said. "When the game was on the line you wanted Leonard to have the ball."

Jim Enright, who was enshrined in the Naismith Memorial Basketball Hall of Fame as an official and later resumed his career as a sportswriter, once wrote this about Slick Leonard.

"That fellow Leonard is to basketball what Robin Roberts is to baseball, Ben Hogan to golf and Eddie Arcaro to horse racing," said Enright who wrote for *The Sporting News* and the *Chicago Evening American*. "Pound for pound, dribble for dribble, pass for pass and shot for shot, Bob is without question the game's greatest individual player in my book."

George McGinnis, an Indiana University basketball legend who played for Leonard in the ABA, said he went back and watched film of Leonard as a college player and it surprised him.

"I didn't realize he was that good of a college player," McGinnis said. "He was really, really good. He was tenacious and a good defender. My memories of him are more of as my coach but when I went back and did a little research on Slick I was surprised at just how good of a player he really was."

Filmmaker Ted Green, who was also a former assistant sports editor with the *Indianapolis Star*, debuted a documentary on Bobby Leonard in the summer of 2014. The debut was in Bankers Life Fieldhouse and attended by former teammates and opponents, family and friends of Leonard. Even five members of Branch McCracken's extended family were on hand.

In the documentary entitled *Bobby 'Slick' Leonard: Heart of a Hoosier*, Green has footage of Leonard all the way back to his high school days. Green admitted that going into the project he was familiar with Leonard as a coach and a broadcaster but not so much as a player.

"We really dug into it and we ended up digitalizing old footage that hadn't been seen in fifty or sixty years," Green said. "What I saw was that Bob was the guy that made that team go. That was no question about that. He ran the show offensively and he was the top defensive player. He was just the spark out there. Every key play went through him."

Green talked to several of Leonard's former teammates from that time period and they all told him the same thing. They said that Don Schlundt was the big scorer for the Hoosiers but it was clearly Leonard's team.

"I had heard those things but when I saw them for myself I was completely convinced," Green said. "I thought he actually got shorted a little bit on how good he was just based on the statistics."

Christie, who saw Leonard play, remembered him as a good all-around player.

"He was a hell of a player," Christie recalled. "He was a great outside shooter. He was called 'Mr. Outside' and Don Schlundt was called 'Mr. Inside.' They were a really good one-two combination back then."

Bobby Leonard (Indiana University Archives – P0043439)

Bill Murphy said that Leonard was moved to the guard position at the beginning of the 1953 season and the nicknames quickly stuck for both players.

"Bob Leonard had a really good two-handed set shot that he could hit from all over the court," Murphy said. "He was a really good outside shooter. And it wasn't long before everyone simply thought of him as Mr. Outside."

Ted Green said it was clear from his research that Leonard was 'The Man.'

"He didn't make every shot in clutch situations but almost every time he had the ball to take the big shots," Green said.

And Christie said Leonard was a great defender as well.

"I think sometimes people forget that Bobby was a great defender as well," Christie said. "Mac would put Leonard on the other team's best guard or forward. It didn't make a difference. He would shut them down."

Jim Schooley was one year ahead of Leonard in school and was a 6-5 senior center on the '53 national championship team. When I asked him about Leonard, the first words out of his mouth were that Slick was "one of a kind."

"He was very cool, very self-assured, a good shooter, a good player, he just had a very good floor sense," Schooley said. "I was sitting on the bench a lot with that team because I wasn't very good. I remember one time I was sitting on the bench. We were playing Minnesota and the score was tied with about a minute to go.

"Leonard was right in front of the bench so we could hear him and the guy was guarding him pretty close. And Leonard looked right at him and said 'You can kiss this ballgame goodbye.' And then he threw in a shot which won the game. But that was vintage Bobby Leonard right there."

Ted Green, the filmmaker of the documentary on Slick's career, said Leonard was not afraid to talk the talk.

"He definitely talked some trash, a lot like his good friend Larry Bird would later," Green said. "But he backed it up."

Green said the other thing that really impressed him about Leonard was his range.

"You really had to see his range to believe it," Green said. "I had heard he took some long shots but I had no idea just how long we were talking about."

Green gave an example of the LSU game in the national semifinals in 1953. He said Leonard made his first six shots in the game.

"Well if you look at the film, at least five and maybe all six of those shots, would have been not just college 3-pointers, they would have been NBA 3-pointers," Green said. "And he missed some long ones, too. But it was never a case where

McCracken was looking to give him a quick hook in a game. Branch rode with Bob and Bob was very confident in his abilities."

Danny Bridges, an avid Indiana fan who was one of the 10 people who gave me lists for this book, said he didn't realize how good of a player Leonard was until he attended the premier of the documentary on Leonard that night at Bankers Life Fieldhouse.

"They had some 8-milimeter high school film of him from Terre Haute and Slick was a stud," Bridges said. "The guy was a hell of a player. I saw Don Fischer as I walked out of there and I said to him 'I didn't realize that guy was that good,' and Fish said, 'Oh yeah.'"

Bridges was impressed with Leonard as a guard. He just didn't ever think of Leonard in that light.

"He was a pretty damn good ball handler and he had pretty good quickness," Bridges said. "The guy could get up and down the floor and he could handle the ball. There was a game where they showed Slick hitting a 40-foot set shot. That was Jimmy Rayl country out there. "

Jim Schooley also recalled that IU coach Branch McCracken once described Leonard as having ice water in his veins.

That story came about in the '53 national championship game against Kansas with the score tied at 68 with 27 seconds to play. Leonard was fouled and got two free throws. He missed the first, but made the second to put IU up 69-68. IU then pressured Kansas all over the floor and the Jayhawks missed a desperation shot at the end as the Hoosiers captured the national title.

In Bill Murphy's book, *Branch*, he retells a story about reporters talking to McCracken in a postgame interview. McCracken said Leonard had ice water in his veins on that final free throw.

Leonard just smiled and said, "If that was ice water, it sure felt warm running down my leg."

•••

Those who knew Leonard back in the day all talk about the fact that Leonard was a local legend, even in college, both on and off the court.

Jim Schooley said that as the lone senior on the '53 national championship team he felt like he needed to try to keep Leonard in check.

"He was a little bit of a problem off the court," Schooley said. "He swung a little wider than most of us did and I was always on his ass about that. The only goods I had on those guys was that I was a year older and I was a good student and Mac (Branch McCracken) kind of looked at me to be a mentor of sorts."

Schooley said Leonard loved to play cards, he liked to drink and he liked to get out and have some fun.

"It never seemed to affect his play and that's all that we really cared about," Schooley said. "As long as he could maintain a good balance then nobody was really going to say much about his extracurricular activities."

Bill Murphy, the IU basketball historian, told a story about an infamous poker game that Leonard was a part of during his playing days at IU.

When Leonard arrived at Indiana, Branch McCracken got him a job as a stone cutter to give him a chance to earn some extra money. He worked there for a while and at one point some of the older workers asked Leonard if he knew how to play poker. He told them had never played poker before in his life and so they invited him to play, figuring they had an easy mark.

They played for a while and Leonard was losing money. Then all of a sudden there was a raid on the poker game by the Bloomington police.

"And as all of these older men were running out of there, Bobby was raking all the money in and stuffing it in his pockets," Murphy said.

Apparently though, Leonard was able to slip out a back door and not get noticed.

The next day in the newspaper, there was a story about the raid and it listed every one that had played in the game – except Leonard.

But the one thing you learn about Branch McCracken is that the IU coach had spies all over town. His former players say he was a master of social media long before it became an official form of communication.

And of course, McCracken found out that Leonard had been at the game.

The next day, he called Leonard to his office and told him to close the door. McCracken proceeded to embark on one of his meetings aimed to straighten one of his players out. Leonard later said that McCracken ripped him up one side and down the other and told him it had better never happen again.

Once inside, Leonard, in the book *Branch* by Bill Murphy, tells the story of what happened next.

"He called me in his office and he told me 'When we get through, if I ever have to call you in again, I'll lock the door and only one of us will come out.'" Leonard said.

Leonard promised his coach he would change, but before he left, Leonard said he "stopped at the door and said, 'I guess I know which one of us will come out' and then I ran down the hall."

Those who know Leonard and hear that story have no problem believing it to be true.

"That's just the character that Bobby Leonard was when he was in Bloomington," Murphy said. "It seems everyone has a story about something Bobby did off the court."

There was another story involving Leonard and Jim Schooley where there was trouble again. Leonard had the bad boy image and Schooley was the guy who never got into any trouble.

The team was on a road trip to Minnesota and had gone out for a nice meal the night before the game.

"They ate at a really nice restaurant because Branch always made sure they got a good meal on the road," Murphy said. "The next morning when they came down with their bags packed and they were ready to leave, Branch said 'Boys, line up and put your bags right in front of you.' It was just like the army. Everybody was in line and their bags were in front of them for inspection."

It turns out that McCracken had learned from the restaurant manager that the night before there had been some pearl-handled steak knives stolen from the restaurant.

So McCracken did an inspection with every player. He would open their bag and go through it looking for the knives that were missing. He got to Leonard's bag and he was certain that's where he would find the knives but when he opened the bag they weren't there. Leonard later said that McCracken was shocked that this was the case.

A couple of players later, McCracken opened the bag of Jim Schooley.

"Branch was always saying, 'Boys, why can't you be more like Jim Schooley. He's a straight A student, he goes to church, why can't you all be like him,'" Murphy recalled.

Yet when McCracken opened up Schooley's bag there were the steak knives.

"And Leonard told me, 'We never heard about how we should all be like Schooley again,'" Murphy said.

Schooley, when interviewed for this book, said it was a low moment in his IU basketball career.

"I was a wide-eyed kid from a small Indiana town and I just had a weak moment," Schooley said. "I actually put one knife in my pocket and asked Don Schlundt to put the other in his pocket. But that one was all on me."

George McGinnis, who played for Leonard in the ABA, said he heard that his former coach was quite the carouser when in college. When McGinnis saw Leonard's college picture from the '53 national championship team, he said he got all the evidence he needed.

"And after watching the old tapes I told Slick, 'Man, I've never seen anyone with a bigger Adam's apple than that,'" McGinnis said. "If you've ever seen that '53 picture of him you know what I mean. I told him, 'That was a crazy Adam's

Apple. That was from all that beer you were drinking down there.'"

•••

Bobby Leonard's first season at Indiana was 1952 when he was a sophomore. Had he arrived at IU one year later than he did he could have played right away as a freshman. For freshmen in 1952, players were permitted to take advantage of the Korean War waiver which allowed freshmen to play right away because the military draft had drained the number of young men on college campuses.

While Don Schundt was able to take advantage of the waiver and play as a freshman, Leonard had to wait until his sophomore season to play.

IU had lost a couple of front line players the year before in Bill Garrett and Bill Tosheff and so at 6-foot-3 Leonard was looked upon to play forward his sophomore year.

His final two seasons he would play guard and form the one-two punch with Schlundt and the inside/outside combo.

"You have to remember that Leonard was 6-foot-3 and in 1952, a 6-foot-3 player could easily play a forward position," Bill Murphy said. "You had Bill Garrett the year before who had played the center position at 6-foot-3. That was not a stretch at all for Leonard to play the forward position."

Leonard's first big scoring game of his college career came against Wyoming in the fourth game of the season. He led IU with 24 points as the Hoosiers rallied to beat Wyoming, 57-55 and improve to 4-0. The next game, Leonard had 18 points in IU's overtime win at Kansas State.

In the Big Ten opener against Michigan, Leonard led IU with 18 points in a 58-46 win over the Wolverines.

Leonard would continue to have double-digit games throughout his sophomore year and finish with a 14.5 per game scoring average in 22 games. The Hoosiers would finish 16-6 overall but just 9-5 in the Big Ten which did not qualify them for postseason play.

The next season, when Leonard would move from the forward to the guard position on a permanent basis, turned out to be a magical year for the Hoosiers.

••••

As Indiana headed into the 1952-53 season, Branch McCracken was in need of some good guards.

Sam Miranda and Bob Masters, IU's starting backcourt from the year before, had graduated. McCracken opted to make Bobby Leonard a full time guard after he had split time between guard and forward the year before.

Burke Scott and Bobby Leonard would form the starting backcourt tandem for the upcoming season.

In the 1953 national championship season, Indiana only played three non-conference games. The Big Ten had opted to go to a complete round robin schedule of 18 conference games.

In the second conference game, Leonard scored a career-high 27 points in a 92-72 win over Iowa in Iowa City.

Indiana picked up another big road win late in the conference season when it knocked off No. 10 Illinois in Champaign. Don Schlundt had 33 points and Leonard chipped in 23. That win gave IU its first outright Big Ten title in school history.

The Hoosiers would finish 17-1 in conference play. IU won its first 16 Big Ten games before losing at Minnesota, 65-63.

Indiana was ranked No. 1 in the nation heading into the NCAA Tournament.

IU's first game of the tournament was a tight 82-80 win over DePaul. Schlundt had 23 points and Leonard had 22 to lead the Hoosiers. Indiana beat Notre Dame 79-66 to advance to the Final Four.

"The regional in Chicago Stadium was the best," Leonard said in the summer of 2014. "Normally, you had to win the conference championship to get into the NCAA Tournament. We had a tough time with DePaul the first night and then the next night we handled Notre Dame convincingly. Don Schlundt scored 41 points that night."

The national semifinal against LSU is when Leonard got hot and hit his first six shots from the field. LSU was sagging in on Don Schlundt and forcing IU to beat them from the perimeter. Leonard was more than happy to oblige. After he hit those shots, LSU went back to a more normal defensive plan and at that point Leonard continually fed the ball inside to

Schlundt. IU won the game 80-67 with Schlundt scoring 29 points and Leonard picking up 22.

In the national championship game against Kansas Leonard had the "ice in his veins" moment when he hit the game-winning free throw with 27 seconds to play. Overall, he was 5-of-15 from the field and scored 12 points. He was one of three players in double figures for the Hoosiers. Schlundt had 30, Charlie Kraak had 17 and Leonard had 12.

In Bill Murphy's book *Branch* about the life of Branch McCracken, Bobby Leonard talked about just how good that Indiana team was in '53.

"It was one of those ball clubs where everybody just fit together like a glove, everybody did," Leonard said. "I think the thing was there was no jealousy, no nothing. We went out with a team concept. I don't think I have ever been with a group of guys in my life that were as close to each other as that ball club.

"That was a great basketball team."

For the season, Leonard would earn his first of two All-American selections with the highest scoring average of his career at 16.3 points.

He also earned all-Final Four honors as well as first team All-Big Ten.

• • • •

Indiana was the favorite to win the national championship in 1954 because basically everyone was back. Jim Schooley was the only player who had graduated and he only averaged 0.8 points per game.

Led by Don Schlundt and Bobby Leonard, the Hoosiers looked primed to repeat as national champs.

Right from the start, the Hoosiers looked in top form. In the opener against Cincinnati, Schlundt and Leonard both scored 20 points in a 78-65 victory. IU had a big non-conference game against Notre Dame and won 66-55. The Irish tried to take Schlundt away and Leonard burned them. Leonard had 21 points to key the IU win.

Indiana went 6-1 in pre-conference play losing only to No. 11 Oregon State in Corvallis, Ore.

In the Big Ten opener, IU beat Michigan State 62-60 on a 25-footer at the buzzer by Leonard. He had 16 points in the game. A few games later, IU went on the road and beat Minnesota 71-63 led by Leonard with 20 points.

Leonard and Schlundt combined for 56 points a few games later in a 90-74 win over Wisconsin. Schlundt had 33 points and Leonard had 23 in the win. That put IU at 5-0 in Big Ten play.

The regular season came down to one game for the title. IU and Illinois were tied with 11-2 records going into the season finale in Bloomington when the Hoosiers hosted the Illini.

Leonard hit several clutch free throws down the stretch and IU prevailed 67-64. It gave Indiana its second consecutive outright Big Ten championship.

Indiana got a tough first round assignment in the NCAA Tournament against a familiar foe. The No. 1 Hoosiers played No. 5 Notre Dame in Iowa City. The Irish again tried to sag in on Don Schlundt and force others to beat them. Leonard had a tough shooting night.

Still, the Hoosiers were right there with a chance to win in the closing seconds, trailing 63-60. In a controversial call, Leonard drove the basket and scored but was called for an offensive foul. The basket counted but the Notre Dame player made two free throws. Leonard came down and scored again but the Irish were able to dribble out the final few seconds and win 65-64 knocking IU from the tournament.

Bobby Leonard still to this day disagrees with that charging call and really believes if IU had won that game it would have gone on to win a second consecutive championship.

"It was a great ball club," Leonard said in the summer of 2014 when interviewed by Justin Albers for this book. "As a matter of fact, we should have won it back-to-back years. We got upset in the regional in 1954. We should have won. We were rated No. 1 the whole year and we won the Big Ten championship.

"We should have won back-to-back championships. That always sticks with me because we knew we were good enough to win it back-to-back. It was a great ball club. Not just the starting five. We had everything covered. All our guys could play, and most of them were Hoosiers."

Ted Green, the filmmaker who did the documentary on Leonard's career, said that Notre Dame game in '54 still lingers with Leonard.

"He still maintains, and I mean maintains, that it was a bad call," Green said. "And having seen a still photo of it I tend to agree with him."

Leonard averaged 15.4 points per game his senior season and once again earned All-American honors for the Hoosiers. He wrapped up his career having scored 1,098 points in 71 career games for a 15.5 career scoring average.

Looking back on his Indiana basketball career, Leonard said he still gets a lot of satisfaction from it.

"The thing that stands out is walking out with two Big Ten championships and a national championship," Leonard said in the interview for this book. "We had a great bunch of guys. Some of them have passed away and I miss them dearly. Branch McCracken was a great coach. It was just a wonderful four years."

Leonard said as is often the case with great teams, it's those teammates he thinks about most when looking back.

"We were a very close-knit group," Leonard said. "We were very close. As a matter of fact, Dick Farley was the best man at my wedding and I was the best man at his. All of the teammates were in the weddings.

"We were a special group, I have to say that. To win championships, you have to be special."

•••

Leonard was a second round selection of Baltimore in the 1954 NBA Draft.

Instead of playing in the NBA, however, he went into the military for two years right out of college. He then played for the Minneapolis Lakers and was with them when they moved to Los Angeles. In fact, he was on the first Los Angeles Lakers team.

"We had Elgin Baylor and Jerry West," Leonard recalled. "We didn't win a world championship. Boston was a powerhouse then. It was really a good career though. It gave me an opportunity to play against the all-time greats."

Leonard played with the Lakers from 1956-61 and then with the Chicago Packers and later Zephyrs from 1961-63. His last season there he was a player-coach.

In seven NBA seasons, he scored 4,204 points for a 9.9 average. He also had 1,217 rebounds and 1,427 assists.

"One year I led the ball club in assists and averaged over 16 points per game," Leonard said. "In today's market, I'd be worth something. But it wasn't that way back then. Look at Gordon Hayward and how he was offered a max contract worth $65 million. His numbers at Utah are almost the same numbers I had back in Chicago. He made $65 million and I made 65 cents."

••••

Leonard still lives in Carmel, Indiana, with his wife Nancy. The couple have five children and seven grandchildren.

He and Nancy met in a health class at IU in the fall of their freshman year of college.

Ask Leonard today to reflect on his favorite memory of his IU career and he has a quick answer.

"Well, the best memory I have was that's where I met my wife," Leonard said.

Ted Green, the filmmaker who did the documentary of Leonard's career, said that when they filmed a segment with Leonard at IU back in the old fieldhouse where he had played he got choked up by some of the memories.

"He got pretty emotional," Green recalled. "You could see it in him. He was looking over to the place where Nancy would sit at every game. And to steal his words, he said 'There are a lot of important people in my life but no one has ever been more important than Nancy.

"I think that's why more than anything he is so nostalgic about that place. In a lot of ways, through Nancy, this is where his life really began."

Throughout these 10 chapters of the top 10 players in Indiana basketball history, one player after another talks about the special relationship they had with their coach at Indiana.

Many of those stories are about Bob Knight, who coached six of the top 10. One is about Lou Watson, who coached one of IU's all-time greats. The other three were all coached by Branch McCracken.

When Leonard looks back on his IU career he always speaks fondly of McCracken and the things he did for him, both as a player and as a man.

In the book *Branch* by Bill Murphy, Leonard relayed one of the most important stories when it came to his coach and mentor.

"He took me as a wild kid off the streets of Terre Haute and taught me a lot of values," Leonard said. "I had never been baptized. Branch took me to a church and had me baptized when I was 19 years old.

"You don't get any greater feeling for a man than I have for Branch McCracken. There is no greater feeling."

6

Number 9
Randy Wittman

With many of the top players in Indiana basketball history, you hear the same kinds of praise over and over.

He was a great scorer. He was a great shooter. This guy could rebound better than any of them. That list goes on and on.

I found it interesting though when talking to people about Randy Wittman what they remembered most about the former IU All-American.

Three different people interviewed said the same thing.

He rarely made a mistake. Yes, he was a great shooter, terrific with fundamentals, extremely coachable and all of those things. But it was the fact that he did what he did best without making errors that really stood out.

Randy Wittman (Indiana University Archives – P0035252)

"He never turned the ball over and never, ever, made a bad decision," was one of the first qualities mentioned by former IU player, coach, and brief interim head coach Dan Dakich. "He was just terrific with the ball."

75

Don Fischer, the voice of Indiana basketball for more than 40 years, said Wittman was just a really smart, intelligent player.

"He just had an incredible basketball mentality, a basketball IQ," Fischer said. "He almost never made a mistake. He was kind of a gangly looking guy at 6-5 but could play the point guard position as well as anybody. He brought the ball up all the time against pressure. He wasn't the fastest guy on the floor but he just had a great basketball mind.

"He didn't make mistakes. He didn't force anything. Honestly, I just thought he was one of the best basketball players you could ever watch and I think most people who ever saw him play would say the same exact thing."

Wittman played at Indiana from 1978-83. He was an All-American for IU as a senior and scored 1,549 points for his career.

Fundamentally speaking, there are few players who ever played basketball at Indiana University that would be in the same league as Wittman.

He had great form, was fundamentally sound, and could flat out play. He was a great shooter. Not a good one, a great one. For his five-year Indiana basketball career he shot better than 52 percent from the field in more than 1,200 shot attempts. And these weren't bunnies, they were mostly legitimate perimeter jumpers.

Brian Evans, an IU All-American in 1996, said when he was growing up the two guys he wanted to be like were Ted Kitchel and Wittman. He said when he watched those guys play they were doing everything that he was being taught as an 8-10 year-old at the Wabash Valley Basketball Camp.

"We were learning how to get our feet set and get our shoulders squared to the basket and do all of the things that Randy was doing at that time at IU playing in the Big Ten," Evans said. "And he was doing it better than everyone else.

"And yes, I saw that when I watched him play."

Ask Pat Graham, the former Indiana Mr. Basketball in 1989 who went on to play at Indiana, who the players were that he looked up to when growing up and the same two names as Evans came quickly off his tongue – Wittman and Kitchel.

"Everybody has their guys that they watched and tried to be like growing up," Graham said. "For me, that was Wittman and Kitchel."

When Graham thinks of Wittman, he remembers a player who was fundamentally sound.

"I remember he was that way at IU and when he was in the NBA with the Hawks," Graham said. "He got by because of his fundamentals and then he took those fundamentals and went overboard with them. That's just how he played. He was almost robotic.

"I can remember watching that as a kid and knowing he was going to shot fake in a certain situation and thinking 'Who in the hell takes that fake?' but opponents always did. He was so robotic on his fundamentals. I remember watching that and then trying to copy that."

Dakich said there were a couple of things that really stood out about Wittman as a player.

"One was defensively, he was really good," Dakich said. "But the other is that he was never, ever, out of position with his body when he shot. He could definitely get his feet set and get his shoulders squared when he shot. He was really good at the mid-range leaner over guys. He could shot fake, one dribble, pull up and was the best I had ever seen at that."

And Dakich couldn't stop talking about Wittman fundamentally, too.

"He was just really strong fundamentally," Dakich said. "He bought in to what everybody taught which is to get your shoulders in front of your feet. He was an unbelievable post feeder. We talk about the Pacers can't get the ball in the post, well Randy Wittman could get the ball in the post. He could bounce pass, or throw it away from the defender. He was just really smart. He was really, really smart."

Because Wittman was a few years older than him, Steve Alford remembers that Witt was one of the first players he really followed closely.

"He went to Ben Davis High School (in Indianapolis) and I got a chance to follow him since he wasn't that far away," Alford said. "And I followed him and watched him probably as much as I did anybody as I got older. He was just really good at a lot of things I wanted to be good at."

One of the things that set Alford apart as a college player was how hard he worked to get open. He was rarely not in motion. He was always looking for a way to get open within the offense. He credited Wittman as helping him in that regard.

"As I got older and really started to understand the game, I watched Randy a lot because I thought he knew how to move without the basketball and how to get himself open," Alford said. "When you're not the fastest guy out there, you need to find ways to create opportunities for yourself. I thought Randy was really good at that."

Alford also said Wittman had great form.

"He always had his feet set which sounds simple but it really isn't," Alford said. "It's an art form in the game that few players have where you can slow the game down enough to get your feet set and be ready to take great shots."

And when you get your feet set, you're not traveling very often either which goes back to the original point of Wittman not making many mistakes.

Jake Query, the Indianapolis sports radio talk show host with WNDE 1260-AM, recalled that he was in the fourth grade when Wittman was in his prime at Indiana. He remembers his fourth grade travel coach using Wittman as an example to the players.

"Our coach would point things out about Wittman because he was good at everything," Query said. "I don't know that he was exceptional at anything but he was just such a complete player. What stood out to me was that he never seemed to focus on just one area of his game and thus neglect the others. He was always working to be at a high level in everything that he did."

Query also remembers his father telling him that he thought the baseline jump shot was the hardest shot to make in basketball because you didn't have the backboard to use for assistance.

"I remember being mesmerized by the fact that Randy Wittman had seemingly mastered what my dad considered to be the most difficult shot in basketball," Query said. "And I would stand in my driveway and shoot baseline jump shots from 15 feet for hours and I thought I was Randy Wittman."

• • • •

Wittman's earliest memories of Indiana were when he would go to Bob Knight's Basketball Camps as a young boy. Wittman said he would go to various camps during the summer including Ohio State and Purdue, too.

The first time Wittman recalls talking to Knight was when he was at Knight's camp between his eighth and ninth grade year. He said Knight had been watching him a lot during that camp and at the end of it approached him.

"He came up to me after a particular afternoon and said 'Would you ever come here and play for me if I offered you a scholarship?'," Wittman said. "And I was obviously intimidated and I said, 'Sure, why wouldn't I?'"

So Wittman felt he was on IU's radar a little bit heading into his freshman year in high school.

Wittman said it was after his sophomore year that Knight offered him a scholarship.

By the time that the Indiana offer came, Wittman was also being recruited by several other schools. Three stood out: Purdue, Notre Dame and Arkansas. In fact, Wittman said Arkansas was really the most intriguing offer of the bunch.

"Arkansas at that time had the great teams with Sidney Moncrief and they had a run there for three or four years where they were always in contention for a national championship," Wittman said. "The thing that was a little bit enticing was that I played baseball, too, and they offered me a scholarship to come to Arkansas to play both sports.

"That was the one that was probably the most intriguing to me because I loved baseball and I thought I was a pretty good baseball player."

But when Knight offered Wittman that scholarship, it pretty much sealed the deal in Randy's mind.

"Once he offered me a scholarship I didn't even take a visit anywhere else," Wittman said. "You had the opportunity back then to make five visits but once he offered me I didn't go anywhere else.

"I told him it was a done deal. Indiana was the only place I really ever wanted to play."

Don Fischer remembers the story exactly the same way. At the time that Wittman was growing up, Fischer was close friends with Wittman's parents, Bob and Shirley. They attended the same church and did a lot of things together.

Fischer remembers that IU's assistant coaches knew that about Fischer and when they were recruiting Wittman gave the radio man a little ribbing on the topic.

"Not Knight, but a couple of assistant coaches told me, 'Well, if he goes somewhere else, it's your fault," Fischer said with a smile. "They were putting a little heat on."

Fischer said he never said much to Wittman about IU. He had lots of good things to say to Wittman's parents on the topic but that was the extent of it.

"I had nothing to do with recruiting Randy Wittman," Fischer said. "The fact of the matter is that once Knight offered him, though, there was never any question that he was going to Indiana."

• • • •

As a boy growing up playing basketball in the state of Indiana, the initial focus is often on two things: winning a state championship and making the Indiana All-Star team.

The All-Star team was always announced on a Sunday morning in the *Indianapolis Star* and Wittman couldn't wait to get the paper that day and read about which of the guys he was following had made the team.

This was long before the Internet or Twitter where the story would leak out and everyone would know it that way. It was a pretty highly kept secret and most people really didn't find out until the newspaper arrived on their doorsteps in the morning.

Wittman, however, had a major advantage over most people and in fact always felt he was among the first to learn who had made the Indiana All-Star team.

That's because he was a newspaper carrier for the *Indianapolis Star* and would get the papers delivered to his house early in the morning. He had the job all the way through high school.

"I had to get up at 4:30 or 5 o'clock every morning to deliver the paper so I would always get the news a little earlier than most people," Wittman said. "And that particular day was always one of my favorite days of the year. I followed Indiana high school basketball and it was always a treat, even as a young kid, to see who is going to make it this year."

Wittman said that was how he found out he had made the Indiana All Star team back in 1978.

Randy Wittman (Indiana University Archives – P0022036)

"Oh yeah," Wittman said. "I was up especially early that morning and went out and looked the paper over before I even folded them up. I'll never forget that moment."

Wittman said making that All-Star team had always been one of his biggest goals. Ben Davis was one of the largest high schools in the state at the time and remarkably there had never been an Indiana All Star come out of that school.

As of the summer of 2014, there have been seven Ben Davis players named to the Indiana All-Star team.

But Wittman will be forever remembered as the first.

"That will always be something that is very special for me, knowing that I was the first one," Wittman said. "I don't know if it's as big of a deal for kids today but back then it was a really big deal."

• • • •

When Wittman arrived on campus at IU in the fall of 1978, the only regular starters returning for Indiana were Mike Woodson and Ray Tolbert.

Wittman recalled later that he came in as a wide-eyed freshman not really knowing what to expect. IU opened that season in the Sea Wolf Classic in Anchorage, Alaska. IU lost the first game by one to Pepperdine and then also lost the second to Texas A&M by five points. The Hoosiers salvaged the trip with an 86-65 win over Penn State, years before the Nittany Lions would join the Big Ten.

IU would then play three more games back in the lower 48 before Bob Knight had some suspicions confirmed that not all was right on the Alaska trip.

Knight found out that several IU players had smoked marijuana during the Alaska trip. According to an excerpt from the book *Bob Knight: The Unauthorized Biography* written by Steve Delsohn and Mark Heisler, it was sophomore guard Butch Carter who had told the coaches that his teammates and been smoking pot.

Knight confronted the players about it back in Bloomington and the following Monday three players were dismissed from the team. Sophomore guard Tommy Baker, sophomore shooting guard Don Cox and senior center Jim Roberson were the players let go. Others were put on probation.

One of those dismissed was Baker, who had started five of the first six games at point guard.

"I remember the next morning, Knight came up to me and said, 'You're going to be my point guard,'" Wittman said. "He said, 'All I want you to do is get the ball over half court without turning it over and get the ball to the people who need to score.'"

Looking back Wittman said that was probably the best thing that ever happened to him.

"It really enabled me to expand and develop part of my game that maybe never would have been developed in terms of ball handling and learning how to run a team," Wittman said. "I ended up my freshman year averaging I think 39.4 minute per game. I think that might still be a record. Having that happen to me as a freshman was invaluable to me."

The move to the point guard spot forced Wittman to be a steady contributor throughout that season. He played in all 34 games, hit 53 percent from the field on 190 attempts and averaged 7.1 points per game. His high game was 16 points at Iowa on Jan. 13.

Before the season was over though, Wittman would be able to hoist the first championship trophy of his collegiate career – the NIT title.

Indiana beat rival Purdue in the championship game 53-52.

IU finished 22-12 in Wittman's rookie campaign and 10-8 in conference play for fifth place.

•••

Wittman's sophomore season will long be remembered as his lost season. Indiana had opened the season with four wins in a row and Wittman had started all four games. His high game had been 10 points in the season opener against Miami of Ohio.

As IU headed to Kentucky on Dec. 15 little did the Hoosiers know what a costly game it would turn out to be.

Wittman, who started for the fifth time in the season, limped off the court in pain early in the second half. It would later be revealed that he had suffered a stress fracture in his foot and would be done for the year.

Things got worse when senior Mike Woodson hurt his back. He stayed in the game and actually played one more game before he ended up having back surgery. Woodson would return late in the Big Ten season to lead his team to six wins in a row and catapult the team to the Big Ten title. Despite only playing six games in the Big Ten, Woodson was named the conference's MVP because of his late season heroics.

As for Wittman, though, his season was over and he would eventually get to take it as his redshirt season.

His season statistics were a 5.8 scoring average and a 46 percent field goal percentage but just in 28 total shots.

"I played on good teams my entire career but I really think the best team I played on was not in '81 but rather in 1980," Wittman said years later. "Woodson had the back injury and I redshirted after the fifth game when I broke my ankle in Rupp Arena against Kentucky and I was done.

"But just the opportunity to know that we had a fighting chance to win it all was worth it that year. We had a really good team. It's too bad the breaks didn't fall our way."

•••

Heading into the 1980-81 season, Indiana was ranked fifth in the nation. The Hoosiers would be ranked in all but four weeks the entire year.

Senior Ray Tolbert was the most experienced returning player and the other focal player was sophomore Isiah Thomas.

Joining Thomas and Tolbert in the starting lineup were a pair of redshirt sophomores – Ted Kitchel and Randy Wittman. Wittman was a 6-6 guard who started alongside Thomas in the backcourt. Landon Turner rounded out the starting lineup.

It was a magical season for Indiana and when it was over, the Hoosiers would hang their fourth national championship banner and second under Knight.

Wittman has plenty of fond memories of that team and is still close with those players today.

He said the best player he ever played with in college or the pros was Isiah Thomas.

"Having the opportunity to play with a Hall of Fame player like that and just the camaraderie we had as a team are the things that stand out about 1981," Wittman said. "We still talk to each other once or twice every two weeks. I just talked to Isiah today and yesterday it was Mike Woodson. Two days ago it was Ted Kitchel and Tony Brown was last week. I talked to Landon Turner when we were playing the Pacers in the second round.

"There was just something about that special bond we had back then and we still have it today even 30 plus years after we played together."

One of Wittman's memories from that team was what happened when it got to the NCAA Tournament. IU had won the Big Ten with a 14-4 record. IU won its final five games to edge out Iowa by one game for the title.

Because IU was 21-9 overall, however, the Hoosiers only got a No. 3 seed in the NCAA Tournament despite winning the Big Ten title. But it was a No. 3 seed in the Mideast Regional. The significance there? IU would have a first round bye and if it could win its second game, would have a chance to play the next two games at Assembly Hall in Bloomington. Assembly Hall was hosting the regional semifinals and finals that season.

So confidence was high when the Hoosiers faced Maryland in that second round game in Dayton. Or I should say confidence was high until the game began.

"In '81 we win the Big Ten and our first round opponent is Maryland and that's Albert King and Buck Williams and I'm thinking 'Holy crap, we win the Big Ten and this is our first round matchup? All of a sudden we were down 8-0. It was in Dayton, Ohio and I'm wondering if this was going to come to a close after one game.

Fortunately, we went on and really demolished them but it was scary."

The final was 99-64.

Another highlight came in the NCAA championship against North Carolina. Wittman had 16 points in the title game on 7-of-13 shooting from the field. North Carolina, though, led the entire first half until Wittman hit a long jumper from half court as time expired in the first half to give the Hoosiers a 26-25 lead.

IU would go on to win the title, 63-50 over the Tar Heels in Philadelphia.

Wittman recalled as a young boy watching the NCAA championship game on television and then going out in his backyard afterward and pretending he was playing in the final game, whether it be against UCLA or whoever the opponent might have been.

Then in 1981, someone asked Wittman what was going through his mind when he walked out on the court for the jump ball in the national championship game?

"And I told him that it really wasn't that big of a deal to me because I had done it a hundred times in my backyard," Wittman said. "That did actually cross my mind in '81 in Philadelphia when I walked out for the jump ball. I even remember saying to myself, 'Heck, I've done this a hundred times. This shouldn't be too hard.'"

••••

Coming back for their junior seasons, Randy Wittman and Ted Kitchel were Indiana's two most experienced players in the 1981-82 season. The IU roster did not have a single senior but Wittman and Kitchel were both redshirt juniors so they were technically seniors academically.

Bob Knight wasn't happy with the way his team looked in a 71-64 season-opening win against Miami of Ohio and so he benched four of his starters for the next game against Notre Dame.

Wittman was one of them. He did come off the bench, though, to help spark IU with 15 points and lead the Hoosiers to 69-55 win over Notre Dame.

The season would be an up and own affair with IU finishing the regular season with an 18-9 mark and a 12-6 conference record which was good enough for a tie for second place with Iowa and Ohio State.

In the NCAA Tournament, the Hoosiers beat Robert Morris in the opener but lost to Alabama-Birmingham in the second game, which knocked the defending champs from the field.

Wittman started 26 games and averaged 11.9 points.

••••

The 1982-83 Hoosiers were a team that resided that season somewhere in the top 10 in the country. IU opened the season No. 9, got to as high as No. 1 for two weeks at Christmas time, and finished the year No. 5.

Randy Wittman shared team captain duties as a collegiate senior with Ted Kitchel and Jim Thomas.

Wittman wasted little time setting the tone for what would end being an All-American season. In the season-opening 91-75 victory over Ball State, Wittman had a career-high 28 points. He also held high-scoring guard and future Indiana assistant coach Ray McCallum to 13 points.

In Wittman's second game of the season, a 75-59 victory over Miami of Ohio, the senior from Ben Davis knocked his career-high numbers up a couple of notches. He scored 31 points that night.

Indiana continued to win. In fact, the Hoosiers would open the season with 10 wins in a row. The first loss came against Ohio State in the Big Ten opener.

During the non-conference run, Wittman took home MVP honors at the Indiana Classic after he scored 30 points against Wyoming in the title game, a 78-65 IU win.

The non-conference also featured a matchup between No. 5 Indiana and No. 2 Kentucky in Assembly Hall. Wittman led the Hoosiers with 17 points and 12 rebounds as IU beat the Wildcats, 62-59.

After losing to Ohio State on the road to open conference play, Indiana bounced back to win five more in a row to up its record to 15-1.

The first game in that stretch was at Illinois and Wittman came up big for the Hoosiers. He scored a game-high 27 points to lead IU.

The Hoosiers continued to be strong in the Big Ten. IU improved to 9-2 in conference play when it went on the road to Madison and knocked off Wisconsin, 75-56. Wittman had 26 points to lead Indiana.

Iowa slowed down the Indiana train in the next game when it shocked the Hoosiers 63-48 in Iowa City. Only one IU player scored in double figures and that was Wittman who had 33 of IU's 48 points.

IU continued what would be an eventual Big Ten championship season but suffered a costly injury in the Feb. 24 game at Michigan. Ted Kitchel left the game with back spasms and didn't return. It turned out he wouldn't return and his season and career was over.

IU lost that game and then the next game, too, at Michigan State, 62-54. Suddenly, IU was no longer in the driver's seat and felt it would need to win out in order to win the Big Ten title. The Hoosiers would close conference play with three home games against Purdue, Illinois and Ohio State.

"It was kind of a devastating loss at Michigan State," Wittman said. "It went down to the wire, I didn't play worth a crap, and I can remember afterwards that Ted is not able to play and this being your last year you don't want to go out that way.

"We were able to come together as a team though and win those three games to clinch the Big Ten title."

Indiana went into the final Big Ten game with a one-game lead over Ohio State in the standings with the Buckeyes coming to town. Wittman led Indiana with 24 points and IU raced to a 81-60 victory to give it the Big Ten title outright.

Wittman was later named the Big Ten's MVP.

IU received a No. 2 seed in the NCAA Tournament and a first round bye. IU beat Oklahoma in the second round but dropped a 64-59 decision to Kentucky in Knoxville, Tenn. in the Sweet Sixteen.

Wittman's senior season was clearly his best statistically. He started all 30 games and averaged 18.9 points. He hit 54.3 percent of his shots from the field.

For his four-year career, Wittman scored 1,549 points for an 11.6 points per game average. He shot 52.4 percent from the field for his career.

"I played in the NBA for nine years and I've been in the NBA now for 30 years as either a player or a coach, but those years at IU were the still the best years of my life," Wittman said, in an interview for this book in the summer of 2014.

•••••

Wittman's college roommate for all five years was Ted Kitchel. They lived in the dorms the first year and then the Fountain Park Apartments off of 10th Street their final four seasons.

Wittman said Kitchel was one of the two toughest competitors he ever played with (the other was Isiah Thomas). When Wittman thinks of Kitchel though, he always thinks of a stubborn player.

He remembered the 1983 season when IU was one of the first teams ever to play in Carver-Hawkeye Arena in Iowa City. He said when IU arrived at the arena and walked into the locker rooms, they weren't even finished yet.

Wittman said that Knight's pregame speech was how it was going to be a wild crowd opening up a new arena. He told his players that they needed to be methodical and take great shots the first five minutes of the game. He stressed that IU needed to take control of the game right from the start.

Knight's final advice when they broke the huddle to start the game was to make sure they got good shots early and definitely not take any hurried or rushed shots.

"So it's the jump ball and we get the tip," Wittman said. "And it was tipped to me and Kitchel was up on the wing and I throw him the ball. And I mean he was closely guarded as you could be closely guarded. And he fires up this shot that hits the side of the backboard. And shortly thereafter Knight calls a timeout and just rips into us.

"So I pulled Ted by the shirt as we were coming out of the huddle as we're coming back out to the court and I said to him 'What the hell are you thinking? Why would you do that the first possession of the game? And he said, 'Man, all I was trying to do was get us off to a good start.'

"And I told him, 'Well, that was a hell of a way to do it.'"

Kitchel told a similar story on Wittman but the result was kind of the same.

"Randy was one of coach Knight's favorites," Kitchel said. "I always tell people, if Knight told us we needed eight passes or 10 passes to start a game before we took a shot, Wittman was counting them out. Where me, if I got an open shot on four, I'm firing. That was the difference between Wittman and I."

With both stories, Wittman said that was vintage Kitchel.

"That's the kind of guy he was," Wittman said. "And you know what, that kind of stuff didn't affect him. A timeout getting ripped by coach wasn't something that was going to go out and bother Ted."

Wittman said Kitchel had a great inner drive. Some of that was because he wasn't what you would consider to be a great athlete.

"He's not the greatest athlete," Wittman said. "He couldn't jump but he could shoot the crap out of the ball and he was smart and knew the things he could do and what he couldn't do and he was a great teammate. We've been great friends ever since that time and we're great friends today."

••••

Wittman said that looking back one of his greatest experiences of playing at Indiana was the opportunity to play for Bob Knight.

"When you're going through it you don't think so because it's not easy," Wittman said. "When you get away from it, and you look back you're grateful that you had the opportunity to go through it. Obviously I stayed in the game but I can tell you just about everything I do today (in coaching) comes from him."

One thing Wittman remembers most about playing for Knight was how he believed you needed to give your best effort every day. It didn't matter if you were tired or not feeling well, because somebody else was outworking you that day and that was not acceptable to Knight.

"He would talk about as you got older and your time at IU was near an end, you might not have had a good practice," Wittman said. "And he would say, 'It's you and somebody else going in for a job interview and are you going to get that job? You've got to get that job and you've got to be prepared.'

"And I don't think people give him enough credit for that. It's the things he does for people now to show them he cares. And people don't see that side of him, the caring side. And that's really too bad."

Wittman's son, Ryan, played college basketball at Cornell from 2006-10. His daughter, Lauren, attended IU. But Wittman said the greatest compliment he could pay coach Knight is that he would be proud to have had his son play for him.

"I'd let my daughter go play for him," Wittman said. "Because I just know that she would benefit from it. I just think what we got out of playing for him lasted with us for a lifetime. And I don't think a lot of people can say that about their experiences playing college basketball."

••••

Don Fischer, the voice of Indiana University basketball since Bob Knight arrived on campus for the 1972-73 season, has seen hundreds of IU basketball players come and go in more than 40 years on the job.

But apparently Fischer plays favorites. He said he does have one all-time favorite Indiana University basketball player and that's Randy Wittman.

Fischer has ties to the Wittman family, too.

"When we first moved to Indianapolis and I became the voice of IU, he was about 10 years old and we went to the same church as Randy and his folks," Fischer said. "Bob and

Shirley, his mom and dad, just befriended my wife and our kids and just made us feel like we were at home at that church."

The church was Our Shepherd Lutheran which is located about 4 miles west of I-465 on 10th Street.

"We went to a lot of functions with them," Fischer remembered. "We went to ice cream socials. We played softball. Randy was actually on our church softball team when he was 10 years old. He was a pretty good athlete even at that time. But it was a family type deal and we had other kids playing, too.

"So we got to know them pretty well."

Fischer said that Wittman was just always a real fun player to watch.

"He was just really good at understanding the game and understanding his teammates," Fischer said. "He was just a guy who knew what to do, when to do it and how to do it. I know a lot of guys who are really good at passing the ball but they often times try to do too much and pass it to the wrong guy in the wrong situation at the wrong time.

"But Randy never did that. Now there were guys that couldn't catch it," Fischer said. "He did play with Uwe (Blab). It's not like he didn't play with guys who couldn't catch it. But he always seemed to put it in the right place for different players."

Fischer said the greatest compliment he could pay Wittman was that he simply proved day in and day out what a great player he was.

"For being a guy that wasn't fast or super quick or anything like that the guy played in the NBA for nine years," Fischer said. "He wasn't a tremendous scorer, he wasn't a tremendous athlete, he was just a great basketball player."

●●●●

Players can be remembered for a variety of different things and Wittman seemed to do a lot of them really well.

Dan Dakich had the opportunity to play with Wittman and see him up close. Dakich was a sophomore when Wittman was a senior in 1983.

He doesn't remember any negatives.

"He was always the first out for practice," Dakich said. "He was just an absolute spectacular leader. I don't admire a lot of people, but Randy Wittman is someone I absolutely admire. I thought he was kind of everything you wanted to be as a guy and everything you wanted to be as a player."

It was the leadership abilities of Wittman that really stood out though for Dakich. He said that Wittman, Steve Alford and Calbert Cheaney are the best three leaders he has ever been around.

"He was a guy that I personally looked up to from the moment I got there," Dakich said. "I didn't know how good he was because coach Knight was always telling me as a recruit that I was better than Wittman and all this stuff. Let me just say that he exaggerated that one a little bit."

When Wittman looks back on his own career, he said the defining thing that he learned was the importance of knowing your role on a team and finding a way to embrace that. He said that helped him as a player in the NBA and continues to help him as a coach.

"With me I got to experience the dynamics of understanding what your role is and how it does change," Wittman said. "You need to be willing to accept a role. That is something that not only helped me as a player in the pros but as a coach. Developing and trying to get players to understand the importance of who they are on this team, this year. And it could be different next year. It's all about trying to get guys to understand that and that was one thing Coach Knight was the best at."

Wittman said Knight was really good at establishing roles for every player on the team and communicating that so that there was no confusion.

"My role changed every year," Wittman said. "I think I averaged 7.5 points as a freshman playing 39 and a half minutes a game because I was playing the point guard. Then I became the main scorer on the team as my years went on and my senior year I won Big Ten player of the year."

7
Number 8
Jimmy Rayl

If you just looked at Jimmy Rayl walking down the street, you might not have guessed that he was a high level college basketball player.

He simply didn't look the part. He was 6-1 but only weighed 148 pounds by his senior year in college. When he was in high school he guessed that he may have weighed closer to 130.

Bob Ford, the sportswriter from the *Kokomo Tribune*, gave him the nickname "The Splendid Splinter."

"He said I looked like a splinter because I was so thin," Rayl recalled. "I used to get banged around a lot."

Jimmy Rayl (Indiana University Archives – P0028401)

That's the way author and IU historian Bill Murphy remembers Rayl, too.

"Jimmy Rayl was all over the court," Murphy said. "He'd get knocked down and then he'd bounce right up and hit a shot. I think you could have punched him and he would have still hit a shot."

Actually, that scenario transpired in Rayl's final college game at home against Ohio State. The *IU Basketball Encyclopedia*, written by Jason Hiner, described the scene like this: 'The game nearly got out of hand in the final seconds of overtime when two Ohio State players flattened Rayl as he received an inbounds pass with 9 seconds remaining and IU clinging to an 86-85 lead. Both benches cleared, and a bunch of Indiana fans poured onto the court to defend their star player. Once the officials had sorted the mess out and got the fans back in their seats, Rayl made one of two free throws. Ohio State then missed a 20-footer to tie in the closing seconds and the home crowd stormed the floor to celebrate.'

"He missed the first one I think because he was really hurt," Murphy said. "But then he adjusted on the second free throw and shot a lot harder and a lot higher and it went in."

That may have been muscle memory taking over, too. Rayl was a strong believer in that and believed shooters could always recall that certain form when they needed it the most.

Rayl tells a story from when he was in high school when he and four buddies were shooting free throws one day in the gym at the Congregational Church of Kokomo. He said they were listening to a baseball game on the radio and while they listened they passed the time by shooting free throws. He said he would shoot 10 free throws and then each of his buddies would do the same. They were there for a couple of hours.

"You want to guess how many I made in a row?" Rayl asked me on a summer afternoon in July of 2014. "I hit 532 free throws in a row. That's a true story. I finally missed one. And that was shooting 10, taking a pretty long break, and then shooting 10 more so it wasn't a matter of getting in to a rhythm and not being able to miss."

Anyone who watched Rayl shoot from the time he was a young boy probably wouldn't have a difficult time believing his tale.

Some say he is one of the greatest shooters to ever come out of the state of Indiana.

A lot of it was repetition. He was constantly shooting and knocking down shot after shot. He averaged 30 points a game in grade school, did the same in church leagues and middle school and in high school was Mr. Basketball at Kokomo in 1959.

But it didn't stop there.

At Indiana he had back-to-back All-American seasons. As a junior in 1962, he averaged 29.8 points per game. The only player who ever averaged more was George McGinnis at 29.9.

Rayl's senior season he averaged 25.3.

Perhaps Rayl's most impressive accomplishment though still sits atop a category in the Indiana basketball record book. It has been over 50 years since Rayl played basketball at Indiana but one record has withstood the test of time.

The most points ever scored by an Indiana player in one game is 56. It has been done twice in history – both times by Jimmy Rayl.

His first 56-point game came on Jan. 27, 1962 against Minnesota. Rayl made 20-of-39 shots from the field and 16-of-20 free throws and hit a 35-footer at the buzzer in overtime that gave the Hoosiers a 105-104 victory at home.

The second 56-pointer came in his senior season on Feb. 23, 1963 in a 113-94 rout of Michigan State. That night, Rayl hit 23-of-48 shots from the field and the home fans at IU booed head coach Branch McCracken when he took Rayl out with just under 4 minutes to play. They wanted to see him break his scoring record but McCracken didn't want to run the score up any more than it was at that point.

"That was an incredible performance," said IU basketball historian Bill Murphy, who was in attendance at that game. "He was out on the fast break getting layups and he was hitting jump shots from all over the court. Jimmy was just a thing of beauty to watch shooting the basketball."

In two games against Michigan State that season, Rayl scored an even 100 points. He had 44 in the first game and 56 in the second.

Years later, Scott Skiles asked Rayl if he would make a phone call to Michigan State coach Jud Heathcote to help him get a basketball scholarship to East Lansing. Rayl remembers making the call and when Heathcote's secretary patched the call through to the head coach, Rayl said that Heathcote answered the call by saying, 'Jim Rayl. Indiana's all-time leading scorer.'

Rayl's response: "No coach, that's not really true. But if I played you guys every game I most certainly would have that record."

Even more impressive about the two 56-point games in Indiana history is the fact that they were accomplished without the benefit of the 3-point line. The 3-point line first came into play for the 1986-87 season, Steve Alford's final year with the Hoosiers.

What is hard to put a finger on though is just how many points would Rayl have scored if there had been a 3-point line back then. Rayl made a living from the outside and was considered a dead-eye long distance shooter.

In that second 56-point game, years later some people around the IU program went back and looked at shot charts of the game. They determined that 17 of Rayl's 23 field goals that game were from beyond today's 3-point line.

So 56 points could have just as easily been 73 in a different day and age.

"There were still 3 and a half minutes to play when I came out, too," Rayl said. "I think I could have gotten 80 but we'll never know. I think what I did was kind of unusual at the time. Nobody is getting those kinds of points even today with the 3-point line."

Rayl had range that some say extended to the parking lot outside the fieldhouse. When asked about that range, he said he felt comfortable from 35 feet and in.

"I always felt I could shoot 35-foot jumpers fairly good," Rayl said. "I'm not sure anyone felt real comfortable from 50 feet but 35 was a good distance for me."

Rayl has a fan club of former players that would get in line to tell stories about his success as a shooter.

Archie Dees, an IU All-American in 1957 and '58, never played with Rayl but the two became good friends when Dees was in the NBA and Rayl was playing at IU. They remain friends today and talk frequently, according to Dees.

"He's the best shooter that I've ever seen," Dees said. "And I've seen a lot of great shooters."

Clarence Doninger, who was in law school when Rayl played but attended every IU home game, said Rayl's range was unmatched by most. Purdue's Rick Mount had similar range but beyond that there weren't many players who could shoot like Rayl.

"The way we described him was he came out of the dressing room and he could fire it from there," Doninger said. "I'm serious. He could really knock down shots. I was there for both of his 56-point games and all I remember thinking years later was I wonder how many points he would have had with that 3-point line."

Bill Murphy said Rayl had unlimited range.

"When he walked on the court he was in range and that's no lie," Murphy said. "You can go through Indiana basketball history and there are a lot of great shooters. But Jimmy Rayl had the furthest range of any of them."

When Rayl was a senior, he played alongside Dick Van Arsdale in the backcourt while Tom Bolyard played forward alongside Tom Van Arsdale.

The Van Arsdales knew all about Rayl's range and his propensity for taking shots, too.

"In jest, Dick used to say it was my job to take the ball out of bounds and throw it into Jim because at that point I never saw the ball again," Tom Van Arsdale said. "But seriously, Dick, Tom Bolyard and I all marveled that when Jim Rayl crossed the 10 second line or the half court line he was truly in range."

Bobby 'Slick' Leonard preceded Rayl at IU by a few years but he followed his career closely. He said he and Rayl have remained good friends over the years.

"Jimmy was one of the greatest shooters going," Leonard said. "Jimmy had all the shots. He had 3-point range. He's one of the great shooters to come out of Indiana high school basketball."

Leonard said some players are really good high school players but don't have enough skills to play at the college level. Some are outstanding college players but don't have the tools to play in the pros. Leonard said Rayl was an outstanding college player.

"Sometimes in the college game, the reason that maybe a Jimmy Rayl or a Steve Alford or a Rick Mount don't make it big in the pro game is they're a half a step or a step slow and they can't get shots up," Leonard said. "But all I know about Jimmy Rayl is one thing and that's that he was a great shooter."

Bill Murphy tells the story of a game of H-O-R-S-E once played between Rayl and Mount. The game was believed to have been played at Rayl's house in Kokomo when the two were in their late teens.

"Mount got ahead and Rayl caught up and they were both at H-O-R-S," Murphy said. "Then Rayl hit a shot from way deep and Mount looked at him and said, 'What do you say we just call it quits?' And Rayl said, 'OK, we'll call it quits."

Archie Dees had his own stories about playing H-O-R-S-E against Rayl. He said they played dozens of times.

"And I never beat him once," Dees said. "He had range that was way outside of anything I could do."

Dees said that Rayl had a big basketball court at his house and was always inviting good players up there to play. That's likely how Mount and Rayl ended up playing H-O-R-S-E. Dees said that Rayl tried over and over to get Dees to come up and play but he refused.

"He just wouldn't let it go and he was always on me to go over there and play, and I just really had no interest in that," Dees said with a smile. "I knew that he was just thinking that he would take me back there and beat the hell out of me."

Rayl could do more than just shoot the ball, too. When he was having fun with his friends, Rayl was known to shoot two basketballs at once from the free throw line. He would shoot one with his right hand and the other with his left.

Both balls would leave his hands at the same time and both would go through the net.

"I used to like to fool around with a basketball a lot," Rayl said. "And I got pretty good with my left hand. And so I would get to the free throw line and I would shoot two balls at the same time. What I would do is I would arch one and line drive the other. A lot of time, both would go through the net at about the same time."

Rayl remembered a time when his daughter was doing her student teaching at a grade school in Kokomo and they had an old gym. The teacher she was working with asked if Rayl would come out and shoot baskets with the kids. He was about 53 years old at the time.

"Normally I would practice shooting two balls at once a few times before I made it but when I arrived the kids all huddled around me as I stood at the free throw so I didn't have a chance to warm up," Rayl said. "But this time I put them up and boom, boom, they both went in.

"And not only did they both go in but they went in just perfectly to where the two balls got stuck in the net. The teacher didn't know a lot about basketball and she just figured that everybody could do that but I thought it was pretty neat."

Tom Bolyard, who was in the same class as Rayl and played with him all three seasons at IU, recalled the first time the two met.

It was in the semi-state round of the 1959 Indiana High School basketball tournament when they were both seniors as Bolyard's Fort Wayne South team faced Rayl's Kokomo squad. The game was tied at 90 with just a few seconds to play in overtime.

"Jimmy hits one from just across the mid court line as the gun goes off to beat us, 92-90," Bolyard said. "So that should tell you right there that he could shoot. That was some first impression I had of Jimmy Rayl."

Rayl had 41 points in the game and Bolyard had 39. Bolyard, who scored 1,420 points in his high school career, went on to have a pretty good career at IU, too. He ranks 28th on IU's all-time scoring list with 1,299 points and a career average of 18 points per game.

••••

I had the pleasure in early July of 2014 to spend a couple of hours in Kokomo with Jimmy Rayl and his wife Nancy. In a living room decorated with IU basketball memorabilia, Rayl sat back in his recliner chair and told story after story about his playing career.

One of the games he remembered most fondly was that Minnesota game his junior season. Minnesota had a 10-point lead with 11 minutes to play in regulation before Rayl got hot and helped send the game into overtime.

With 7 seconds to play in overtime, a Minnesota player had two free throws with IU clinging to a 103-102 lead. The first free throw was good and Rayl remembered telling one of his teammates and fraternity brothers, Jerry Bass, that if the player made the second one to call timeout. Rayl figured that McCracken would want to set up a final play or something.

Instead, when the free throw went through, Bass quickly handed the ball to Rayl and told him to go.

"He handed the ball to me and I knew the clock was moving and so I started racing down the floor, weaving in and out past players," Rayl said. "I got to the 10-second line and I figured there couldn't be much time left. I took two or three steps at the most and I knew I had to shoot it. The worst thing that could happen would be to let the buzzer go off without getting off a shot.

"So I stopped and took a shot. It had to be a 30-35 foot jump shot and it went right through the bottom of the net. It was unbelievable."

Interestingly, the Indiana University Basketball Media Guide describes Rayl's end of game heroics like this: His 20-foot shot with 2 seconds remaining lifted IU to the victory.

But Rayl said the shot was well over 30 feet. Author and IU basketball historian Bill Murphy laughed out loud when he heard the media guide description.

"It had to have been at least 35 feet," Murphy said. "He was only a few steps beyond the midcourt line. There's no way that was a 20-foot jump shot."

After the game, McCracken called it one of the greatest exhibitions of outside shooting he had ever seen.

I asked Jimmy about the 39 shots and if he felt like his arms were going to fall off after the game.

He said with a smile, "Well it did go overtime."

Later, when he would take 48 shots against Michigan State in '63, Rayl didn't have the overtime excuse.

"I was just really feeling it that night," Rayl said.

Those still rank as the two highest field goal attempts by a player in IU history. They are just two more examples of the legend of Jimmy Rayl.

Tom Bolyard, said he and his teammates knew that Rayl was really feeling it that night, too.

"We fed him the ball that night like no other team in the country would have," Bolyard said. "We got the ball to him every time we possibly could. And he was in one of those zones."

• • • •

Bolyard also got to know Rayl a little on the recruiting circuit. They were both being recruited by many of the same schools like Michigan State, Illinois and Purdue and the two ended up making several recruiting trips together.

Eventually they both decided to attend IU and Bolyard said they were like brothers once they got to Bloomington.

"We were so close it was unbelievable," Bolyard said. "In fact I feel like I raised Jimmy to a certain extent. Jimmy was a little bit insecure growing up and even a little bit in college. But Jimmy and I are extremely close even to this day. In fact, he named his second son after me and his first son after himself."

Rayl and Bolyard arrived in Bloomington in the fall of 1959. At that time, freshmen were not permitted to play on the varsity. Rayl said looking back, from a basketball standpoint, it was really a lost year.

"There were 25 guys on the freshman team and we didn't play anybody," Rayl said. "There would be two freshman teams and you would scrimmage each other before the varsity game. You would basically practice all week and then have a scrimmage once a week. It was a wasted year is what it was. It was a joke. We couldn't play any other teams."

His sophomore season he played but sparingly. Rayl played in 20 games, attempted a total of 112 shots, and averaged 4.0 points per game. Bolyard remembers that Rayl considered leaving Indiana on a few occasions that season but Bolyard would always try to encourage him and tell him he would definitely play the following year.

Rayl's sophomore year he played with an outstanding senior named Walt Bellamy. Bellamy had career averages of 20.6 points and 15.5 rebounds. His senior season, in 1961, Bellamy averaged 21.8 points per game and 17.8 rebounds. He earned All-American status for the second year in a row.

Bellamy's final two games of his college career were epic. The games were against Wisconsin and Michigan, both in Bloomington. Against the Badgers, Bellamy scored 27 points and pulled down a school-record 28 rebounds. A few days later, in his career finale against Michigan, Bellamy had 28 points and 33 rebounds. The rebound total was a Big Ten record.

The 33 rebounds is still an IU school record and the 28 rebounds is tied for second all-time for one game. Alan Henderson also had 28 rebounds in a game.

While Rayl didn't play much his sophomore year, he remembered Bellamy's 33-rebound game really well.

"I wasn't playing much that year and I remember I was at the end of the bench and Walter came down with a couple of really aggressive rebounds early in the game," Rayl said. "I had an old Juicy Fruit wrapper that I turned inside out and I had a small pencil that looked like a golf pencil. But I started keeping track of his rebounds. Every time Walter would pull one down I would make a mark on that Juicy Fruit wrapper.

"And he was getting just a load of rebounds. It got to the point where Branch would holler down 'How many does he got now Jimmy?' I'd rattle 'em off. 'That's 25, now 26.' Well that was the night he got 33 and that's still the IU record. I wish I had kept that Juicy Fruit wrapper. What I remember most about Walter was that he was like a man among boys."

Rayl's two big seasons at Indiana were his junior and senior years.

Rayl gave an early glimpse of what he was capable of in the second game of his junior season against New Mexico State. IU trailed by five at halftime before Rayl got hot. He scored 21 of his game-high 34 points in the second half as Indiana rallied for a 74-68 victory.

Early in Big Ten play, Rayl had another big second half performance that again rallied IU. This time he scored 21 of his 28 points in the second half as IU came back to beat Michigan State 76-71.

The next two games, Rayl scored 32 against Minnesota and then 41 against DePaul. That set up the second matchup with Minnesota in a three-game span and this would be Rayl's 56-point performance.

Rayl had scored 129 points in a three-game span, a cool 43 points per game average.

For the season, he averaged 29.8 points per game on a team that clearly lived up to the Hurryin' Hoosiers nickname. IU averaged a school record 87 points per game and scored 100 points or more four times.

One thing with Rayl was that in Branch McCracken's system he always had the green light. He remembers it that way, and his teammates did, too. He was one of those players that McCracken didn't worry about how many shots he missed because he was always certain that Rayl would hit the next one.

Rayl was quoted on that very topic in the book *Branch* by Bill Murphy.

"I had some pretty good games my junior and senior years, but there again it was because Branch let me do some crazy things on the floor that a lot of coaches would take you out of the game for," Rayl said. "You shoot a lot of shots, you're going to look bad once in a while. I might miss six or seven shots in a row, but Branch would never take me out."

As a senior, Rayl would be joined on the Indiana team by sophomores Tom and Dick Van Arsdale as well as Jon McGlocklin. Tom Bolyard returned to give IU a pretty solid starting five.

Rayl continued to pour in points as a senior but the team struggled to a 3-6 record in pre-conference play. Rayl had 35 against Virginia and 32 against Detroit.

IU then opened Big Ten play with three wins in a row and once again Rayl was a major contributor. He had 44 against Michigan State in the conference opener and then led IU with 25 in a win over Purdue. The third win was also against Purdue as Rayl had a game-high 25 points for the second time in as many games against the Boilers.

One problem with shooters is that there are always going to be off nights. Rayl had one of those against Northwestern where he went 9-for-30 from the field. The next game IU lost to Illinois 104-101 as Tom Bolyard had 35 and Rayl chipped in 31.

Indiana would win six of its final eight games to finish in third place in Big Ten play but IU's overall record in Rayl's final season was 13-11.

Rayl enjoyed playing with the Van Arsdales, players he described as "really good guys and very good ballplayers."

He even credits the Vans with one of his nicknames. Not the 'Splendid Splinter' but something else. He said the Vans were the first ones to call him Ginger.

As in Ginger Rayl.

Jimmy and Nancy liked the name so much that when they had a daughter they named her Ginger.

"And no one ever forgot her name," Nancy Rayl said. "She was Ginger Rayl."

Tom Van Arsdale said one thing he remembered about Rayl as a player was just how determined he was to win.

"Jim was a type A player," Tom Van Arsdale said. "He was very nervous before each game because he wanted to win so very badly. Jim was the most sincere of ball players. He just loved the game so much."

••••

There are varied reports of how Rayl got along with legendary IU coach Branch McCracken. Some say the two butted heads on more than one occasion.

Rayl even said the two had their moments.

But Rayl said he had the utmost respect for his coach.

"I liked Branch," he said. "If you didn't like Branch, there was something wrong with you. He was a little rough at times at practice but he was someone that you also knew cared very much."

When Jimmy Rayl married his high school sweetheart, Nancy in 1966, they had invited McCracken and his wife to the wedding but wasn't real sure if the IU coach would come.

"When I came out and looked, one of the first people I saw was Branch," Rayl said. "He was in the second row. I just about fell over. He was a big man and very, very strong. It meant a lot to us that he came for the wedding."

Jimmy met Nancy in high school in 1957. They dated for more than nine years before getting married. When Rayl was at IU, there were times after practice when he would hop in his Pontiac and make

Jimmy Rayl (Indiana University Archives – P0028398)

the 100-mile drive to Kokomo to see Nancy. Rayl's dad was a Pontiac dealer and Jimmy always had a Pontiac from his freshman year on.

"It might be 7 o'clock at night after practice and I would just get in my car and drive to Kokomo," Rayl said. "I might get back to Bloomington around midnight or 1 in the morning."

It was in these times that Rayl would learn of the well known information system that existed with McCracken. Everyone said the IU coach had spies everywhere feeding him with information. If someone saw a player out too late at night, they would report it to the coach. IU basketball players didn't dare miss a class because they knew McCracken would find out.

And when players drove to Kokomo and returned late in the evening, somehow the Sheriff would find out.

"The next day after coming home late I would go to practice and I would step up on the raised floor of the old fieldhouse and coach McCracken would walk by me and say, 'So how was Kokomo last night?'

"And for the life of me, I have no idea how he knew. But that's the way he was. He was something. He had spies everywhere. But it wasn't just me. Branch knew what everybody did."

Rayl said that was one of the things he learned very quickly after arriving in Bloomington. He said you made sure you did the things you were supposed to do.

"You had to be very punctual with Branch," Rayl said. "And being on time meant you were there 15 minutes early or you were considered late. He had Lombardi time before Vince Lombardi.

"But again, you knew that before you got there."

● ● ● ●

Rayl has followed Indiana basketball closely over the years. He said he has really enjoyed the job that Tom Crean has done with the Hoosiers the last several years.

Rayl said Crean has always gone out of his way to make him feel welcome around the program.

"Tom Crean has really treated me nicely," Rayl said. "I had heart surgery three years ago and I had three Get Well cards in the mail from him. I received one from him, one from his coaches and one from the players. I got a birthday card from him this year where he said I was welcome any time."

Rayl had the birthday card in close reach to his recliner and was quick to pull out his prized possession.

Rayl remembered the first time he met the Indiana coach. He went down to Bloomington shortly after Crean had taken the job to meet the coach and to tour the new Cook Hall practice facility.

He said there were five of them in his party including Archie Dees and Jeff Sagarin, who does the Sagarin rankings that have appeared in USA Today since 1985. Sagarin lives in Bloomington, Ind.

"Everybody went up and was introducing themselves to coach Crean and I was kind of hanging back," Rayl said. "He walked over and said, 'Hi, I'm Tom Crean.' And I looked at him and said, 'What do you do?' He wasn't sure if I was serious or not until everyone broke out laughing.

"That was the first time I ever met Tom Crean."

Archie Dees smiled when that story was retold to him in an interview in Bloomington in the summer of 2014.

"Jimmy would do that," Dees said. "He loved to have fun messing with people."

Dees recalled a day in March of 1962 when Rayl called him up and asked if he would like to drive with him to Louisville for the NCAA Final Four. Rayl had just completed his junior year at Indiana and had earned his first of back-to-back All American team honors.

The first thing that Dees recalled was that the car they drove in was rather small and at 6-8, Dees had a difficult time climbing into it. The other thing he remembered was the way Rayl drove he wasn't sure if he was going to survive the trip.

"I've never been so happy to get out of a vehicle before," Dees said. "The only hard part was when I had to get back in when it was time to go home and do it all over again."

When they arrived in Louisville, the two didn't have tickets but instead showed up and got behind members of one of the teams when they were walking into the arena. No one asked them for tickets and they were in.

They walked around, first up in the higher seats but there was nothing available. They eventually ended up down by the playing floor, standing off to the side at one of the tunnels that led on to the playing surface.

At some point they got to talking to a young man who appeared to be an Indiana fan as they were watching the two teams warm up and Rayl pointed to one of the players and said 'That guy right there is the best shooter I've ever seen.'

This guy wasn't buying it. Dees said the guy quickly said, 'No way. There's a little skinny kid that plays for IU and he's the best shooter I've ever seen.'

Rayl smiled on the inside and decided he would have some fun with the guy.

Dees said that Rayl argued with him for a minute or two and tried to bait him into defending him even more. All the while, Rayl had a sheepish grin on his face.

Finally, Dees stepped in and asked the guy a question.

"I said, 'What does this guy look like?'" Dees recalled. "He said, 'Well, he's thin and kind of scrawny and ...' right about then he looked over at Jimmy and made the connection and he knew he had been had. We ended up talking to the guy for quite a while and he knew an awful lot about basketball.

"But Jimmy is just that kind of guy. He has always enjoyed having fun."

8
Number 7
Mike Woodson

When Mike Woodson arrived in Bloomington in the fall of 1976, he admitted he hadn't paid a great deal of attention to the personnel on Indiana's '76 unbeaten national championship team.

What he knew about Indiana was that it was one of the best college basketball programs in the nation and he wanted to be a part of it.

He also knew that Indiana had lost most of its team from the national championship year. Gone were All-Americans Scott May and Quinn Buckner as well as players such as Bobby Wilkerson, Tom Abernethy and Jim Crews.

Mike Woodson (Indiana University Archives – P0022043)

The one thing Woodson was thinking going into his freshman season was that if he performed well, he might have a pretty good shot at playing time.

One thing he hadn't given any thought to was what number he would wear. He had worn No. 43 and No. 44 in high school so those were his first choices.

When it was time to pick out his uniform number, Woodson went to the equipment man at the time, a man he called 'Red', and said he wanted either 43 or 44.

"Red said, 'Well, you can't get 43 because Jim Roberson already has that number and Derek Holcomb just got over here and he scooped up No. 44'," Woodson recalled. "So now I'm steaming. Those were the numbers that I wore in high school.

"So I asked him what numbers did he have left?. He said, 'Well, I've got 42 and 41.' So I asked him if 45 was gone and he said that belonged to Rich Valavicius. So I said to give me 42 because it was the closest thing to 43 and 44 that he had."

Woodson said he never had the slightest idea who had worn No. 42 the past three seasons for Indiana – the reigning national player of the year, Scott May.

"I had just never paid any attention to what number different guys wore," Woodson said. "I wasn't naïve about it, I just didn't think like that. The only number I had ever been concerned with was the number that Mike Woodson wore which was either 43 or 44."

Woodson took 42 and then found out that Butch Carter wanted that number. Woodson told him, "You can have 42 if you can get Holcomb to give me 44."

"We tried to get Holcomb to switch with me but he wouldn't do it so I stayed with 42," Woodson said. "The next year Holcomb was gone and the number came open but by that time my new number was staying 42. I wasn't about to change at that point."

From the fall of 1973 when Scott May came on campus until Mike Woodson graduated in 1980, No. 42 claimed four All-American awards at IU – two from each player.

Woodson hadn't grown up idolizing any Indiana players. In fact, he said he hadn't really paid that much attention to the college game. His favorite player growing up was Roger Brown of the Indiana Pacers.

"I didn't really look at any IU players, I looked at the program," Woodson said. "How uniform they were, how professional they were, their approach and how well they were coached. And they won.

"I looked at professional players. Roger Brown was my idol growing up. When I would practice by myself I thought I was Roger Brown."

Woodson tried to pattern his game off of that of his idol.

"He had a tremendous jump shot, a beautiful jump shot, with great rotation on the ball," Woodson said. "From a one-on-one standpoint he could go get his shot pretty much any time he wanted to. And he knew how to use the glass. Over my career I became this great glass shooter and a lot of it had to do with the fact I watched (Brown) and how he used the glass when he played."

George McGinnis remembered how much Woodson looked up to Brown and tried to pattern his game off of that of Brown.

"They both had this really sweet jump shot," McGinnis said. "You could tell at an early age that Roger really had a great influence on Mike Woodson."

When Woodson was in high school, he cut his teeth in the summer playing basketball in the evenings at Douglas Park Rec Center in Indianapolis. Tuesday and Wednesday evenings in particular were a treat because several members of the Indiana Pacers would come over and play.

By the time Woodson was a senior in high school, the Pacers would actually let him play a little bit in their games. Then throughout Woodson's days in college he would try to find a way to get there on summer nights and match his skills against the pros again.

Roger Brown would be there. So would McGinnis, Bob Netolicky, Mel Daniels and Freddie Lewis along with others.

"I truly believe that's when my game started to evolve and how I got better as a basketball player in my younger days," Woodson said.

McGinnis said there were two things that he remembered about Woodson, even at that stage of his life: He was confident that he could play with that level of competition and that he could really shoot the basketball.

"When this guy put the ball in his hands and put it up you almost never thought it was going to miss," McGinnis said. "He had a really sweet shot."

McGinnis said it was unusual then that a kid either late in high school or early in college would be able to compete with a bunch of professional athletes.

"He could his hold his own and you could tell that right away," McGinnis said. "He wasn't intimidated, he just played. He shot the ball well and we all knew, 'This kid is going to be a player.' He worked hard and played hard but the one thing you saw right from the start was that Mike could really score the ball."

• • • •

When Woodson was recruited out of Broad Ripple High School in Indianapolis, he was courted by dozens of schools but had three he was most interested in: Indiana, Purdue and Cincinnati. He said Indiana was always the leader but he did take a visit to Cincinnati, too. He had one planned to Purdue but canceled it after visiting IU.

"My recruiting visit to IU was a tough visit in terms of coach Knight was on point and up front and basically wondered why would I even consider going to another school to potentially play when I could play at IU?" Woodson said. "He said these are all of the things we can do for you here and they all held true."

Woodson said Knight told him he could get three things if he came to IU: a good education, great basketball and Knight would help him get a summer job.

"I couldn't ask for more than that," Woodson said. "I just had to do my part."

Woodson said one thing that Knight made clear in the recruiting process was that academics would come first.

"When coach Knight recruited me, it was class first and then concentrate on playing basketball," Woodson said. "And he promised me a summer job. And all three of those things happened throughout my four years. I was able to graduate on time, I played for what I thought was the greatest university as far as college basketball in the country, and I was able to secure a job every summer to be able to help out with my mom and my family back in Indianapolis.

"For me, I look at all the games, and all the accolades and all of the accomplishments along the way, but what stood out to me more than anything else was that I was able to graduate on time thanks to some tremendous people that helped me like two ladies named Buzz Kurpius and Anitra House, who were my academic advisors and my tutors."

Woodson felt like he had it all at Indiana. Good basketball, a good education and a good summer job.

His first summer in Bloomington, he worked for a construction company in town. The second summer he worked for a company called Flashers Barricade in Indianapolis and the summer following his jun-

Mike Woodson (Indiana University Archives – P0022044)

ior year he worked for Detroit Diesel Allison in Indianapolis in a big factory job.

"I didn't work after my senior year because I was fortunate enough to get drafted," Woodson said.

Looking back, Woodson said he was able to do just about everything he hoped for at Indiana. The only thing he missed out on was a national championship. That happened at Indiana the year before he arrived and the one after. While he was at IU, he was on a team that was ranked No. 1 in the nation early in his senior year but he would have to settle for that.

"We didn't get to win the big one but we won a Big Ten title, and there was a gold medal that came along during the Pan Am Games and there was an NIT championship," Woodson said. "And the main one we were chasing was my senior year. We were ranked No. 1 but unfortunately a lot of things went against us. One was Randy Wittman breaking his foot. And then I went down with the back surgery even though I was able to come back.

"I thought that team our senior year was as good as any team that coach Knight ever coached."

••••

Mike Woodson had an interesting ride in his four years at Indiana.

His freshman year, IU was coming off the unbeaten national championship season and the only returning starter was Kent Benson. The only two players with much experience were juniors Jim Wisman and Wayne Radford.

Beyond that three sophomores and six freshmen battled for the remaining spots. The other freshmen were Butch Carter, Bill Cunningham, Glen Grunwald, Derek Holcomb, Mike Miday and Woodson.

Woodson had a solid camp leading up to the start of the season and was in the starting lineup in his opening game of his freshman campaign. IU dominated South Dakota, 110-64 and Woodson was one of five players in double figures with 16.

In IU's sixth game of the season, the Hoosiers beat Utah State with Woodson scoring 26 points. He would have a few other 20-point plus performances for the season with a high game of 34 at Iowa on Feb. 28. He also had 32 against Michigan on Feb. 3.

Woodson scored 500 points as a freshman and averaged 18.5 points per game. The 500 points was the most scored by a freshman at that point in Big Ten history.

The season was a rocky one and in fact IU needed to beat Ohio State in the season finale to avoid finishing with a losing record. The Hoosiers finished 14-13 overall and 9-9 in Big Ten play. If you look back at IU's record for the season it will show the final record as 16-11 and 11-7 in conference but that was only after Minnesota was forced to forfeit two games to IU after incurring NCAA violations.

The significance of IU not making the postseason in the 1976-77 season was that it would end up being the only season in Bob Knight's 29-year coaching career at Indiana where he didn't make postseason play.

It didn't take long for the Hoosiers to right the ship. The Hoosiers bounced back in Woodson's sophomore season to go 21-8 including a 12-6 mark in Big Ten play. The Hoosiers made the NCAA Tournament, beating Furman in the first game and losing to Villanova in the second.

Woodson started 28 of 29 games his sophomore season, averaging 19.9 points and shooting better than 52 percent from the field. By the time his sophomore season ended he was a member of IU's 1,000-point club. In fact, he got to 1,000 points in 54 games which still ranks as the fifth quickest total in IU history.

Woodson's junior season in 1978-79 was an up and down affair.

IU opened the season at the Sea Wolf Classic in Anchorage and lost the first two games to Pepperdine and Texas A&M before beating Penn State. After six games, IU was 3-3 but Knight had been sensing something had been amiss with his team for a few weeks.

After the Bradley game on Dec. 9, Knight learned while on the Alaska trip some of his players had allegedly smoked marijuana. Knight confronted the players about the incident and the following Monday kicked three players off the team. He put several others on probation and threatened immediate dismissal if it happened again.

"You go through tough times in life and that was a tough time for Indiana University in basketball and for a lot of players," Woodson recalled years later. "But we were able to weather the storm. Coach Knight refused to let us quit. And we were able to accomplish something that probably no one thought we could do."

Randy Wittman, who was a freshman on that team, was moved to point guard by Knight. He said that he had a lot to think about but it was made easier knowing that there was really one priority above them all.

"When I was a freshman point guard playing 39 ½ minutes my job was to basically make sure Mike got the ball in the right place to score," Wittman said. "He was a great scorer of the basketball."

It started with the very next game. IU, with a depleted roster, played host to No. 6 Kentucky at Assembly Hall. Woodson scored a game-high 27 points and hit two free throws with 5 seconds remaining to give the Hoosiers a 68-67 victory in over-time.

The Big Ten season was more of the same up and down play. Indiana had a 9-8 record in Big Ten play entering the final regular season game against Illinois in Champaign.

Mike Woodson would have the single greatest individual performance of his career as he scored 48 points on 18-of-27 field goals and 12-of-14 free throws. IU won the game 72-60 to finish 18-12 overall and 10-8 in conference.

For Woodson it was the third highest scoring game in Indiana basketball history (Jimmy Rayl holds the top two with 56 points twice) and that point total still ranks as No. 3 all time in school history today.

Indiana managed to sneak into the NIT field and played Texas Tech in Lubbock, Texas on March 8. The Red Raiders were coached by Gerald Myers. Interestingly, years later when Knight took the head coaching job at Texas Tech after he left Indiana, Myers was his athletic director.

Woodson scored 30 in the NIT opener and IU won easily. The Hoosiers beat Alcorn State in the second game to advance to Madison Square Garden for the NIT Finals. IU beat Ohio State in the semifinals and would face Purdue in the NIT title game in '79. Butch Carter hit the game winner from the top of the key with 6 seconds remaining to lift IU to a 53-52 win.

"I'll admit there was something special about beating Purdue on a national stage like that," Woodson said. "That was a rollercoaster year but after we qualified for the NIT that was the best way it could have ended."

That took Woodson to his senior year and the Hoosiers were loaded with talent.

IU returned all five starters from the '79 team and added Glen Grunwald and Ted Kitchel, who had both redshirted the year before. The incoming freshman class was highlighted by Isiah Thomas. The Hoosiers were ranked No. 1 in the nation heading into Woodson's senior season.

IU won its first four games before a demoralizing loss to Kentucky in Lexington on Dec. 15. It wasn't the fact that IU came out on the short end of a 69-58 decision that was so bad, it was how much the Hoosiers lost in the game.

Randy Wittman limped off the court early in the second half. He didn't return for that game or the remainder of the season for that matter. He had suffered a stress fracture in his foot and would take a redshirt season. Then it got even worse for the Hoosiers when Woodson hurt his back. He stayed in and finished the game.

The next game, Woodson actually led all scorers with 19 points in an easy win over Toledo on Dec. 18. But after the game his back was giving him all kinds of trouble. He was diagnosed with a herniated disc that would require immediate surgery. Woodson was hopeful he could come back by the end of the year but that seemed optimistic.

Don Fischer said the majority opinion at the time was that he probably would not be back.

"I always thought he might be able to come back but I really wasn't sure if he would be any good and be able to contribute because he had missed so much time," Fischer said. "That's tough when you have to spend so much time rehabbing an injury and just trying to get back. You also lose your conditioning. I just wasn't convinced how effective he would be or how much of an impact he would be able to make.

"That turned out to be a mistake on my part."

When IU played at No. 20 Iowa on Feb. 14, the Hoosiers were 7-5 in Big Ten play and one game out of first place. It had been less than two months since Woodson had back surgery. But he was back in the Indiana lineup that day against Iowa.

This is how Jason Hiner in the *IU Basketball Encyclopedia* described Woodson's return.

"Most observers looked at Woodson with a wary eye and doubted he could be very effective after missing two months while rehabilitating for major surgery. However, a minute into the game, Woodson peeled off a screen, caught the ball in rhythm and buried his first jump shot. Then he buried his second shot. Moments later he drained his third straight jumper. He eventually scored 18 points and helped carry the Hoosiers to a 66-55 win over one of their main rivals for the conference title."

Fischer said what impressed him the most was that Woodson never acted like he was tentative with the injury when he came back. Sure everyone is going to feel their way back a little bit, but Woodson came back a confident player.

"When he came back he never acted like there was going to be a problem," Fischer said. "He acted like he was going to have a good ending to his senior year no matter what happened. He had that kind of purpose to what he was doing.

"From his first game back you could tell he was going to make an impact. He really believed that he was going to be a factor and once he was back he really was the old Mike Woodson. It wasn't like there was anything missing."

Next up was Minnesota and Woodson scored a game-high 24 points in the Indiana win. IU would go on the road and sweep a pair of games from Michigan State and Michigan. Woodson had 20 against Michigan State and 24 against Michigan. IU won its fifth game in a row, beating Wisconsin at home. Woodson *only* had 16 against the Badgers but IU was able to post a 61-52 victory.

That set up a regular season finale with Ohio State in Bloomington with the winner taking the Big Ten championship. Two free throws by Butch Carter forced overtime and IU won the game there, 76-73. Woodson had 20 points for the Hoosiers.

After going 3-3 their previous six games without Woodson, the Hoosiers had bounced back to go 6-0 over the final six games with him. The average winning margin was 6 points a game but that wasn't the important thing. What was important was that IU had found a way to win when it needed to the most.

Woodson had put the Hoosiers on his back and led them to the Big Ten championship. It was an incredible comeback story. And when the Big Ten announced its annual awards, Woodson was rewarded for his efforts.

Despite playing only six games in Big Ten play that season, Woodson was named the Big Ten's most valuable player based on his heroic comeback from back surgery. In those six games, Woodson averaged 20.5 points per game. In 14 games overall that season, Woodson averaged 19.3 points.

"I just think Mike was really a tough kid," Fischer said. "He was tough mentally and physically. He was a great shooter but he was an even better scorer. He found a way to get the ball in the basket. If they were guarding him on the perimeter he would drive the basketball. If they were permitting him to sit out there and shoot it, he'd knock it down.

"He was just an absolute tremendous scorer. He had that mentality where missing a shot or two or even three never bothered him. But you rarely saw him do that, too. He was one of those guys where when he shot it you thought it had a pretty good chance of going in."

Fischer said there was one other thing that really stood out about Woodson while at Indiana. This was especially true in that six-game stretch to wrap up his regular season career as Woodson was more determined than ever.

"For a guy who was as rail thin as he was throughout his playing days at Indiana, he was one of the best finishers I've ever seen," Fischer said.

As for the Hoosiers, IU earned a No. 2 seed in the Midwest Regional of the NCAA Tournament. IU had a first round bye in the tournament before beating Virginia Tech to reach the Sweet Sixteen.

That's when the storybook quality of the 1979-80 season came to an end.

In fact, it wasn't simply how Indiana lost but who they lost to and where the game was played. The Sweet Sixteen that season was played in Lexington, Ky., which earlier in the year had been the place where IU had lost Wittman for the season, and ultimately Woodson for a seven-week stretch.

And making it even worse was that for the second season in a row IU would face Purdue on the national stage. As much as Woodson had enjoyed beating the Boilers the year before for the NIT championship, it was Purdue that would use the Hoosiers this season as a springboard to the Final Four. Purdue won the game 76-69 and IU's season came to a close.

"That one hurt a little bit more because of who we lost to," Woodson said. "But when I look back that was an amazing finish from a good group of guys."

Woodson ended his career as just the second player at that time in IU history to eclipse the 2,000 point mark for his career. Woodson finished with 2,061 and a four-year scoring average of 19.8 points per game. The only player with more points at the time was Don Schlundt with 2,192.

Since Woodson played at IU, three players (Calbert Cheaney, Steve Alford and A.J. Guyton) have all scored more points than he did. But Woodson still ranks fifth all-time in scoring at IU despite a back injury that cost him 15 games in his senior season.

"We had some things going for us early my senior year but then again, hey, sometimes things happen in basketball and you have to play through it," Woodson said. "For me, it's the guy that can get up and keep it going. We were able to still bounce back and win the Big Ten and move on from there."

After leaving Indiana, Woodson was selected in the first round of the 1980 NBA Draft by the New York Knicks, the 12th player selected overall. He would play in the NBA for 11 years, scoring 10,981 points, a 14.0 points per game average.

His first two seasons he played in New York before being traded to the New Jersey Nets. He would play there just seven games before he was traded to the Kansas City Kings. He averaged 18.3 points that first season there and later moved with the team when it went to Sacramento. In the final few seasons of his NBA career, Woodson bounced around with several teams, playing in Los Angeles (with the Clippers), Houston and Cleveland.

From 1996-2004, Woodson worked as an assistant coach in the NBA with Milwaukee, Cleveland, Philadelphia and Detroit. He was a part of an NBA championship staff in the 2003-04 season under Larry Brown with the Pistons.

Woodson's first full time head coaching job came in 2004 with the Atlanta Hawks. He was with the Hawks through the 2009-10 season and compiled a 206-286 record.

He took Atlanta to the playoffs his final three seasons. In fact, Atlanta won more games every year under Woodson. His first season, the Hawks were 13-69. His last they were 53-29.

Woodson's next stop was with the Knicks as an assistant under head coach Mike D'Antoni for the 2011-12 season. In

March of that year, however, D'Antoni resigned and Woodson was named interim coach. On May 25, 2012, Woodson was named the full time head coach.

He served in that capacity through the end of the 2013-14 season.

Early in the summer of 2014, Woodson accepted a position as an assistant coach on Doc Rivers' staff with the Los Angeles Clippers.

••••

Ted Kitchel played with some great players in his Indiana basketball career. He played on the '81 national championship team that featured Isiah Thomas, Randy Wittman, Ray Tolbert and Landon Turner.

But he said Mike Woodson stood above the others.

"He was probably the best player that I ever played with," Kitchel said. "The best team I ever played on was not the '81 national championship team but the 1980 team. It's kind of interesting, if you look at coach Knight's best team, the 74-75 team was much better than the 75-76 team because they could score so many more points. They were a much more dominant team, yet they didn't win.

"It was like the same thing with us. When we first started in 1980, we were a dominant team. We played the Russians who had just won the Olympics because we had boycotted the Olympics and not gone. The Russians won the Olympics pretty handily and they came over and played us, and we beat them by 20. We were a dominant team. Woody had to have back surgery and he still came back at the end of the year and we were able to win the Big Ten title."

Kitchel said, the truth about Woodson was that he was more than just the best player he had ever played with.

"As a college player, I think he was the best player in the country," Kitchel said. "He wasn't the most well-known player, but I think he was the best. I watched the Pan American Games tryouts, watched practice and he was such a dominant player and a great scorer and slasher. The most important thing about Woody is he's one of the finest people that you would ever want to know. He's just a great, great individual."

On that final point, Steve Alford said he couldn't agree more.

"Mike is just class all the way," Alford said. "Since he was a little before my time at IU, I've gotten to know him more away from Indiana. He's just a really classy individual. He has always taken time not to just help me but help others."

Randy Wittman feels the same way. He said when he was a freshman at IU (Woodson's junior year) that Woodson took him under his wing.

"He made me feel like I was a part of the family," Wittman said. "And he being an Indianapolis kid as well made it special. The thing about Mike is that he not only was a great player but he was a better person. He was one of the best people that I played with in terms of caring for another individual. That always sticks out with me with Mike."

Bobby 'Slick' Leonard isn't one to just hand out compliments. In fact, he's often critical in his assessment of players at the college and pro level. But he said only good things about Woodson.

"Well, Mike's special," Leonard said. "He's a special guy. He played all those years, he had a great college career and an excellent pro career, too. He played a lot of years. I'll tell you one thing. Phil Jackson just fired him as the head coach of the New York Knicks (in the summer of 2014). And Phil hired one of his buddies, Derek Fisher as the new coach.

"Mike Woodson is a better coach than Derek Fisher."

Quinn Buckner, one of the key ingredients on IU's 1976 national championship team, had high praise for Woodson, too.

"Of the guys that I know, Mike may have been the best scorer at Indiana from Indiana," Buckner said. "He was just that good. He was tough, he had back surgery and still came back to play. He had a very soft touch and used the glass. He just had a really good understanding of how to play.

"To me, I think he was the best player from Indiana in the era that I saw."

••••

From the very beginning of my interview with Mike Woodson in July of 2014, the former Hoosier great made it clear that he owed a great deal of his success to the coaching he received at Indiana from Bob Knight.

"The one thing you learn when you go to Indiana University to play for Bob Knight is that you're going to do it right all of the time," Woodson said. "At least you're going to attempt to do it right all of the time. He's going to make sure of that. Coach Knight was a disciplinarian which was fine with me."

Woodson said Knight taught him many things but first and foremost he learned how to play the game beyond high school.

"He taught me how to play college basketball," Woodson said. "Yes, I could score the ball and I could do a variety of things on the floor but he taught me how to defend. I don't think I was ever a great defender in coach Knight's eyes but I got better as a defensive player as the years went on."

Woodson said Knight taught him other things, too.

"He taught me how to respect others and how to work," Woodson said. "A lot of young players think they know how to work hard. If you went in with the idea that 'I really busted my ass' you learn that there's always another level. And Knight seemed to always push those buttons to find that level. If a player was slow at the start of the year, just look at that player when the Big Ten started, and then again when the Big Ten was over. It was the same way with his teams. They always got better. And to me that's the sign of a great coach."

Woodson said a lot of the lessons he learned as player he has tried to instill in his players in his own coaching career.

"I try to be a disciplinarian but I try to be open minded on how I approach a player and his style of play," Woodson said. "And I like to teach. That was the big thing that coach did a lot – he taught. I don't know how much teaching goes on today but I love to teach the game. I really do. I think if you can find players who are willing to learn and accept coaching then you've got something. Sometimes coaching is tough love."

Woodson said looking back he owes a great deal to Knight.

"When I look at Bob Knight and how he helped me better my game, on and off the court, you couldn't ask for nothing better," Woodson said. "He was the best in terms of being able to do that."

9
Number 6
Alan Henderson

When I did my daily blog series of the top 50 Indiana
University basketball players of
all-time for my previous employer in the summer of 2012,
Alan Henderson was one of the
most difficult players to rank.

As I did with this project, I
had polled a large group of
people who had close ties to the
IU basketball program from
media members to former players and a few others in between.
What I found was that people
had Henderson ranked all over
the board.

Eventually, he settled into
the No. 16 spot on that list although if I were to do it over
he would likely have moved up.

*Alan Henderson (Indiana
University Archives – P0020239)*

The reality is that when you look at Alan Henderson's total
body of work there's no doubt he needs to be ranked high on a
list like this one.

He was an All-American in 1995, a season where he averaged 23.5 points and 9.7 rebounds per game. In 24 of IU's 31
games that season, Henderson scored at least 20 points.

Henderson is part of an answer to an IU trivia question involving Indiana head coach Bob Knight. The question: What player averaged the most points under Knight in his 29 seasons as the IU coach?

Depending on how technical you want to be the answer is two players: Scott May in 1976 and Alan Henderson in 1995. The technicality is that May's average was an even 23.5 while Henderson was technically 23.516.

Either way it's an impressive accomplishment.

But there are other impressive statistics, too.

For his career, Henderson recorded 49 double-doubles, third most in Indiana basketball history.

His rebounding total – 1,091 for a career average of 8.8 per game – ranks first all-time in Indiana basketball history.

No, Henderson clearly deserves to be on the list of IU's best players, especially those players who hail from the state of Indiana.

It should be noted that while Henderson did grow up in Indiana and played high school basketball at Brebeuf Jesuit in Indianapolis, he technically was not born in the state. His birthplace is listed as Morgantown, W.V., but anyone that knows Henderson thinks of him as being a Hoosier Through and Through.

He initially took on Hoosier legend status in high school where he was the runner up in the state's Mr. Basketball voting behind Glenn Robinson of Gary Roosevelt. Robinson and Henderson also met in the state championship game that year when Gary Roosevelt defeated Brebeuf for the title.

At the time of his graduation from high school, Henderson ranked as the all-time leading scorer in Indianapolis High School basketball history and No. 6 all time in the state's basketball history. Henderson scored 2,419 points in high school.

As a high school senior, he averaged 27.4 points and 15.4 rebounds. As a junior, he averaged 29.7 points and 14.1 rebounds.

He was considered a top 10 recruit nationally coming out of high school.

All of those numbers and accomplishments just added pressure to the Indiana University basketball staff when it came to Henderson's recruitment.

In fact, former IU player, assistant coach and interim head coach Dan Dakich, who was on IU's staff when Henderson was being recruited, called the recruitment of Henderson incredibly intense.

That's because the two gems in the state that year from a high school standpoint were Robinson and Henderson and IU coach Bob Knight had made it clear to his staff that IU needed to get at least one of them.

Robinson had actually played on a Bloomington-based AAU team but eventually chose Purdue.

Pat Graham, the Indiana Mr. Basketball in 1989 who played with Henderson at IU, said Knight really wanted Henderson. He said when Robinson went to Purdue he doesn't think Knight was that upset about it.

"That's because he had Alan," Graham said. "If he could have had his choice, obviously he would have wanted both but I don't think that was going to happen. From what I was told and the feeling that I had being in the program, was that coach Knight got his top choice in Alan."

Dakich said Henderson was a high priority.

"Coach Knight made a big push for Alan for a number of factors," Dakich said. "One was his grades and the fact we knew he was going to be eligible was the most important factor. But I remember that coach Knight pulled out all the stops on that one to recruit both Alan and his parents."

The academic side of things was never in question when it came to Henderson. He was a member of the National Honor Society throughout high school. After college, he was accepted into medical school at Indiana University and the Howard University School of Medicine. He was a member of Kappa Alpha Psi Fraternity and graduated from IU with a degree in biology.

So academics wasn't going to be an issue as Henderson was a poster child for the term 'student-athlete'.

But Knight wanted to do everything he could within the rules to make a good impression when Henderson and his family came to visit Bloomington.

"I remember that the Henderson's stayed in the Union on his visit and they were put up in a suite that I had never even seen before," Dakich said. "I was an assistant coach and I didn't even coach the day he visited. Instead I sat in the stands with the Henderson's and explained every drill and answered every question.

"He was a huge, huge, huge recruit for Indiana University basketball. Because we had lost (Eric) Montross (to North Carolina) a few years before and here's another kid out of Indianapolis who is perfect for Indiana with the way he plays."

All of that just put the pressure that much more on Dakich and the staff to land the recruit.

"We had to have him," Dakich said. "And it was as nervous as I've ever been in recruiting because we were calling different people every day to try to get a pulse. It was a hectic time."

Henderson obviously ultimately committed to Indiana and the rest, as they say, is history.

Henderson would go on to have a four-year career at IU where he just missed becoming the sixth player in IU history to score 2,000 points or more. Henderson finished with 1,979 in 124 career games. Had he not gotten injured and missed some games his sophomore year, he would have easily surpassed the 2,000-point mark.

In four seasons at IU, his teams would go 98-32 including a Final Four appearance his freshman season, a team that Calbert Cheaney would later say was the best team he played on at Indiana.

••••

Henderson's first two seasons at Indiana he played in the shadows of Calbert Cheaney in terms of being the go-to player. This isn't to say he didn't contribute because he was a significant contributor at IU all four seasons.

His freshman year, he started 26 of 33 games, averaged 11.6 points and 7.2 rebounds per game.

Greg Graham, a junior when Henderson came to IU, said that the addition of the big post player made a huge difference with that IU team.

"He was a great rebounder, just a wonderful piece to that team," Graham said. "When he came in there, it was a great complement to what we were trying to do."

Todd Leary, who had redshirted and was a sophomore in Henderson's freshman season, said the rookie forward simply gave the Hoosiers a player they didn't have up until that point.

"It wasn't that he was a freakish athlete from a jumping standpoint but he was tall, and he was really long, and pretty athletic and he had the ability to shoot the ball a little bit," Leary said. "He just gave us a little different dimension. At that point our big guys were Eric Anderson, who was extremely talented, but not that athletic. And with the other guys you were not talking about a whole lot of athleticism.

"So Alan gave us that 4/5 guy that is athletic and physical and can play out a little bit."

Pat Graham said the same thing regarding Henderson and his athleticism.

"Alan was not a great athlete," Graham said. "As far as running and jumping and speed and quickness, I never considered Alan to be a great athlete. Greg Graham was a great athlete. Matt Nover was a great athlete. Alan Henderson was more of an Eric Anderson type, not a great athlete.

"But man did he have hands. And man, could he see things early. He had a quick response. I would say he was the best I've ever seen at that. He had the little intangibles and that was the reason he was good. He had a gift with his hands, I will say that. A basketball came off the rim, and he had it."

Brian Evans came in with Henderson as a freshman and was his roommate right away at IU. He said IU had some experienced veterans at the time but no one quite like Henderson.

"We had rebounders on that team but nobody like Alan," Evans said. "He was a blue chip, McDonald's All-American guy that brought a different element to the team immediately. It only took one open gym for Alan to leave his mark on the team. He was able to do that from the first day we arrived on campus."

Evans said Henderson was able to take advantage of the ways he was different.

"He wasn't like Eric (Anderson) who was a great shooter and a great scorer, he was just different," Evans said. "Alan gets 10 rebounds in his sleep. He just had a nose for the ball. There was just something about Alan all through AAU and high school growing up, he really just had great instincts for the ball. And then he just had a big heart and spirit when it came to tracking it down.

"He was just always a great rebounder and guys like that are going to play. Even though we had guys that were of a similar size as Alan on that team, he was the best rebounder from the day he showed up."

Jake Query, the radio talk show host in Indianapolis on 1260 WNDE-AM, once asked Dewey Williams, who played center at Northwestern at the time that Henderson was at Indiana, just what was the scouting report on Henderson.

"He said, 'The first thing it says is: LOVES EVERY RE-BOUND,' and it was in all capital letters," Query said. "He was relentless in terms of rebounds number one. He was a better shooter I believe tham people remember. He was a better passer than people remember. He could block shots, he could defend. I remember the blocked shot he had on Chris Webber to win at Michigan. Alan could really do it all.

"I think he's the most underrated player in Indiana history."

Mention Alan Henderson to Don Fischer and the first words out of his mouth were, "He could rebound like nobody Indiana has ever had."

"The one thing that he brought to the table that we needed and he had it from the day he walked on the floor was the ability to rebound the basketball," Fischer said. "To me it looked like he loved to rebound. He had a great sense of where the ball was going to come off, that kind of thing, and he always seemed to be in the right spot to get rebounds. He was not afraid to mix it up and he wasn't the physical specimen coming out of high school that a guy like Glenn Robinson was.

"But he had no fear of mixing it up inside."

Query agreed that Henderson wasn't afraid to mix it up. In fact, according to Query, Henderson in effect tried to change his image on how he was thought of between his freshman and sophomore years at IU.

"In Henderson's sophomore year all of a sudden (longtime IU public address announcer) Chuck Crabb changes the introduction of the starting lineup from 'Henderson, who is from Carmel, Indiana' in Alan's freshman year to 'Henderson, who is from Indianapolis, Indiana'," Query recalled. "My understanding is that Henderson, partially because of the image of the Fab Five from Michigan at the time, didn't want the soft image of being the suburban, privileged kid.

"He wanted to be thought of more as being a city guy, more of a hard guy."

The Indiana University media guides from that time period support Query's claim, too. In the media guide from Henderson's freshman year in 1991-92, he is indeed listed as being from Carmel, Ind. But in the 1992-93 media guide, Henderson is listed as being from Indianapolis and it stayed that way throughout his IU career.

Leary said another big key with Henderson was what he was able to do in the weight room.

"Alan really developed his body," Leary said. "You take a look at a picture of Alan at Brebeuf, I mean he was tiny. Skinny was a great description of him. But he got big at IU. He got a big chest and some big arms. He really worked out hard in the weight room."

Evans said the weight room piece was mandatory for every-

Alan Henderson (Indiana University Archives – P0020243)

body so it wasn't that Henderson was doing something that he didn't necessarily have to do. The difference, Evans said, was the commitment Henderson showed once he got there.

"It was just the approach he took," Evans said. "It wasn't like we were excited to be getting out of bed at 5:30 in the morning, I'll tell you that. But when Alan got out of bed and we walked into the building and got to the weight room, he got down to business. He worked at it. He knew that if he was going to continue to play basketball beyond college that he was going to have to beef up and add muscle.

"And he did. He worked at it. It was his approach more than anything else. Any time he went in there, he clocked in and he worked at it and he never took days off."

• • • •

Calbert Cheaney's first game of his college basketball career, he scored 20 points on 9-of-11 shooting against Miami of Ohio.

Henderson's college debut came against a little better opponent. IU faced UCLA in Springfield, Mass. in the Hall of Fame Tipoff Classic. The Hoosiers dropped an 87-72 decision that day but Henderson, like Cheaney a few years before, shined in his collegiate debut.

Henderson came off the bench to play 28 minutes and lead Indiana in scoring with 20 points. He also pulled down eight rebounds. Henderson hit 8-of-12 shots from the field.

Don Fischer said Henderson's first game as a collegiate player really surprised him. To Fischer's way of thinking, Henderson was even better than advertised right from the start.

"To me it was stunning to see him play that way," Fischer said. "I knew he was good coming out of high school. I had seen him play a couple of times and I liked what I saw but I just thought he would be a typical freshman in college where he would barely get his feet wet and not really contribute all that much.

"But I'll tell you what, as a college player playing his first game after that I thought 'Oh my God am I wrong about this guy.' Because he was a factor from the day he stepped on the floor."

And again, the thing Fischer liked more than the fact Henderson had the 20-point game to open his career was that he was a rebounding presence on a team that needed that piece.

"I remember he had a phenomenal first game and the thing that impressed me so much about him was how he loved to mix it up inside," Fischer said. "He had no fear and he wanted to get the rebound. He loved to rebound the basketball and of course, his career showed that he did that."

Henderson's first double-double came in the second game of his collegiate career. He had 16 points and 11 rebounds in 26 minutes off the bench.

A few games later, against Vanderbilt, Henderson had 13 points and 14 rebounds in an 88-51 victory.

Henderson eventually started all but seven games his freshman year. His high was 24 points at Ohio State in a February win over the Buckeyes.

The highlight of his freshman season, obviously, was the run that his Hoosiers were able to make. IU finished second in the Big Ten at 14-4, one game behind conference champion Ohio State. IU won six of its final eight games, which included an 86-80 win over Ohio State at Assembly Hall, to earn a second place finish.

That gave IU the No. 2 seed in the NCAA Tournament's West Regional.

There, IU opened with a 94-55 win over Eastern Illinois in a game where Henderson led the way with 19 points and 11 rebounds. He was 7-of-12 from the field.

That set up a second round matchup with an LSU team that featured Shaquille O'Neal. O'Neal got his points (36 to be exact) but Henderson and Calbert Cheaney took it to the big fella all day long. Cheaney led the way with 30 points but Henderson had 19 on 8-of-14 shooting including numerous 10-12 foot jumpers after Cheaney would force the action and then kick the ball back out to Henderson. IU won 88-79 to advance to Alburquerque where it would face Florida State.

The Hoosiers beat Florida State 85-74 and then knocked off UCLA 106-79 to advance to the Final Four where they would play Duke. Calbert Cheaney and Damon Bailey combined to score 45 points to lead IU, but Henderson had a double-double, too. He had 10 points and 12 rebounds in 26 minutes.

IU's season would end in Minneapolis in the Final Four with an 81-78 loss to Duke, a game that is revealed in more detail in the chapter about Calbert Cheaney.

One thing people remember about Henderson in this game though was what he was able to do defensively against Christian Laettner. He limited Laettner to eight points on 2-of-8 shooting. Henderson had 15 points hitting 6-of-9 shots.

Jake Query remembered one play in particular in that game that really stood out with the Henderson/Laettner battle.

"Henderson had clearly outplayed Laettner for the first half of that game," Query said. "And he had a follow up dunk early in that game and then gave that Henderson scowl where his nostrils flared up like Secretariat. Henderson had a nastiness about him on the floor."

••••

As a sophomore, Henderson looked bigger and stronger and poised to have a breakout season.

In the second game of the year against Tulane, Henderson posted a career scoring high with 28 points on 10-of-12 shooting from the field. He had a 19-rebound game to go along with 14 points in a 90-48 rout of Butler in late December.

But when people talk about Henderson and his sophomore year, however, there's one incident that is always remembered. Some say that along with Scott May's broken arm in 1975 that this may have been one of IU's most heart-wrenching injuries. It was difficult because it was a significant injury to a star player.

In this case, the star was Henderson. That season his numbers were much like they had been his freshman year (he averaged 11.1 points and 8.1 rebounds) but he was considered the glue in many ways. And he was an inside presence that a lot of IU's opponents simply didn't have an answer for.

"Alan was really their only true interior defensive rebounding presence," Query said. "Henderson was 6-9 and he had size. He could guard on the wing, he could guard inside. I think his defense was versatile. He could score outside, he could score in the post. He was just an anchor for them. And he was the only one they had.

"He was their only true definition of a big that year so when he got hurt, I mean, it was over."

IU won the first 13 games of the Big Ten season that year, but in terms of how that team would ultimately fare in the season, it was the events in practice leading up to the 13th game against Purdue that would always be remembered.

In practice the day before IU played Purdue, Henderson went into the air to catch a long outlet pass and came down awkwardly on his right knee. It turned out Henderson tore his ACL and would require knee surgery when the season was over.

IU would finish Big Ten play at 17-1 and still earn the No. 1 seed in the Midwest Regional of the NCAA Tournament but eventually not having Henderson in the middle would catch up to them.

IU made it to the regional final, one game away from the Final Four, before falling to Kansas 83-77 to end its season. Henderson attempted to play in the NCAA Tournament but was ineffective. In the four NCAA Tournament games, Henderson scored a total of four points, all against Wright State in the opener.

Against Kansas, he played 3 minutes and missed his only shot attempt.

"He looked like a deer with three legs that day," Pat Graham recalled. "He wanted so much to be able to pull it off but he just couldn't go."

Bob Knight was quoted at the time as saying he thought that Indiana had the best team in the nation when it had Alan Henderson on the interior. Without him, however, the Hoosiers had a major hole inside, one that a team like Kansas was able to exploit.

"I think we had the best team in the country," Knight said. "Without Henderson, we were stuck as we were without Scott May in 1975 – we went on, we still had a very good team, but we had lost a key component. Maybe Kansas would have beaten us anyway, but I don't think so. I don't think anyone would have."

Greg Graham, a senior on that '93 team, summed it up like this:

"To be honest with you, we're one Alan Henderson ACL away from winning the national championship," Graham said. "We were probably one of the better teams that went through IU that didn't win a national championship. (Alan) was an extremely important part of that.

"He had an opportunity to come back, but he wasn't the same when we lost to Kansas after he came back from the ACL. He just wasn't the same."

Todd Leary is one of those people that while agreeing that Henderson was an important piece still believed that the '93 team had the ability to win it all even without him.

"If you went back and watched the game film (against Kansas) when it got down to the end, we didn't play our best and we didn't do a lot of things that we were used to doing or comfortable doing," Leary said. "Everybody blames it on Alan's injury and obviously it would have helped us if he had been in there.

"But I don't look at it as it ruined our whole year and we didn't have a chance after that all happened. I still thought we had a chance even after that happened."

Calbert Cheaney said you can never understate what Alan Henderson meant to those first two Indiana teams he played on.

"He was the backbone of our team," Cheaney said. "He was in my mind probably the most valuable player on our team because of what he brought to the table. His rebounding, his blocked shots, and just all the things he did defensively. And then he was a premier offensive player as well."

• • • •

With Cheaney and company gone, Henderson was looked upon as more of a go-to player as a junior.

Considering he had just had knee surgery to repair ligament damage in May, some may have thought he would have needed to ease back into that role but that was never the case.

136

Henderson was ready to go when the Hoosiers tipped off the season with Butler on Nov. 27.

Looking back, Don Fischer, the radio voice of IU basketball, said it was an amazing accomplishment.

"That was stunning," Fischer said. "Generally, as a rule it's a year rehab before you can get back. And it took him very little time to get back to where he was his old self again."

Brian Evans agreed that it was a remarkable feat.

"I give him a ton of credit because he delayed the surgery initially because he wanted to come back and try to make himself available in the tournament," said Evans, Henderson's teammate and roommate at IU. "That pushed his recovery back into the start of his junior year. What it did was it shortened his window."

What it also did was increase the amount of time he spent in the weight room.

"I remember that once he had his knee operated on and he couldn't do a lot of the other things that we were doing, I know that he spent a lot of time on the bench press and a lot of time working on his upper body," Evans said. "And then once he got three months into his recovery when he could start working his legs, he worked really hard. I think he kind of transformed his body that summer and that was a big leap that he took toward strength."

Pat Graham, who had taken a redshirt year along the way and was a senior the year that Henderson was a junior, said people were skeptical that Henderson would be able to return to be the player he was before.

"I remember talking with Jeff Oliphant, who was a senior when I was a freshman, and he said he was really worried about Henderson knowing the nature of his injury," Graham said. "He said 'I don't believe he'll be able to do this and this and this and that', and the list went on and on. Well, none of that turned out to be the case."

Graham said the thing that still amazes him, however, is how quickly Henderson was able to come back.

"I know it was something like it wasn't that his knee was shredded or anything but it's still amazing that he could come back like that," Graham said. "If it's your knee it's simple, if it's my knee it's severe. That's just the way it always is. I think it was something simple but man, he did make a good recovery. I remember he worked his tail off though. He absolutely worked his tail off."

As for Henderson's junior season, IU still had Damon Bailey and Pat Graham in the starting lineup but Henderson's role was increasing. Bailey went on to be named first team all-Big Ten that season and was named an All-American.

Henderson started 29 of 30 games and averaged a double-double with 17.8 points and 10.3 rebounds.

IU opened the 1993-94 season figuring they might be looking at a split. After facing Butler in the opener in Indy, IU would square off against No. 1 Kentucky. As it worked out, the Hoosiers got a split. They lost to Butler 75-71 and then after an intense week of practice came back to beat the Wildcats 96-84.

Early in the conference season, Henderson got another rematch against his old nemesis, Glenn Robinson, now playing for Purdue. Henderson had a double-double with 24 points and 12 rebounds but Robinson had 33 points to lead the Boilermakers to an overtime victory.

Henderson also had his highest point total game of his career late in the '94 season. In a game at East Lansing, Henderson had 41 points and 13 rebounds but the Hoosiers lost to the Spartans.

Henderson would also have a big game in a winning effort during the NCAA Tournament. In an 84-72 win over Ohio University in the first game of the tourney, Henderson scored 34 points and pulled down 13 rebounds.

Indiana would make it to its fourth Sweet Sixteen in a row by beating Temple but then the Hoosiers lost to Boston College in the regional semifinals and the season came to a close.

Looking back on the junior season as a whole and how well Henderson was able to come back and be effective did not surprise his teammates at all. Brian Evans said that Henderson was always a man on a mission.

"With Alan it wasn't that he didn't want to have a fantastic career in Bloomington, because obviously he did that, but Alan had a great belief in himself," Evans said. "It was borderline wild arrogance. He knew he was going to play in the NBA and that was his dream and he was going to get there.

"I grew up playing with him, against him and living with him. He was arrogant about it but it wasn't that he talked about it all the time. Alan Henderson knew he was going to play in the NBA because he knew he was willing to pay whatever price it took to get there and he did. To his credit, through that injury, that was his vision and he stayed after it and ultimately realized that dream."

••••

Prior to his senior season, Henderson was a key contributor for Team USA in the Goodwill Games.

Early in the season, in the Maui Invitational, Henderson had 28 points and 10 rebounds in a win over Chaminade. Teammate Brian Evans led the Hoosiers with 37 points.

Indiana got off to a rocky start, opening the season 1-3 and then 2-4 before righting the ship a little bit with a six-game win streak. But after that IU could just never get another streak going. The longest winning streak from that point on was two games.

Henderson had some big games down the stretch. In his final matchup against Purdue, he had 26 points and 10 rebounds. In his final game in Assembly Hall, Henderson had 35 points on 16-of-19 shooting from the field in a lopsided win over Iowa. He also had nine rebounds.

Indiana finished in third place in the Big Ten and was given a No. 9 seed in Boise against Missouri. The Tigers brought an end to Alan Henderson's college career that day with a 65-60 victory.

Henderson did get 10 rebounds in his final college game which was significant because it gave him 1,091 for his career, a school record that still stands today. With 1,091 Henderson was able to edge out Walt Bellamy who had 1,088 rebounds in three seasons.

But Don Fischer doesn't think there should be any kind of asterisk affixed to Henderson's rebound record even if he did get an extra year to accomplish it. Fischer said people need to remember the difference in the two eras that the feats were accomplished in.

"When Bellamy played there weren't that many guys that were his size," Fischer said. "When Henderson played everybody was that big – or bigger. I just think about how tenacious he was on the boards and for me that puts him in that iconic group of players in Indiana history. There's no question about it."

Henderson's senior season was a memorable one and he was rewarded when he was named an All-American. He started all 31 games, averaged 23.5 points and 9.7 rebounds per game. He also shot 59.7 percent from the field.

Henderson was elected to the Indiana University Hall of Fame in 2008.

Talk to former Indiana players about Henderson's success at IU and many weighed in that they thought he deserved to be high on a list among the all-time greats.

"I thought Alan was a really smart player who really understood how to use his body," said IU forward Ted Kitchel, a member of the '81 national championship team. "He wasn't a guy that was going to out jump you but he really knew how to use fakes and work down inside. He was a very good athlete, and ran the floor very well."

Henderson was a first round draft pick of the Atlanta Hawks, the 16th selection overall. He would play 12 seasons in the NBA, including the first nine with the Hawks. He finished his career with more than 5,000 points.

"He was just really a solid player," Kitchel said. "He had a great NBA career. He was a solid individual from a very solid family background. You could always count on him. He was always there each and every night."

I was unable to reach him in doing research for this book but the last time I talked with Henderson was the summer of 2012. At that time he was living in Naples, Fla. with his wife, Maxine and their four children.

In fact, at that time Henderson and his wife had four children under the age of five and Henderson was a stay-at-home dad.

"It definitely makes you appreciate all of the stay-at-home moms out there and also just makes me that much more thankful for what my mom did for us," Henderson said. "It's time consuming and requires you to be on your game all of the time. At the same time it's very rewarding."

Jake Query graduated from high school the same year as Henderson. They both attended Allisonville Elementary School together, but Henderson eventually went to Brebeuf and Query attended North Central. They were both at IU at the same time, too. The point is that Query followed Henderson's career closely.

"It has only been 20 years since Henderson left Indiana but I think people forget how damn good he was," Query said. "He finished in the top five in like five different categories. You would be hard pressed to find a statistical category in IU basketball history that doesn't have Henderson in the top five, certainly in the top 10.

"I just thought he was a great player."

So how close was Query on his statistical prediction? Extremely close.

Consider this. As of the start of the 2014-15 Indiana basketball season, Henderson ranks sixth in career scoring, first in rebounding, fifth in steals, second in blocked shots, fourth in field goals made, ninth in field goal percentage, fourth in free throws made, second in free throws attempted and third in double-doubles.

The only significant categories where Henderson didn't show up were assists and 3-point shooting. He had averaged a little over one assist per game for his career and was 6-of-26 all-time from 3-point range.

But as a 6-9 beast inside, Henderson can get a free pass there.

10
Number 5
Kent Benson

As a three-time All-American in Indiana University basketball history, Kent Benson is part of a very select club.

Only Don Schlundt, Calbert Cheaney and Benson accomplished that feat in their Indiana basketball careers.

Only Benson and Schlundt also took home national championships in the process.

If you ever did a Mount Rushmore of Indiana basketball history, the big red head would have to be in the conversation.

Kent Benson (Indiana University Archives – P0043376)

I've often thought about what four faces would be on Mount Rushmore. It would be easy to go with two players and then Bob Knight and Branch McCracken.

But who would the two players be? Don Schlundt? You could certainly make that case. Calbert Cheaney? He is both Indiana and the Big Ten's all-time leading scorer. Isiah Thomas? I'm sure he would get votes. Scott May? He was the college player of the year on the last undefeated national champion in 1976. George McGinnis? Steve Alford? You could make arguments for any of them.

Still, Benson would be an intriguing choice as well.

Benson had career averages of 15.3 points per game and 9.0 rebounds. He shot 53.6 percent from the field for his career including a 57.8 percent season when the Hoosiers won the national championship in 1976.

He finished his career with 1,740 points, which at the time was second all-time in IU history behind Don Schlundt.

Today, he still ranks eighth all-time but that's because players like Cheaney, Alford, A.J. Guyton, Mike Woodson, Alan Henderson and Damon Bailey all passed him by later in their careers.

Benson is also part of another exclusive two-man club in IU history when it comes to playing at the next level. Scott May, Archie Dees, Isiah Thomas and Victor Oladipo all were the second players selected overall in the NBA Draft.

But when it comes to IU players in NBA Draft history, only Benson and Walt Bellamy can stake claim to be the first overall selection. For Benson it came in 1977 when he was selected first overall by the Milwaukee Bucks. Bellamy was the first pick of the Chicago Bulls in 1962.

Here is Benson's resume:

- Indiana's Mr. Basketball in 1973 at New Castle High School

- Second leading scorer on undefeated national champion team in 1976 at IU

- A three-time All American selection in college

- The first pick in the NBA Draft by Milwaukee in 1977

That's a resume for an Indiana basketball player that is going to be awfully tough to top.

••••

Think of Benson and the first thing most people remember is the hook shot. It was deadly. He could shoot with great accuracy and it became one of his most prolific weapons.

Archie Dees, a two-time IU All-American in the late 1950's, was impressed with Benson's abilities around the basket. He said he always wished that he could have done some of the things that Benson could do.

"I thought Kent was a very, very good college center," Dees said. "He was so much better inside than I was. He had a nice little baby hook and he had a great career at Indiana.

"I have a lot of respect for Kent Benson."

Bobby 'Slick' Leonard echoed Dees' remarks.

"Kent had a great college career," Leonard said. "He was going along pretty well in the NBA and all of a sudden, I don't think playing in the NBA was a big desire of his. I think he had other things on his mind. But you're not going to find many more dominant college players than Benson."

Ted Kitchel played a few years after Benson had graduated but he said he remembered that hook as well.

"I just remember he was a great college player and a very good professional player, too," Kitchel said. "He was a big body and obviously he learned to swing that hook. He was very dominant with that little hook shot that he had.

"At Indiana you had Scotty May shooting jumpers and Kent Benson was swinging the hook. But he was also a good defender. He was big and strong."

Randy Wittman had high praise for Benson. He said he thought the 6-11 center was in a league of his own in terms of IU big men.

"In my estimation, Kent Benson and Steve Downing were two of the best big men that ever played at Indiana in terms of straight, basic centers," Wittman said. "To do what Kent did in his college career and then to be the first pick in the NBA Draft was incredible.

"When you talk about the great players in college basketball across the country you probably wouldn't think of Benson. But when you think about his accomplishments at IU and then being the first player selected it makes you think about that again."

Wittman said he couldn't think of many others that were in Benson's big man class. Players like Don Schlundt, Archie Dees and Walt Bellamy were more before Wittman's time but in the period that he was most familiar with it was those two big men that had impressed him the most.

145

"I really believe that Benson and Downing, in terms of pure post up big men, were two of the very best we ever had at Indiana," Wittman said.

Bob Hammel, sports editor of *The Herald Times* in Bloomington, agreed with Wittman's assessment in the period he was referencing.

"They were different in style but they were both dominant big men as players," Hammel said. "And Bob (Knight) relied on that a lot."

One of those differences may have been Benson's ability to do more than just rely on post moves.

Don Fischer, the voice of Indiana football and basketball for more than 40 years, said with Benson he was far from one-dimensional offensively.

"The thing I always remember about him is that he had a variety of ways to score the basketball," Fischer said. "He wasn't just a post guy and a back to the basket type guy. He could do that very well. He had a good right-handed hook and he had a decent left-handed hook. But he could also go out and knock down the 15 to 18 foot jump shot.

"And he utilized all of those skills in almost every game that we played in. He was really a talented offensive guy."

Downing said Benson was a special player.

"He could do so many things and he could do them well," Downing said. "He was the focal point in the middle of a great basketball team. When you think of the 1976 undefeated national champions, Bennie is one of the first players you think of."

Hammel said in many ways Benson's game reminded him of Don Schlundt, the three-time All-American who starred on the '53 national championship team. Schlundt had a good inside game but he could knock down the perimeter shot, too.

"Kent was the first big man I can recall who was like Schlundt in that sense," Hammel said. "Schlundt was a really good shooter and he had a little hook. I don't think it was as good as Bennie's but it was effective. But they had similar post skills."

Quinn Buckner, who was a starter and senior on the 1976 national championship team, also talked about Benson in terms of being exceptionally talented offensively.

"Kent was somewhat unusual because he was so big and could really shoot the ball," Buckner said. "He had a great scoring touch, and that make him very, very difficult to play against."

Buckner said he thought Bob Knight deserved a lot of credit with Benson developing as he progressed in his career.

"I thought coach Knight did a terrific job of getting Kent the ball in positions where Kent would have success with it," Buckner said. "He could knock down the jump shot, he had his hook shot, and he was big and strong and could go get some rebounds."

Steve Alford had a little different perspective on Benson. He was coming from the place where Benson had attended his high school and now he was there trying to break Benson's records.

In high school, Benson scored 1,496 points and pulled down 1,585 rebounds in three seasons with the Trojans.

"Kent was somebody where as I got into the New Castle thing and learned about who he was, Kent was just someone I looked up to," Alford said. "We were from the same home town. As a player you're always driven to be the best and for me the measure of being the best often times meant trying to break his records.

"And Kent just set such a high standard at New Castle and it was fun growing up trying to compete and get to that level. I appreciated Kent at my high school setting the bar extremely high and not just for individual and team records but who you are as a person, too."

• • • •

Kent Benson was well known in Indiana circles long before he came to IU. His high school team his sophomore season made the state's Final Four which helped put him on the radar.

When it came time for his recruitment, a lot of schools were interested but Benson seemed to be interested in three in particular: Indiana, Notre Dame and Kentucky.

Archie Dees was a two-time All-American big man in 1957 and again in '58, but years later he had a hand in recruiting Benson.

When Benson was on his recruiting visit to Indiana, the IU staff asked Dees if he could come over and spend a few hours with him.

Dees remembered the first thing he asked him was where he thought he would end up going to college?

"He said, 'I'm going to Kentucky'" Dees said. "I told him 'Well, I don't think that's really a good idea for you. What do you think about IU?'

"He said, 'I don't think I could play there. They have a complicated system.'"

Dees said he passed on a little advice to Benson at that point.

"I told him if he went to Kentucky nobody was even going to know who he was and he was going to have to make a name for himself," Dees said. "I told him it would be a hell of a lot easier to take what he had already built up in Indiana and go up with it rather than start at the bottom."

Dees said he didn't remember much after that except that a few weeks after that visit he learned that Benson was coming to Indiana.

Dees, who was living in a nursing home as of the summer of 2014 after he had fallen and broken his hip a few years back, said that Benson still comes by and visits him from time to time.

"He tells everybody that I kept him from making a horrible mistake," Dees said with a smile. "I'm not sure if it would have been a mistake for him to go to Kentucky but I certainly thought it would have been at the time."

Hammel called Benson a major recruit. And he remembered those three schools in particular being the ones that were most in the mix for the big red head.

"I know Kentucky was attractive to him and so was Notre Dame," Hammel said. "He's Catholic and that had something to do with it, too. Ultimately he chose Indiana which turned out to be a big get for Bob (Knight) and the program."

• • • •

One of Don Fischer's first memories of Benson was in his sophomore season when he began to get more significant playing time. Fischer said one of Benson's biggest deficiencies at that point was that he wasn't physical enough.

"He had to learn how to become a more physical basketball player," Fischer said. "And I'll give him credit, it didn't take him long to learn it once he was put in that role. But Knight, to my memory about him, was always on him about that. He told him he had to be tougher and more physical."

Hammel said part of Benson's troubles in that area was that he needed to bulk up.

"He really hadn't filled out yet," Hammel said. "There was

Kent Benson (Indiana University Archives – P0041428)

an enormous physical breakthrough for Kent between his freshman and sophomore years. I do remember when he came back in August, and I saw him in a T-shirt up watching football practice and I couldn't believe how much he had filled out through his chest and upper body.

"He was never thin but there was a considerable difference between those two years."

Hammel said another reason Benson hadn't been real physical early was simply that in high school at New Castle he never really had to worry about that because he was so much bigger than the other players.

"He was used to not having to do a great deal of blocking out or fighting for post position when he was in high school," Hammel said. "It was a big transition for him."

Fischer said that Knight believed that Benson needed to be tougher both mentally and physically.

"There were a lot of times that he had to be talked off the ledge," Fischer said. "I know he thought about leaving many times in his IU career.

"Father Higgins was a part of the basketball program at that time, at least he was part of it in the sense that players went to him and talked to him and those kinds of things. And Bennie had to be talked off the ledge many times by Father Higgins. I know that for a fact. "

In his book, *Tales from the Hoosier Locker Room: A Collection of the Greatest Stories Ever Told,* John Laskowski confirmed what Fischer had said. Laz remembered Benson wanting to quit several times.

"When he got here, Bennie was the only freshman on the team but he also was the only 6-foot-10 guy we had," Laskowski wrote in the book. "We needed to have a center, so Coach was really on (Benson) to get going from day one. He was the missing part.

"But Bennie took it hard. He couldn't understand why he was getting picked on. Obviously he was a star and had been the biggest kid around his whole life and now things had changed."

Laskowski remembered a day when he saw Benson in the locker room after practice and he could tell the freshman had something on his mind.

"He said 'Laz, I'm going to quit the team. I'm going to get in the car and drive back to New Castle. I just can't handle this.' And I said, 'Let me walk you back to your room.

"We walked back to McNutt Quad, a very short trip, and by the time we got there I'd convinced him that coach really liked him and the reason he was yelling at him was that we needed him on the team and he needed to do some things differently. I told him if he'd just stick it out everything would pay off."

Laskowski said that conversation would be replayed a few times in the future.

"He'd say, 'All right, I'll stick it out' and then two weeks would go by and he'd say, 'I'm quitting,' and we'd do it all over again. I bet we did it three or four times, but each time he was able to come back, and I know today that he's glad he did."

Fischer said as Benson's career progressed he got better and better in the toughness department.

"He developed those skills, he was a tougher player and he was better defensively as his career progressed," Fischer said.

• • • •

Kent Benson was the only freshman on the 1973-74 team but he was looked at in terms of filling a big void in the IU lineup.

Steve Downing had graduated and the Hoosiers needed a big man in the middle. Benson would start 25 of 27 games his freshman season and make a solid impact.

He averaged 9.3 points and 7.9 rebounds per game. He shot 50.4 percent from the field.

In the first game of his college career against the Citadel, Benson scored eight points on four field goals.

His first double figure scoring game came five games into the season on Dec. 15 when he had 14 points at Ball State.

His first 20-point game came against Michigan Jan. 5 when he scored 20. After that he had 18 against Illinois, six versus Wisconsin, and then 18 at Minnesota and 19 against Michigan State.

From a team standpoint, the Hoosiers finished 12-2 in Big Ten play and co-champions with Michigan. The Hoosiers then played in the CCA where they beat Tennessee and Toledo by one point each before dropping an 85-60 decision to the University of Southern California.

That loss would be significant because over the next two seasons IU would suffer the exact same loss total combined – one game.

In the postseason, Benson had 18 points against Tennessee, 14 versus Toledo and 17 against the University of Southern California.

Those that saw Benson play the final seven or eight games of his freshman season believed they saw a player who was just warming up for what potentially could be an outstanding college basketball career.

"By the end of his freshman year you could see signs that this kid was going to be special," said Bill Murphy, IU historian and author of the book *Branch* about the life of Hoosier legend Branch McCracken. "As far as consistently blossoming into the star he was going to be and the All-American player, that would begin in his sophomore year."

••••

Indiana returned everyone Benson's sophomore season and optimism was high in Bloomington.

The IU starting lineup included Benson in the middle, Steve Green and Scott May at the forward positions and Quinn Buckner and Bobby Wilkerson at the guard spots.

In the *IU Basketball Encyclopedia*, Jason Hiner had this to say at the beginning of the 1974-75 chapter of Benson.

"At 6-11, Benson was a space-eater on the inside," Hiner wrote. "Although not a great athlete, he was a hard worker and probably the most improved player on the team. After winning the MVP award as a freshman in the CCA tournament in the spring of 1974, Benson was ready to carry more of the offensive load as a sophomore. He used a hook shot, a reliable face-up jumper and a variety of post moves to provide the Hoosiers with a solid presence in the paint."

Benson had 17 points in IU's season opener, a 113-60 thrashing of Tennessee Tech.

Two games later, he had 26 points and 13 rebounds as Indiana would beat Kentucky, 98-74 in Bloomington. He also had double figure points when IU beat number 11 Notre Dame 94-84 in South Bend the next game.

IU was a perfect 11-0 in the non-conference season and then followed that up with an 18-0 Big Ten record.

In Big Ten play, Benson had three 20-point plus games. He had 20 against Northwestern, 22 versus Wisconsin and 20 against Illinois.

It was the 15th Big Ten game at Purdue when Scott May broke his left arm in the first half, though, and that would end up being a red letter day for the Hoosiers.

IU beat New Mexico State easily in the first game of the NCAA Tournament 78-53 and then Benson dominated in the middle in a 81-71 win over Oregon State. Benson had 23 points and Steve Green led the Hoosiers with 34.

In the rematch with Kentucky, Scott May tried to play with a cast but was ineffective.

Benson put the Hoosiers on his shoulders and IU hung around but eventually dropped a 92-90 decision to the Wildcats. Benson had career highs with 33 points and 22 rebounds and was named the MVP of the regional but it was to no avail and Kentucky came away with the win.

Benson finished his sophomore season averaging 15 points and 8.9 rebounds per game. He shot 54 percent from the field and 74 percent from the line.

He was first team All-Big Ten and an All-American selection. It would be his first of three All-American nods.

• • • •

Benson's junior season was his most memorable simply because Indiana went a perfect 32-0 and captured the national championship, Bob Knight's first of three with Indiana.

Benson would average 17.3 points and 8.8 rebounds. He would be named the most outstanding player in the Final Four.

Indiana's first game of the 1975-76 season was against UCLA on a neutral floor in St. Louis. The Bruins were the defending national champions and ranked second in the nation in '75-76. Indiana was ranked number one.

IU posted an easy 84-64 victory. Benson had a double-double with 17 points and 14 rebounds. A few games later, IU played at Kentucky and needed a tip in by Benson in the closing seconds to force overtime. In OT, the Hoosiers prevailed 77-68.

It was an impressive tip-in because Tom Abernethy had missed the shot and it came off at about waist level for Benson. He gave it an underhand tap as if he was trying to help it get to the rim. Instead, the ball went straight up in the air and came back down through the hoop to force overtime.

Benson had some other good games and IU finished up non-conference play with a 9-0 record. He had 22 points against Florida State as he hit 10-of-15 shots from the field. He also had 15 against Virginia Tech and Columbia and then 19 against Manhattan.

IU was 9-0 heading to Big Ten play where it faced a pesky Ohio State squad. IU would win 66-64 and Benson had 23 points and 12 rebounds.

The next game he had 22 points against Northwestern and then 33 points at Michigan in an 80-44 win over the Wolverines. That game was particularly special for Benson because he hit 16-of-18 shots from the field.

His next game, Benson had 23 points and nine rebounds against Michigan State.

IU needed another tip-in by Benson against Michigan on Feb. 7 in Assembly Hall, again to force overtime. This time Quinn Buckner missed a shot in the closing seconds, Jim Crews got the rebound and missed a shot and Benson tipped it in at the buzzer. IU would win 72-67 in the extra session.

Benson had a couple of 16-point games against Illinois and Minnesota and then had 23 points and nine rebounds against Wisconsin. He had 21 points and 15 rebounds in the rematch with Michigan, and would close the Big Ten season with 21 points and 11 rebounds against Ohio State.

IU would finish 18-0 in Big Ten play for the second consecutive year in conference play.

IU beat St. John's in the first NCAA Tournament game as Benson had 20 points and 13 rebounds. That advanced IU to the Sweet Sixteen where it beat Alabama 74-69. Benson had 15 points and five rebounds in that game. His rebounds were low because Scott May had 16 and Bobby Wilkerson 12 in that game.

That set up a matchup of the top two teams in the nation, No. 1 Indiana and No. 2 Marquette. Benson had 18 points and nine rebounds in IU's 65-56 win that advanced the Hoosiers to the Final Four.

Benson would score 16 points and pull down nine rebounds in the first game of the Final Four, a 65-51 win over UCLA. That advanced IU to play Michigan for the third time in the season in the title game. Benson had 25 points and nine rebounds in the championship game to help lift IU to an 86-68 win. Scott May led the Hoosiers with 26 points.

• • • •

In Benson's senior season in 1976-77, all of a sudden the big red head was the focal point of the team.

Gone were Scott May, Quinn Buckner, Tom Abernethy, Jim Crews and Bobby Wilkerson. Those five players had combined to average more than 53 points the year before.

So now Benson was the lone senior on the current Indiana team.

Bob Hammel said Benson's senior year was clearly a difficult one for him.

"It was an odd year for him because he was not a natural leader and now he was put in that position," Hammel said. "Bob (Knight) has always second-guessed himself for not doing what wasn't common

Kent Benson (Indiana University Archives – P0023273)

then which would be redshirting Jimmy Crews for a year or Tommy Abernethy for a year. Not the same years but one year along the line. They wouldn't both have been missed that much and they would have been valuable the year that Bennie was a senior."

Don Fischer said Benson struggled with being "the guy."

"When Kent was surrounded by a great cast he was another great player," Fischer said. "But when he was the main man it was a much more difficult role for him. I'm not saying he didn't have a good year because obviously he was an All-American and he would get picked first in the NBA Draft.

"But you could tell he missed that supporting cast that had been so vital to Indiana's success."

Bill Murphy agreed Benson clearly missed his supporting cast. Murphy said Mike Woodson was a freshman and a player like Wayne Radford was called upon for a bigger role but Benson was clearly the focal point.

"He was the man that year, no question about it," Murphy said. "Benson drew the attention of everybody. Actually Benson really helped Woodson and Radford and Butch Carter an awful lot because they were able to do some things that they normally couldn't have done right off the bat because everybody was really, really keying on Kent.

"In some ways you felt bad for Kent because it would have been poetic justice for him just to be able to graduate with May, Buckner and Wilkerson and begin the next chapter of his career."

Benson would end up with the highest individual scoring average of his career at 19.8 points. He averaged a double-double with 10.5 rebounds, too.

But the bottom line is that IU would finish the season 14-13 overall and 9-9 in Big Ten play. Later, the schedule would show two more victories as Minnesota had to forfeit two games to the Hoosiers that season which made it look more respectable at 16-11 overall. But the 14-13 mark was the actual reality.

Benson had 17 points and 11 rebounds in the opener against South Dakota but then IU dropped three games in a row to Toledo, Kentucky and Notre Dame. That three-game losing streak was three times as many losses than Indiana had total the previous two seasons.

Benson would open the season with seven double-doubles in the first eight games. He had 17 and 13 against Toledo and 21 points and 13 rebounds against Kentucky. Against DePaul, Benson had 18 points and 16 boards. He had 16 points and 11 rebounds against Utah State and then 26 points and 15 rebounds against Miami of Ohio.

His final game in that streak was when he scored 19 points and pulled down 11 rebounds in a victory over Georgia.

In Big Ten play the Hoosiers were up and down as a team but Benson had some big games individually.

IU jumped out to a 4-2 record and beat Ohio State in Columbus, 79-56. Benson had 29 points and 12 rebounds in the win and Mike Woodson had 22.

Benson also had 25 points and 14 rebounds against Minnesota.

The Hoosiers would steal an 81-79 win at Michigan State later in conference when Benson had another big time performance. He had 35 points, nine rebounds and four blocks against the Spartans. Benson also had 24 points and 12 rebounds in a 73-64 win over No. 5 Michigan.

As the Big Ten season went on Benson started having trouble with an ailing back. He was still able to put up some big games though. He had 19 points and 13 rebounds in the first game against Purdue. Against Illinois, he had a double-double with 17 points and 11 rebounds. Against Northwestern, Benson scored 32. He had 23 in Madison against Wisconsin and then 25 points in Champaign against Illinois.

Benson's senior season didn't end well though after he aggravated a previous back injury in the Purdue game Feb. 20 when he collided with Joe Barry Carroll and was knocked out of the lineup. Benson did not play in the final four games of the season against Wisconsin, Northwestern, Iowa and Ohio State. IU finished 2-2 in those games.

For his Indiana career, Benson averaged 15.3 points, 9.0 rebounds and shot 53.6 percent from the field.

"Benson shouldered the responsibility that he was given really, really well," said IU basketball historian Bill Murphy. "And he did the best he could to make IU as good as they could possibly be after they lost as much as they lost.

"Benson really stepped up and did as much as he could his senior year."

••••

Kent Benson was selected with the first pick in the NBA Draft by Milwaukee. Houston's Otis Birdsong was taken second, followed by UCLA's Marques Johnson, Oregon's Greg Ballard and North Carolina's Walter Davis.

Benson would play 11 years in the NBA for four different teams. He started with Milwaukee, then played for Detroit, Utah and Cleveland. He also spent one year after his NBA career ended with Vismara Cantu in Italy.

But what a lot of people remember about his NBA career occurred in his first professional game on Oct. 18, 1977 in Milwaukee Arena against the Los Angeles Lakers.

There are different accounts of exactly what happened but Benson reportedly hit Kareem Abdul-Jabbar with a pretty hard elbow. Jabbar retaliated with a punch that broke his hand and cost him 20 games.

Benson explained what happened in a 2012 interview with Mark Montieth on 1070-The Fan in Indianapolis.

"Let's back up and tell the story as it really is," Benson said in the interview. "First of all, I out-jumped Kareem at the tip-off. I'm not supposed to do that. Second, we come down the floor. Brian Winters takes a shot, misses it. I go up over Kareem, get the rebound and score."

Benson claimed that Abdul-Jabber initiated the elbowing and he then gave the Lakers center an elbow to the stomach.

"I run down to our defensive end, their offensive end of the floor to set up on the spot where Kareem likes to shoot his hook shot on," Benson said. "And in doing so he comes down the floor and drives his elbow into my chest. I take it and elbow him back while we are jostling for position.

"I'm watching the ball come up the floor," Benson said. "He falls back about 10 feet away from me and runs up and sucker punches me from behind. All you see on these videos or whatever is me elbow him first and then him retaliating that way. They don't show what started it."

Benson said the punch from Jabbar did not break his jaw as some have reported. But it hurt. No question about that.

"He knocked me silly, no doubt about that," Benson said. "He hit me so hard he broke his hand. He hit me in the temple. I had a black and swollen (right) eye. I didn't have a concussion, but I missed a couple of games because of it."

Montieth asked Benson if that first punch had an impact on his career.

"You know, the critics say that it did, it took everything away from me, yadda, yadda, yadda," Benson said. "But I don't buy that. Did it have an impact on me? Yeah, I think it had some impact, not a devastating one. I showed I could stay in the league for 11 years."

11

Number 4
George McGinnis

There are two major difficulties when putting together an all-time list like this one.

One is comparing players from different eras. For example how do you compare a player like Everett Dean, who was IU's first All-American in 1921 and the first Indiana player to ever score 20 points to someone who averaged double figures all four years on a team in the last 20 years?

The other is how do you handle players who only played one or two seasons? When I did a countdown of the top 50 players all-time in IU basketball for my previous employer in the summer of 2012, that question was hotly debated with players like Isiah Thomas and Eric Gordon.

George McGinnis (Indiana University Archives – P0020277)

And George McGinnis.

When you just look at what he was able to accomplish in his one and only season at Indiana and the way he impacted the game, it stops you in your tracks.

In the 1970-71 season, the season before Bob Knight took over as the Indiana coach, McGinnis averaged 29.9 points and

14.7 rebounds per game. Several people interviewed for this book have described him as having been a man amongst boys.

McGinnis was the model of consistency. He scored 20 or more points in 21 of his 24 college games, including an IU record 14 times in a row. In 12 games, he scored over 30 points which is also an Indiana school record.

He had 45 points and 20 rebounds against Northern Illinios. He had 38 points and 23 rebounds against Northwestern. He had 37 points against Michigan State. The list goes on and on.

He sat out his freshman season at Indiana in an era when freshmen were not allowed to play on the varsity. His only season as a sophomore he was an All-American.

He went on to an incredible 11-year professional career in both the ABA and the NBA. Six times (three in each league) he was named to the All-Star team. For his career he scored more than 17,000 points and pulled down more than 9,000 rebounds. His career averages are a double-double at 20 points and 11 rebounds a game.

If he had stayed at Indiana and not went quickly to the ABA, most people believe there would be at least one more national championship banner hanging at Assembly Hall.

But how does one year – one incredible year – of play stack up against players that scored more than 2,000 points in their Indiana careers?

We can probably assume that if McGinnis had played all three of his possible seasons at Indiana that he would have put up gaudy numbers but we also know what happens when people assume, too.

Bobby 'Slick' Leonard was a two-time IU All-American who would go on to coach McGinnis at the professional level. If he was the lone voter in compiling IU's top 50 list, there would be no debate on who was the No.1 player all-time: it would be George McGinnis.

"The best player that ever came out of Indiana is George McGinnis," Leonard said, matter-of-factly. "He was a true talent. George could do everything. He could score, he was a great rebounder. He tore the Big Ten up. The numbers he put up as a sophomore were fantastic."

Leonard's bias came from coaching McGinnis daily at the professional level.

"I had great years with him," Leonard said. "I've seen him dominate games. Here's the way I look at it: What players could dominate a ball game? George can absolutely dominate a ball game, just like Larry Bird could. When it went to the wire, Larry could dominate a ball game.

"There are three guys from Indiana that could dominate ball games. Oscar Robertson could dominate. George McGinnis could dominate. Larry Bird could dominate. Those are the three most outstanding that have come out of the state of Indiana."

Tom Bolyard averaged 18 points per game at Indiana in a three-year career that went through the 1963 season. He was a first team All-Big Ten selection that year. Later, he returned to his alma mater and spent six seasons as an assistant coach to Lou Watson on the IU staff.

Bolyard was the man who recruited McGinnis to Indiana.

"George McGinnis was as good a player that has ever played here," Bolyard said. "For a high school and college player he was unbelievable."

Bolyard remembered that McGinnis would always be the first player on the floor for practice. The coaches would be out there but McGinnis would be the first player to arrive.

He said one day at practice, McGinnis yelled over at him that he wanted Bolyard to come over and try to take the ball from him. McGinnis started dribbling the basketball and Bolyard tried to steal it. And then he tried some more. On and on he went.

"I tell you, you couldn't get it away from him," Bolyard said. "He was so big and so strong you couldn't get close to the ball. He was just unbelievable. He was clearly a man amongst boys. That's the only way you can describe him."

Bill Murphy, author of the book Branch and an IU basketball historian, said McGinnis was simply unstoppable.

"The only person who could ever stop George was George," Murphy said. "Every once in a while he would pull up and take a real outside jumper but that wasn't his specialty. But if he decided he was going to score on you, he went down inside and no one was going to stop him."

Murphy said McGinnis had it all.

"He was fast and strong and had a body that Greek Gods were envious of," Murphy said with a smile. "He was a great, great player."

• • • •

As a young boy growing up in Indianapolis, McGinnis remembers his first real basketball memory was as a 6-year-old boy going to the state championship game with his dad at Hinkle Fieldhouse and watching Indianapolis Crispus Attucks play.

It was 1956 and Oscar Robertson scored 39 in the title game to lead his team to a 79-57 victory over Lafayette Jeff. It was the second consecutive state title for Attucks which had beaten Gary Roosevelt in the title game the year before.

"I saw them play again in '59 when they won the state again," McGinnis said. "Those were my first two impressions. And Oscar Robertson was the guy everyone looked up to, especially in the black community."

But watching Robertson had McGinnis hooked at an early age.

Steve Downing first met George McGinnis when they were young boys playing football on the west side of Indianapolis. McGinnis grew up near Military Park on the west side of Indianapolis. When he was in high school his family moved to the Haughville area which is where Downing lived. Haughville was located just west of IUPUI.

McGinnis came by his height naturally. His mother was almost 5-10 and his father was 6-6. When McGinnis was a high school freshman, he was about 6-4.

"I was always a fairly tall kid and I was always the tallest kid in my class," McGinnis said. "When you're tall you get teased a lot. I was pretty clumsy. It took me a while to gather myself. By the time I was in about the eighth grade I was pretty well coordinated. But early on from the time I was 8 to about 12 or 13, I was pretty clumsy.

"The kids would say 'Oh here comes old goofy George.' I got a lot of that when I was growing up. It kind of made you close up a little bit. You would just walk around with your head down hoping people wouldn't notice you."

Downing didn't remember the goofy part but he certainly remembered his friend's height. Downing's growth spurt came later. When he was a freshman in high school he was 5-10. By the time he was a senior, he was 6-8.

"I knew of George because he was always the biggest kid around," Downing said. "We used to play football over there at a little park where the V.A. Center is now in Indianapolis. And so we would play pickup football most every Saturday. At that time, I really didn't know much about him other than he was a really big kid."

Downing and McGinnis became close friends when they went to high school together at Washington High School in Indianapolis.

"His family ended up moving out to Haughville and I met him as a freshman playing football in high school," Downing said. "He just played on offense and he was a tight end. He was really a good football player. He could have played either professional football or basketball. He always wanted to play basketball."

In an interview for this book in the summer of 2014, Downing was asked to retell his favorite memory of watching McGinnis play basketball.

There was no hesitation. The site was Freedom Hall in Louisville, Ky. for the second Indiana-Kentucky high school All-Star game following McGinnis' senior year of high school. McGinnis had been named the state's Mr. Basketball and would wear the coveted No. 1 jersey in the two-game All-Star series.

In the first game of the series, played in Indianapolis, McGinnis scored 23 points and pulled down 14 rebounds in Indiana's win at Hinkle Fieldhouse. Kentucky All-Star Joe Voskuhl guarded him that night and in the newspapers the next day said he thought McGinnis was good but nothing special.

"I think he's overrated, I really do," Voskuhl told the Louisville *Courier-Journal.* "Oh, he's good, but he's overrated."

Those comments found their way to McGinnis. When the two teams played again the following week at Freedom Hall, the Indiana big man was looking to show what he could do on the basketball floor.

McGinnis scored 53 points and pulled down 31 rebounds in Indiana's 114-83 win over Kentucky in the 1969 All-Star finale.

"That was the best I've ever seen him play," Downing said.

After Voskuhl's comments made the rounds after the first game, Downing said that McGinnis was really hurt by what had been said. He pulled Downing off to the side just before the second game in the series and had a message for his buddy.

"He told me, 'Just help me get the ball. Help me get the ball'," Downing said. "He said he knew that I would be in the game and I would be able to do that. And whenever he was like that, well, you got him the ball."

McGinnis said that later in life he and Voskuhl have become pretty good friends. He said Voskuhl is in the oil business and lives in Oklahoma. He said they have had several discussions about it and that Voskuhl laughs about it now.

McGinnis said at the time he took what Voskuhl said as "a personal dis." He said he was determined the next game to show Voskuhl just how good he was.

"He was just an OK player," McGinnis said. "He was big but he was slow. And back then I could take advantage of that because I could put the ball on the floor and get around him. In those days most of the big guys couldn't dribble the ball. They were more of bangers. But I was good with the ball, and had a big advantage on him offensively."

McGinnis felt that if he could get off to a good start he could have a big game. He also remembered the quote that Downing retold about 'Just get me the ball.'

"Yeah, that's what I told him," McGinnis said with a smile. "I said just get me the ball early and if I'm rolling keep feeding me. And that's what happened but not only him but my entire team. We had some great players on that team and every one of them sacrificed and gave up shots that they gave to me because I was so hot. I couldn't miss. I was hitting everything.

"And it went that way for the entire game. Afterwards I went to each guy and hugged them and told them how much I appreciated that."

Another side of McGinnis's legendary evening against Kentucky was that at one point he actually tore the top of his basketball shoes as he made a cut to the basket. He had to have a second pair to get him through the game.

McGinnis said the story was accurate.

"I had some Chuck Taylor Converse and I made a cut and just ripped them completely apart," McGinnis said. "That happened twice."

McGinnis said that in 2008 he was playing in a golf outing at Fuzzy Zoeller's course in Southern Indiana, Covered Bridge. McGinnis was walking on the course and a spectator, behind the ropes, caught up with him and said 'Hey George, I've got something here for you.'

"And I walked over and it was the tennis shoe, it was the Converse shoe I wore," McGinnis said. "It was the first one I tore out of. He said, 'I was at that game and I was five rows behind your bench. When they took it off they just sort of set it there behind your bench. I asked the trainer what they were going to do with it and they said they were going to throw it away. I asked if I could have it and the guy said yes so I took the shoe.'

"So he told me he wanted to give me the shoe back and I told him that no, he had had the shoe all of these years. I said that I would sign it and he could just keep it."

• • • •

From a recruiting standpoint, McGinnis may have been one of the highest recruited athletes ever.

He was being recruited in both football and basketball and in fact said he may have had more offers in football.

Randy Wittman remembered the first time he ever saw McGinnis and it was in a football setting. Wittman's father, Bob, played football at Washington High School and Wittman remembers as a child going over to Washington to see high school football games.

"At that time there was this huge tight end playing for Washington High School by the name of George McGinnis," Wittman said. "So George McGinnis and Steve Downing were two of the guys at that time that I kind of gravitated towards as far as following them when they got to IU."

When the highest level athletes today talk about the number of scholarship offers they've received it can sometimes reach into the high double digits. As for McGinnis, you may not believe the number of scholarship offers he received.

"I think I had somewhere around 500 schools that offered me a scholarship," McGinnis said. "My mom kept all those letters. I still go over to her house and she has a trunk where she kept all of them in. But it was all the major schools. UCLA and Houston and all of the powers back then. I know it was all of the schools in the Big Ten. Pretty much you could name a school and I had a scholarship offer there."

McGinnis had a fabulous high school career at Indianapolis Washington. As a senior, he became the first player in the state's history to score more than 1,000 points in a season. He had 1,019 points for an average of 32.8 points per game. That still ranks as the No. 3 single season scoring effort in the history of high school basketball in the state.

As a senior, he scored 49 points against Jac-Cen-Del in the semi state championship game which set the tone for what he would do in the final two games. In the afternoon game, a 61-60 victory over Marion, McGinnis scored 27 points. In the championship game that night, he had 35 in a 79-76 victory over Gary Tolleston.

Washington finished 31-0 and won the 1969 Indiana one-class state championship led by head coach Bill Green.

So when it came around time to decide where he would go to college, McGinnis had plenty of options.

There were several things that played into the reason he ultimately chose Indiana. Proximity to home was part of it. He also wanted to play with Downing somewhere, plus his one-time high school coach, Jerry Oliver, had taken a job as an assistant at IU, too.

"Steve and I decided that we wanted to go to the next level together and pretty much by our junior year we had narrowed it down to between IU and maybe one or two other schools," McGinnis said.

Downing said Purdue was one of them. He also mentioned Oklahoma and Southwest Louisiana.

McGinnis said he and Downing were beginning to lean heavily toward IU by the time their senior year had arrived. Oliver, now at IU, was then recruiting them pretty hard as well.

McGinnis smiled when he thought back to the fact that Oliver all of a sudden ended up at IU a year or two before McGinnis and Downing arrived.

"Coincidence?" McGinnis said with a smile.

"We took some trips but I think it was more of a fact that we got to ride in an airplane than actually being sincere about going somewhere else and attending another school other than IU."

Downing said Jerry Oliver being at IU was pretty much the trump card in his opinion.

"I think the biggest factor was going to be Jerry Oliver," Downing said. "Jerry Oliver did a lot for both of us as players and as young men helping us grow up. He was almost a father figure along the way. We knew him very well. I would say that Jerry Oliver was almost the equalizer."

The other event that McGinnis said became the overwhelming factor about attending IU later was that his father, Burnie McGinnis, died tragically in a construction accident in the summer after George's senior year of high school.

McGinnis' dad was a construction worker and was working at a building at Eli Lilly and Company in Indianapolis. He was working on a scaffold and the end that he was on gave way. He fell and died. A worker on the other side of the scaffold managed to reach out and grab something and hold on until he was rescued.

"My dad was a healthy, hard-working man who worked two jobs and was just a good guy and a good father," McGinnis recalled. "He goes to work one day and he's dead. It was pretty devastating. It was tough for my mom. It was tough for all of us."

One interesting detail is that the last game his father ever saw George play may have been his best game ever.

"That happened right after the second Kentucky All-Star game so the last game my dad saw me play was probably the best game I ever played in my life," McGinnis said. "After that happened, I wanted to be closer to my mom because she was having a tough time. That pretty much solidified the fact I was going to be heading to IU."

••••

One of the problems at that time about going to college was that freshmen were not eligible to play on the varsity squad.

And so kids that have played basketball every year to that point all of a sudden have to, in essence, sit out a full season of high level competition. Sure, players still would play on the freshman team or play intramurals but it just wasn't the same as playing big-time college basketball.

McGinnis came to Indiana after playing on a talented World University Games team where he was the second leading scorer at 16.6 points per game and helped lead the United States to a silver medal performance.

Then he basically took his freshman season off.

"It was really hard," McGinnis said. "You play ball your whole life. If I wasn't playing basketball I was playing football. And then in the summers I would play basketball all summer long and now all of a sudden you're told you can't play. So that was really hard."

Downing said that the two played a lot of pickup ball that year at the HYPER building. He said the experience did help in one way though.

"What it did do was it made us focus on school," Downing said.

When McGinnis and Downing arrived in Bloomington at the start of their freshmen years they lived in the McNutt dormitory.

"It was the wildest dorm at IU back then and it still is I think," McGinnis said.

Downing said he and McGinnis were inseparable in their Bloomington days.

"We did everything together," Downing said. "He had a car and I didn't and so that was part of it but we were close any way. We were like that in high school also."

McGinnis said those days in Bloomington with Downing just cemented what has been a lifetime friendship. He said the two still talk to each other at least a few times a week today and often go out to eat during the week.

"We would lean on each other back then and we still do," McGinnis said. "We're very good friends. He meant a lot to me. He was a guy who sacrificed a lot. I got all of the individual glory for when we played growing up and in high school and college, but Steve was such a tame guy. He didn't care about any of that.

"He was consumed with winning. He's still that way. He just loves to win but I'll tell you this it's just an honor for me to be able to call him my friend. Steve Downing is about as loyal of a friend as you could ever have."

••••

When his freshman year was in the rear view mirror, it didn't take McGinnis long to make his mark at IU in basketball.

In the season opener that year, a 99-82 victory over Eastern Michigan, McGinnis had his first double-double. He scored 26 points and pulled down 11 rebounds.

It would clearly be a sign of things to come.

For the season, in 24 games, McGinnis would record 22 double-doubles including 13 in 14 Big Ten games. Twenty of his 22 double-doubles were 20-point/10-rebound games. He had 12 games where he had 30 points or more and 10 or more rebounds.

He was both man and machine. When he made up his mind to score or rebound the basketball, there was nobody at the college level that was going to stop him.

With McGinnis, it was news if he didn't score at least 20 points and pull down 10 rebounds. He was that good.

"I was very good in high school and there were all these predictions that I was supposed to be great in college, too," McGinnis said. "And sometimes you live up to that and sometimes you don't. I think I lived up to the expectations that were expected of me. I was the first sophomore to lead the league in scoring and rebounding. So, it was good."

McGinnis made news for all the wrong reasons one time in his IU career when the Hoosiers played host to No. 3 Kentucky.

With the game tied at 80 in the closing seconds, John Ritter put up what was described as a 55-foot desperation heave at the buzzer that went in to give IU what appeared to be an 82-80 win.

Unfortunately for IU, just before Ritter let the ball go, McGinnis had asked for a timeout so that Indiana could set up a play. The official awarded it, the shot didn't count and Ritter missed his next attempt to win it. Kentucky won the game in overtime 95-93.

McGinnis had 38 points and 20 rebounds for the Hoosiers. But he struggled to a 13-for-31 shooting day.

A few games later, McGinnis and the Hoosiers played in the Far West Classic in Portland, Ore. In the second round, in an 86-76 win over San Jose State, McGinnis had 41 points. It was his first of two 40-point games that season.

IU opened Big Ten play with a 101-90 win over Northwestern. McGinnis started his conference career off on a good note that day, too. He had 38 points and 23 rebounds.

After three conference games, the Hoosiers had a non-conference matchup with Northern Illinois in Bloomington. IU won a crazy game, 113-112 and McGinnis had one of his biggest games of his college career. He scored 45 points and pulled down 20 rebounds.

Interestingly, only one other player in Indiana history is a member of the 40-20 club and it's McGinnis's close friend and former teammate, Steve Downing. Downing had 47 points and 25 rebounds in a game against Kentucky in 1971.

In a game against Michigan State in mid-February, McGinnis had 37 points.

IU's biggest victory of the season came against No. 12 Michigan on Feb. 23, 1971. The Wolverines were 8-0 but the Hoosiers knocked them off 88-79. That put IU one game back of Michigan in the standings at 7-2. McGinnis led Indiana with 33 points but the most remembered statistical occurrence from that day was Downing recording the only triple-double in IU history when he had 28 points, 17 rebounds and 10 blocked shots.

IU fizzled at the end of the year though, losing three of its last four games, to finish fourth in the Big Ten with a 9-5 conference mark.

In those days, the NCAA Tournament field was small and a fourth place team, despite a 17-7 record, had no chance to get in the tournament.

George McGinnis (Indiana University Archives – P0020284)

"I had some good games at Indiana and I was happy with what I was able to accomplish there in a short time," McGinnis said.

When you look at the way McGinnis dominated college basketball, you get the feeling that perhaps the college game was simply too easy for the former Washington High School standout.

"No, it wasn't too easy, it was fun," McGinnis said. "I enjoyed it. I enjoyed being at school. I enjoyed the environment there. I just enjoyed my two years of college."

Quinn Buckner, who arrived at Indiana just a year or two after McGinnis left, said when he thinks of McGinnis in that time he thinks of a player who is dominating the pro game today.

"Mac was that era's LeBron James because they were virtually the same size," Buckner said. "Mac could just flat out play."

••••

One of the disappointing parts of his Indiana experience, however, when McGinnis looks back is the way Lou Watson was let go as the IU coach after McGinnis's sophomore season.

The IU Basketball Encyclopedia, written by Jason Hiner, described what happened like this:

"Following the Iowa game (March 6), several Indiana players met with IU professor Dr. John Brown to air some dirty laundry. They leveled a number of charges against Watson, including not teaching them enough about basketball, having a lack of team discipline, and showing favoritism toward John Ritter and George McGinnis."

A few days later after Ohio State beat IU and clinched the Big Ten title, Dr. Brown took the players' grievances to the administration.

According to *The IU Basketball Encyclopedia*, here is what happened next:

"The next day, a meeting was convened with athletic director Bill Orwig, IU president John Ryan, Coach Watson, and the Indiana players. At the meeting, Watson, who had already been considering retirement and was deeply hurt by the diatribes of the fans and the machinations of his players, resigned. The resignation was effective immediately."

Watson said the resignation was done "for the best interest of the team, the university and my family. I am proud of my 22 years as a player and a coach. I will do all in my power to help my successor and wish him and each member of the squad every success."

McGinnis still to this day thinks Watson wasn't treated fairly at the end.

"We had some guys on our team who were not happy with him and at the end of the season they boycotted," McGinnis said. "That kind of helped my decision to go ahead and turn pro. I wasn't a part of that but I thought he got a raw deal. He was a good man, a good honest man and he was a true IU guy.

"He played there, he was an Indiana guy from Jeffersonville and I just loved him. I thought he was just as good as they get as a person. I have a lot of respect for Lou."

McGinnis said Watson's resignation and the actions of his teammates left a bad taste in his mouth.

"That was a real negative for me," McGinnis said. "I just don't think players should be able to do that. Lou was a good guy and he had been down here forever. He played there and he was a good coach and he worked with Branch (McCracken). I loved sitting there talking with him and hearing all the stories and experiences he had with Branch McCracken.

"I just thought he got a raw deal."

●●●●

McGinnis went on to a heralded 11-year professional basketball career.

He won back-to-back ABA Championships with the Indiana Pacers his first two years after leaving IU.

He was a three-time ABA All-Star in 1973, '74, and '75 and was the ABA most valuable player in '75.

He was with the Pacers from 1971-75 and later played on a Philadelphia 76ers team that also included Julius Erving. That team made it to the NBA Finals in 1977. He was traded to the Denver Nuggets in 1978 and two years later, the Pacers reacquired him in a trade for Alex English.

After the ABA disbanded, McGinnis was named an NBA All-Star three times as well in 1976, '77 and '79.

He scored 17,009 points in his professional career for an average of 20.2 points per game. He also had 9,233 rebounds for an 11.0 career average there.

McGinnis is one of only four Pacers players to have their jersey numbers retired. Along with McGinnis's No. 30, the Pacers have also retired No. 31 (Reggie Miller), No. 34 (Mel Daniels) and No. 35 (Roger Brown).

Today, McGinnis still lives in Indianapolis where he owns his own business, GM Supply Co, Inc. He has owned that business for more than 20 years.

●●●●

I asked both Downing and McGinnis if they ever thought about what would have happened if McGinnis had stayed at Indiana rather than turn pro after his sophomore year.

Most believe that Indiana's first national championship banner under Bob Knight would have been hung in 1973. As it was, IU made it to the Final Four before losing a tough game to UCLA.

"There's no doubt in my mind," Downing said. "UCLA would have had a tremendous matchup problem like we had trying to guard (Bill) Walton. Defensively, UCLA would have had real problems with him in the lineup. They wouldn't have had anyone to guard him."

Another interesting possibility had McGinnis stayed would have been the fact he would have played for Bob Knight, who took over the Hoosiers after Lou Watson resigned.

McGinnis remembered sitting in a hotel room when he was with the Indiana Pacers watching IU play UCLA that night.

"I can remember vividly sitting in my room, I think we were on the road, watching that game and just kind of putting myself on that team," McGinnis said. "You end up with a lot of 'What if's'. You know what I mean?"

McGinnis said that over the years he got to know coach Knight pretty well and they talked on a few occasions about how things could have been different.

"I became good friends with him," McGinnis said of Knight. "Everybody said I couldn't have played for him but I think I could have. He was hard but you know what, I've had hard guys coach me before and I think I could have got through that."

Downing is also a believer that McGinnis could have survived just fine under Knight.

"George would have changed his game," Downing said. "Coach Knight tells him that whenever he sees him. He would have made him better as a defensive player."

12
Number 3
Steve Alford

Steve Alford lost the first game of his college basketball career at Indiana. It was a six-point decision to Miami of Ohio no less.

Not the opening game that legends are made of that's for sure.

Still, more importantly, Alford won the final game he ever played in an IU uniform.

Most people would take that trade in a heartbeat.

Especially if they knew that the final game was for the NCAA championship in 1987 when Indiana beat Syracuse 74-73 in New Orleans.

Steve Alford (Indiana University Archives – P0030877)

In between, he experienced the highs and the lows that often are associated with a big time college basketball program.

As a freshman for example, Alford played on a young, inexperienced unit that won enough games in conference play to earn an NCAA berth. Once there, the Hoosiers knocked off the No. 1 team in the nation, North Carolina, to earn a spot in the Elite Eight. That UNC team was loaded with talent including Michael Jordan, Kenny Smith, Sam Perkins and Brad Daugherty.

His second year IU struggled to a seventh place finish in the Big Ten and didn't make the NCAA Tournament. Given new life in the NIT, however, IU won four games in a row and got to the title game in New York before losing to Reggie Miller and UCLA.

As a junior, Alford's Hoosiers were better and earned a No. 3 seed in the NCAA Tournament's East Regional. There IU would face No. 14 Cleveland State. Every IU fan knows what happened next. The Vikings stunned the Hoosiers, 83-79, giving Indiana a quick first round exit.

Then as a senior, Alford and his teammates put it all together. The Hoosiers were co-Big Ten champions along with Purdue. IU picked up a No. 1 seed in the Midwest Regional and were rewarded by playing the first two games in Indianapolis.

IU had to face Duke, LSU, UNLV and Syracuse in the four games from the Sweet Sixteen and beyond, but Alford and company found a way to secure the fifth national championship in school history and the third for head coach Bob Knight.

When you take a step back and look at it all as a body of work, Alford's four years were action-packed to say the least.

"I felt like we were able to put our niche, our statement if you will, on Indiana basketball," Alford said when interviewed for this book. "We had to try to continue to build. There was the first round loss to Cleveland State to playing in the NIT one year. But it was all about experiences we needed to have collectively so that we were best prepared to go win a national championship.

"I think if you told anyone ahead of time that this was the way the script would play out, anybody would jump at the opportunity to be along for that ride."

••••

Don Fischer, the radio voice of Indiana football and basketball for more than 40 years, remembers that he probably saw Steve Alford play a handful of times in high school.

One of those was in the afternoon game of the 1983 Hinkle Semi-State when Alford put on a show in New Castle's 79-64 win over Broad Ripple.

Alford scored 57 in the game, hitting 16-of-27 shots from the field and all 25 of his free throw attempts. And this was before the 3-point line was in effect. It's still a record-setting performance in Indiana high school state tournament annals.

"It was probably the one time where I saw him where you just didn't think he was going to miss," Fischer said. "And I thought, 'Oh my God, this kid is coming to Indiana and I get to watch this for four years.'"

Alford *was held* to 37 points in the Semi-State title game later that evening against eventual state champion Connersville.

Brian Evans, an IU All American in 1996, remembered watching Alford while Evans was in junior high school and marveling at his ability to shoot the ball.

"I just remember thinking 'That guy doesn't miss,'" Evans said. "He was great to watch at my age in the junior high years because it made me think 'That's how great you have to be to play at Indiana. You have to be able to shoot the ball like he does.'

"He was always a guy I looked up to and whenever I was in my driveway or a gym I was thinking I had to get to that point. I had to get to that point where you just don't miss shots. I was a big Larry Bird fan growing up too and I thought of Alford and Bird in the same breath when it came to shooting the basketball."

Quinn Buckner thinks of Alford and the first thought that came to mind was that he was money as a shooter.

"He was an outstanding shooter," Buckner said. "He was not very big, but if he was open, he was making shots."

Joe Hillman played his first two seasons at IU with Alford, including the '87 national championship team. Hillman came to IU from Glendale, Calif., where as a high school senior in 1984 Hillman led the state of California in scoring with a 41.3 points per game average.

But when he saw Alford shoot for the first time, he was left shaking his head.

"He was just ridiculous," Hillman said. "I thought I was a pretty good shooter but then we would do shooting drills after practice and he would hit 23 out of 25 or 24 out of 27. I mean it was a joke. I've never seen a guy make shot after shot after shot like Steve Alford could.

"As far as just a pure shooting stroke, I've never seen anyone like him."

Randy Wittman said Alford was the epitome of Indiana basketball, both in college and high school.

"You would look at him and you say 'How is this kid going to beat me?' and then he would," Wittman said. "Obviously his shooting ability and his ability off of one or two dribbles was incredible."

Jake Query, the Indianapolis sports radio talk show host for WNDE 1260-AM, said he always felt with Alford being able to shoot from long range the way he did that it just gave IU an edge.

"I thought IU had a chance in virtually every game because Alford had the ability to score from so many different places on the floor," Query said.

The thing that Fischer saw in Alford that day and into his IU career was simply how graceful he looked with his shot.

"Steve was probably quicker than people gave him credit for but he was so smooth he didn't look all that quick. He was a glider type of a guy," Fischer said. "I would equate Jay Edwards as being the same way. He never looked super fast or super quick and yet he was so smooth that it didn't matter.

"But Alford had that same quality and every time he shot the basketball you thought it was going in. I don't think I ever saw him take what I would consider a bad shot. Now coach Knight might disagree, but I never saw him take a shot that I didn't think he could make."

Another thing that stood out about Alford from Fischer's point of view was simply how hard the former Indiana Mr. Basketball from New Castle worked to get open.

"Everybody knows what a tremendous shooter Steve was and what a great stroke he had, but I'm not sure I ever saw anybody work harder to get open than Steve Alford," Fischer said. "He was unbelievable in that sense. He knew what his strength was and so he worked to get himself an opportunity to use his strength which was shooting the basketball.

"He worked his butt off, running through screens and it was amazing how hard he worked to get himself open to shoot a shot."

Query said that it was also clear that the IU offense was set up for that kind of player.

"He was the hit man," Query said. "It was unbelievable how hard he worked to get through the screens and then it just seemed that the offense rewarded players like Alford who could take advantage of that."

Randy Wittman agreed that IU's motion offense was designed with a player like Alford in mind.

"He was probably by far one of the better guys when you think of the fact he never created anything for himself," Wittman said. "He was obviously made to play at Indiana in the motion offense, using screens, reading screens and being in constant movement. That was something that Steve probably did as good as anybody."

In the *IU Basketball Encyclopedia*, written initially by Jason Hiner, Bob Knight is quoted on his thoughts of Alford.

"I'll tell you a remarkable thing about Alford," Knight is quoted as saying in the book. "He's not big, he's not strong and he's not quick. It's hard for me to imagine how a kid like that can score as many points as he does. He doesn't post up, he doesn't get rebound baskets, and he doesn't really take the ball to the basket to score. He just has to work like hell to get the jump shot."

Todd Leary followed Alford closely when Leary was in high school at Lawrence North and said Alford was always someone he looked up to. He said he went to at least three camps where Sam and Steve Alford would teach their shooting drills and Leary said he soaked it all up.

"I definitely loved the way he played and everything he did," Leary said. "I learned a

Steve Alford (Indiana University Archives – P0044907)

lot by watching him. He was kind of the Reggie Miller of college basketball before Reggie Miller was the way he was in the NBA. He was really good at coming off screens and reading the defense and all of those kinds of things."

Leary said it was clear with Alford that he needed to do the extra things to get open and get his shot.

"I'm not ripping him obviously, but Alford was no more athletic than 90 percent of the guys I see in the gym every week," Leary said. "But he was able to get himself open and he worked hard and he had that quick release. I think I learned a lot from him about getting my shot off faster because I saw what a fast release he had. It was that and getting his feet set and where he caught the ball and those types of things."

But even with Alford being not the fastest guy on the floor, Jake Query said he came to realize it really didn't matter.

."Even at a young age while I understood the fact that Alford was smaller and less athletic than others, to me it did not factor in because teams could not stop him," Query said.

Query said that Alford *was* Indiana basketball.

"To a kid from Indianapolis, Indiana who was born in the 70's and raised in the 80's, Steve Alford was *Ozzie and Harriett* or *Leave it to Beaver*," Query said. "He was the squeaky clean, perfect role model guy for kids to look up to. I know he wasn't perfect but in the eyes of an eighth grader ... he was perfect.

"I was convinced that Superman went to bed wearing a number 12 jersey."

••••

With great, natural shooters like Steve Alford I've often wondered how many points a player like that would have scored if he had the benefit of the 3-point line for his entire career?

I felt that way when I interviewed Jimmy Rayl, a player that some call the greatest outside shooter in IU history. And you had to feel that way about Alford, too. He just had incredible range.

Alford's senior year in the 1986-87 season was the first year the NCAA went to the 3-point line in college basketball.

And Alford wasn't shy about shooting them. He took 202 3-point field goals that season, almost as if he was trying to make up for lost time. But it was never like he was forcing them. He made 107 of them, a 53 percent 3-point field goal percentage. That percentage ranks fourth for one season in IU history and first for career 3-point percentage.

He still holds IU's single season record for most 3-pointers made in a season at 107 and the most 3-pointers made in one season in Big Ten games only which was 54.

The most 3-pointers he made in a game was eight against Princeton, and he also hit seven on three occasions including the national championship win over Syracuse. The other times were against Auburn and Wisconsin. Against the Badgers, he made 7-of-8 from beyond the 3-point arc.

But really, how many extra points could that have added to Alford's total? It added more than 100 as a senior. He finished with 2,438 career points which at the time had broken the school record set by Don Schlundt which had stood for more than 30 years. It still ranks as the No. 2 scoring total of all time. A kid name Calbert Cheaney came along and broke it between 1989-93 when he poured in 2,613 points for his career.

Still, the addition of the 3-point line makes you wonder what he could have done. Alford's career scoring average was 19.5 including 22.0 his senior year.

"He could have easily averaged 30 points a game," said IU radio voice Don Fischer. "To his credit he didn't shoot shots that he had no chance of making. He was very selective. A lot of people say that as soon as he got the basketball he was going to shoot it but he was always in a position to shoot it.

"I think if he had had the 3-point line all the way through his career he easily would have ended up with the highest scoring average in Indiana history."

Probably, the most points, too.

Joe Hillman, who played with Alford for two years including on the '87 national championship team, said there's no question in his mind that Alford would be IU's all-time leading scorer today if the 3-point line had been there his entire four years.

"He got more than 100 extra points that way as a senior so you just have to figure he would have done it," Hillman said. "My guess is he would have scored probably another 250 points in those other three years and that's a conservative estimate."

Cheaney is IU's all-time leading scorer by 185 points over Alford.

Alford said he has never given much thought to it.

"No, because I'm sure there were a lot of guys that played before me that thought the same thing," Alford said. "Obviously I would have loved to have had it in high school and I would have loved to have had it in college but I tell you what, I wouldn't change a thing."

Alford said he feels blessed to have played in the era of Indiana basketball that he did.

"I'm glad I got to come through the era that I came through and got to play for the people I played for, my dad and coach Knight," Alford said. "I played high school basketball in Indiana when there was only one class and you basically played on Friday and Saturday nights.

"I'd rather not have a 3-point line and play in that era than to have a 3-point line and played in multi-class basketball."

••••

Steve Alford seemed like one of those Indiana high school basketball players that was always going to be headed to Indiana University. It was his destiny.

The boy who grew up in Martinsville and later moved to New Castle, attended his first Bob Knight Basketball Camp when he was 9 years old. And he was hooked. As a young boy he constantly dreamed about wearing the candy-striped pants and running on to the floor someday at Assembly Hall.

Clearly, Alford always looked up to Bob Knight from the time he was a young boy. But he said it was the promises that Knight made in the recruiting process that all came true that sold the deal for him. Mike Woodson, in another chapter in this book, had a similar story. Knight not only had the claim, but he backed it up later.

"The honesty of what he told me and my family in the recruiting process is what meant the most to me," Alford said.

"It probably makes even more sense to me since I've gotten into coaching myself.

"He came in our home in New Castle and promised me I would play with really good teammates, he promised we would have a championship caliber team and play for championships every year, which we did even in our sophomore year when we went to the NIT and played for a championship. He said I would get my degree, which I did, and the fourth thing he said was that I would have a friend for life and he has definitely been a friend for life."

He didn't promise that Alford would start or score so many points per game or be an All American or anything like that. He made promises that could all be attainable.

"For him to be able to say those four things when I'm being recruited and then for me to live the experience out and it all comes to fruition you just have a great appreciation for it," Alford said. "Then to have an Olympic experience on top of it, a national title experience on top of it, an overseas trip on top of it that was three weeks long, I just still feel to this day extremely blessed that I was able to do that with him."

••••

When Steve Alford arrived at Indiana in the fall of 1983 the Hoosiers were in a bit of a rebuilding mode after Randy Wittman and Ted Kitchel had graduated the year before.

The lone returning starter for IU was Uwe Blab.

IU had a great recruiting class coming in including Alford, Daryl Thomas, Todd Meier and Marty Simmons. But the one thing the entire roster lacked was college basketball experience.

That showed right from the start when the Hoosiers dropped their season opener to Miami of Ohio in Assembly Hall on Nov. 26, 63-57.

His second game had a better result. After coming off the bench in the opener, Alford started his second game and scored 14 as IU beat Notre Dame, 80-72.

Five games into the season, the Hoosiers sat at 2-3 after a road loss at UTEP.

The Hoosiers would bounce back against the cupcake portion of their schedule that always included their two tournaments, the Indiana Classic in Assembly Hall and the Hoosier Classic in Indianapolis. IU won its final five non-conference games.

Indiana got off to a nice 2-0 start in conference play, too, beating Ohio State on the road and Illinois at home. In the second win, over the No. 9 ranked Illini, Alford had a career-high 29 points.

The problem for the Hoosiers as they went through the conference season though was inconsistency. They were up and down, up and down.

They would win 10 of their first 12 Big Ten games for example, beating good teams along the way but then would have some hiccups. They lost to a Northwestern team on the road. The Wildcats would finish with a losing record. And late in conference they lost to Michigan State in Assembly Hall in a game where Alford scored 30. But the Spartans were tied for last place in the Big Ten coming in.

Steve Alford (Indiana University Archives – P0044926)

IU finished third in the conference with a 13-5 record and received a No. 4 seed in the NCAA Tournament and a first round bye. In the second round, the Hoosiers beat Richmond, 75-67, to earn a spot in the Sweet Sixteen.

That's when Indiana would run in to the vaunted No. 1 team in the nation, North Carolina. Dean Smith's squad had been steamrolling opponents.

Some remember the game for the heroics of Dan Dakich who limited Michael Jordan to 13 points on 6-of-14 shooting. It was a performance that is etched in Hoosier lore.

But what gets lost sometimes is the performance by Alford, who scored 27 points pulled down six rebounds and dished out three assists. IU won the game 72-68 and it's still considered one of the biggest upsets in NCAA Tournament history.

Jake Query, said people in Indiana in particular still think back on the game as being the 'Dakich/Jordan Game' but Alford's performance was equally stellar.

"I'm not taking anything away from Dan because he certainly deserves credit for that," Query said. "But Steve Alford was a freshman in that game and scored 27 freaking points. That was unheard of back then. Now, freshmen lead teams to Final Fours. In 1984, freshmen didn't do that. He scored 27 points against the No. 1 team in the nation in the Sweet Sixteen.

"Things like that just didn't happen."

The inconsistency bug bit the Hoosiers in the regional final when they lost to No. 7 seed Virginia, 50-48, to miss a shot at the Final Four. But a 22-9 record was far more than most expected going into a season where IU had so little experience.

As a freshman, Alford averaged 15.5 points per game and hit 59.2 percent of his shots from the field.

••••

The summer prior to Alford's sophomore year he was selected to play on the U.S. Olympic team coached by Bob Knight.

He was only 19 years old and yet more than held his own. He averaged 10.3 points per game, was second on the team in assists and shot 64.4 percent from the field.

He and his teammates went on to win the gold medal at the 1984 games played in Los Angeles. He was teammates with players like Michael Jordan, Patrick Ewing, Sam Perkins, Verne Fleming, Alvin Robertson, Waymon Tisdale and Chris Mullin.

It would be one of those experiences that Alford would cherish forever.

When Alford's sophomore season rolled around, Indiana looked primed to take the next step. Just about everyone was back from the year before and IU had added Indiana's Mr. Basketball in Delray Brooks from Michigan City Rogers.

Indiana was ranked No. 4 in the preseason poll and had high expectations. Over the course of the season though, it was clear that this IU team was going to struggle.

For the second year in a row IU dropped it season opener at home. This time it was Louisville that beat IU 75-64 on a night when the Hoosiers turned it over 25 times.

For the remainder of the non-conference season IU still looked the part of a team that could do some damage in the NCAA Tournament. The Hoosiers only lost one other non-conference game and that was a 74-63 loss to Notre Dame on the road, in a game where the Irish simply made it clear that they weren't going to let Steve Alford beat them.

Notre Dame used a box-and-one defense with Alford basically wearing Scott Hicks wherever he went. Alford ended up 1-for-4 from the field and scored four points.

The next game, against Kentucky, Alford had 27 points, six rebounds and seven assists in a 81-68 win over the Wildcats.

In Big Ten though, the level of inconsistency that had dogged IU the year before, reared its ugly head again. Three times in conference play, the Hoosiers lost at least three games in a row. One time it was four.

The one thing that had always saved IU then and still does today is the Hoosiers are really good at home. In 1984-85, IU's final five home games were against Ohio State, Illinois, Purdue, Michigan State and Michigan.

And Indiana lost all five games.

The Hoosiers finished 7-11 in the Big Ten and in seventh place. IU's overall record was 15-13 but based on its tradition, Indiana was invited to play in the NIT.

IU got hot at the right time and would eventually win four games in a row to reach the NIT final. There, the Hoosiers fell to Reggie Miller and UCLA, 65-62.

In another up and down season, IU rallied at the end to salvage something and the next season the Hoosiers would be back on their game especially in conference play.

Alford's scoring average increased to 18.1 points as a sophomore.

••••

As a junior in 1985-86, Indiana was better. IU glided through the non-conference season with an 8-2 record.

One of those wins came against Notre Dame, a team that had bottled up Alford the year before. This time it was a different story. Alford scored 32 points and IU knocked off the No. 10 Irish 82-67.

Another Alford moment in that non-conference season came when he was suspended for one game by the NCAA for appearing in a sorority calendar that was done to help raise money for a camp for handicapped kids.

Sam Alford, Steve's dad and high school coach, was quoted in a story that appeared in the Louisville Courier-Journal as being very disappointed in the NCAA's decision.

"My initial reaction is very sour. I just don't understand it," Sam Alford said at the time. "I guess the bottom line is that straight kids are the ones that get shot down. With all the stuff going on in college basketball today, to penalize a kid for something like this makes me very sad.

"As a father, I'm upset. As a coach, I'm upset. And as a dues-paying member of the NCAA for more than 20 years, I'm really upset."

Bob Knight was upset, too. He was mad at the world. He was mad at Alford, mad at the sorority, mad at everyone. In fact, he was so upset, that he didn't let Alford even make the trip to Lexington. Alford stayed home in Bloomington.

Kentucky won the game, 63-58, though the Hoosiers played the Wildcats tough.

For the second year in a row, IU entered Big Ten play with an 8-2 record.

The start of Big Ten play didn't go well though. IU had back-to-back home games with Michigan and Michigan State and lost them both.

But that's when Indiana turned the season around. Over the next 11 games, the Hoosiers would win 10 of them. It started with a five-game win streak, then a loss at Iowa, and then five more wins. Alford had 38 in a game against Wisconsin. Later in the year in the rematch in East Lansing, Alford had 31 as the Hoosiers would knock off the No. 17 Spartans, 97-79.

That put IU in a Big Ten season finale against Michigan with both teams entering with 13-4 records. The winner would take the Big Ten title outright. It wasn't close though as the Wolverines slammed the Hoosiers by nearly 30 points, 80-52.

That would be the first of two losses IU would suffer to end the 1985-86 season. The second one was a colossal upset when the Hoosiers, seeded No. 3 in the NCAA Tournament, were eliminated in the first round by No. 14 seed Cleveland State.

IU finished the season 21-8 overall.

The '86 season would be Alford's first All-American campaign. He averaged 22.5 points per game, which would end up being his highest scoring average in his four years.

It would also be the final season where Alford's long distance bombs would only count for two points. That was about to change, too.

•••

The biggest additions for the 1986-87 Indiana basketball team were both from the junior college route. Dean Garrett was a 6-foot-10 center who would end up averaging 11.4 points and 8.5 rebounds per game. The other player was 6-foot-1 guard Keith Smart and what he would end up doing by the end of the year would be legendary in Indiana basketball lore.

They haven't forgotten it in Syracuse, N.Y. either.

IU's starting lineup that year was Alford and Smart, Ricky Calloway, Daryl Thomas and Garrett. IU also got help off the bench from Joe Hillman, Todd Meier and Steve Eyl in particular.

IU opened the non-conference slate by going 9-1, the only loss coming to Vanderbilt. Alford had some big games in the non-conference season. He had 26 against Princeton and in doing so made 8-of-11 3-point shots.

The 3-point line had just been introduced to college basketball that season and Alford, as was chronicled earlier in this chapter, took full advantage of it.

But the Hoosiers didn't slow down this time when they got to the Big Ten.

IU opened conference play by winning 14 of its first 15 games. The only loss was to No. 1 Iowa in Iowa City. Later, IU knocked off Iowa at home 84-75.

The Hoosiers finished tied for first in the Big Ten with Purdue, both with 15-3 records.

Indiana earned a No. 1 seed in the NCAA's Midwest Regional which meant it got to play its first two games in the Hoosier Dome. IU beat Fairfield in the opener 92-58 and then beat Auburn in the second game, 107-90. Alford had seven 3-pointers in that game and led IU with 31 points.

IU then dispatched Duke in the first game of the Sweet Sixteen, 88-82 and then rallied from a nine-point deficit with under 5 minutes to play in the regional finals to beat LSU 77-76. Alford had 20 points and seven assists.

The first matchup of the Final Four was between No. 1 UNLV and No. 2 Indiana. Alford scored 33 and IU ran with the Runnin' Rebels and posted a 97-93 victory to advance to the NCAA title game against Syracuse.

Jake Query said the IU/UNLV matchup was a classic in terms of perception.

"When you grew up in Indiana it was just kind of ingrained in you that there was a way you did things," Query said. "There was a way you played the game of basketball and there was a respect you had for the game of basketball. Steve Alford represented everything that Indiana fans saw as the good in Indiana. And when they played UNLV in the Final Four in '87 it was good versus evil.

"UNLV represented everything that we in Indiana were led to believe was horrid about college basketball. They didn't go to class, they were all 30 years old, they were getting paid. And then Alford goes out and drops 33 on them. I remember as a kid thinking that flashy, dynamic dunks are still just two points and a shot from 19 feet, 9 inches is three points and Steve Alford does that better than anybody."

In the national championship game against Syracuse it was the Keith Smart show for the Hoosiers. Yes, there was his little floating jumper with 5 seconds to play that will always be etched in the memory of Indiana basketball fans, but Smart did so much more just to keep IU in it.

Bob Knight would later say that Smart made as many critical plays in that final 12 minutes of the national title game than he had ever seen.

Smart finished with 21 points, six assists and five rebounds and was named the most outstanding player of the tournament.

Alford had 23 points and was named to the all-Final Four team.

And Indiana knocked off Syracuse 74-73 to capture IU's fifth national championship.

Alford finished the season averaging 22 points per game and hitting an incredible 107-of-202 shots from 3-point range, 53 percent. He earned All-American honors for the second time in his career.

For his career, he scored 2,438 points, a 19.5 career average.

Looking back on the '87 national championship team, Alford said it was just a great team to be around.

"They were terrific guys for one," Alford said. "They were great guys that worked hard and worked together. We had great chemistry on that team. We just had all the parts. We took care of the ball, we had good shooting, and our assist-to-turnover ratio was good. We did what good Coach Knight teams do and that's get to the free throw line."

Alford remembers that team had a lot of close games. The last four victories that year were by a combined 12 points. IU had eight regular season wins that year by five points or less.

"The thing I really remember about that team is that we didn't run away from a lot of people," Alford said. "But in the last five minutes we were just really, really good. And that's usually a pretty good characteristic of a really good basketball team. It was just a lot of fun to be a part of that."

•●••

Jake Query had a couple of interesting stories about Alford.

One came when Query was getting ready to play eighth grade basketball at Eastwood Middle School in Indianapolis and when it came time to distribute jerseys that year there was clearly a problem.

Everyone wanted to wear No. 12, the number that Alford wore at Indiana. In the end, coaches decided that in the interests of world peace at that time it would probably be better if no one wore the number.

"No one was allowed to wear No. 12 because all 12 of us on that team wanted to wear that number," Query said. "There was such a huge fight over it among us all of us that they finally just decided that none of us could be number 12."

His other Alford memory of something that had nothing to do with the IU star playing basketball was when Query was in the seventh grade at Eastwood Middle School. Alford's aunt was Query's middle school guidance counselor. And his dad set it up for Alford to call Query on his birthday – collect – to wish him a happy birthday.

"And as a seventh grade kid in Indiana in 1986 that was like the president calling you at the Daytona 500 if you were Richard Petty," Query said. "Maybe it's because we romanticize a lot of things from our childhood but I've had a lot of debates with Pat Knight over whether at the time they played if Damon Bailey or Steve Alford was the most popular player in Indiana history.

"I can't imagine any kids admiring or just having the total genuflecting over a guy that those of us who were of adolescent age did when Steve Alford played at Indiana."

13
Number 2
Calbert Cheaney

When you talk about the best recruiting classes in Indiana basketball history, the class of 1989 is generally among the first that rolls off the tongue.

In fact according to the *Indiana University Basketball Encyclopedia*, written by Jason Hiner, there were some commentators at the time that believed it was the best class in the history of college basketball.

It was a seven-man class including five players from the state of Indiana.

Indiana Mr. Basketball and McDonald's All-American Pat Graham was in that class and so was Greg Graham, who would be a first-team all-Big Ten selection before he was

Calbert Cheaney (Indiana University Archives – P0039773)

through and would go on to be a first round draft pick of Charlotte in the NBA Draft.

Lawrence Funderburke was a 6-8 McDonald's All-American out of Columbus, Ohio. Bloomington's own Chris Lawson, a 6-9 center was in that class, as was 6-1 guard Chris Reynolds out of Peoria, Ill. and 6-2 guard Todd Leary from Lawrence North High School in Indianapolis.

And then there was Calbert Cheaney. The 6-6 forward from Evansville Harrison would go on to become the all-time Big Ten leading scorer before his days in Bloomington were done.

The funny thing, though, going in was that Cheaney said he was in awe of many of the other players in that class.

"Pat Graham was a McDonald's All-American and Todd Leary was just coming off a state championship," Cheaney recalled. "Lawrence Funderburke was another McDonald's All-American so I was just kind of in awe at the time. I had only played half of my senior year in high school because I broke my foot so I was coming off an injury and I really didn't know how I would stack up with those guys."

Todd Leary agreed that Cheaney was one of the lesser known players in the class going in. Leary said the perfect example of that for him was one morning when Leary was reading the Indianapolis Star and was looking in the notes section on the scoreboard page.

"I remember reading that section one day and it said that Calbert Cheaney had signed with IU," Leary said. "And I was like, 'Who in the world is that?' I had no idea who Calbert Cheaney was. I obviously knew Pat Graham who was Mr. Basketball and Greg Graham because we played them all the time, but I did not know Cheaney at all."

Pat Graham grew up an hour away from Cheaney and he had a similar memory.

"When he signed at Indiana and committed, I didn't know who he was," Graham said. "When I walked in, I was the guy. It was me and Greg Graham and Lawrence Funderburke, and Calbert was just this guy over here."

Jake Query, the Indianapolis radio talk show host on WNDE 1260-AM, said it's not all that surprising that a lot of people didn't know who Cheaney was coming out of high school.

"He had a broken foot as a senior in high school plus he was playing in Evansville, which let's be honest is like the big toe that has been removed from the state of Indiana any way," Query said. "There's no easy way to get there. There's just not a great connection between Indianapolis and Evansville."

Brian Evans said part of Cheaney not being a heralded player was that he broke his foot that year in a game against Evans' Terre Haute South team.

"But he was that good then but I just think he was down in that southern pocket of the state and then he broke his foot and you add all of that together and people just didn't see enough Calbert Cheaney," Evans said.

During the recruiting process, Cheaney said there were really four schools who were heavily involved: Indiana, Purdue, Kentucky and Evansville.

"Kentucky was in there but then they got caught up in that situation and put on probation," Cheaney said. "So at that point I had to let them go. Ultimately, though, Indiana just seemed like the best place for me to go."

Dan Dakich, who was an IU assistant coach at the time, recalled that when Bob Knight first went and saw Cheaney play he came back unimpressed. He told his assistants to never send him out to see someone like that again.

But over time that opinion began to change and one weekend Cheaney was on campus and playing in a game in the Fieldhouse and IU assistant Ron Felling found Knight and told him he needed to go up there and watch Cheaney right then.

"Felling told coach that if he didn't go up there and offer Cheaney a scholarship right then, he would be making a huge mistake," Dakich said. "So Coach Knight went and watched Cheaney play and when the day was over, the scholarship offer had been extended."

Cheaney remembers that he was one of the last players to sign in the class of '89. He was actually the sixth player to sign in the class and Leary was the seventh. Leary's scholarship became available when Jay Edwards declared for the NBA Draft.

When Cheaney did sign it wasn't in some elaborate ceremony like players often do today. In fact, it was basically the polar opposite of that.

"When I did sign I signed on a piece of paper on the hood of a car at the airport," Cheaney said. "Coach Ron Felling brought the scholarship papers down to Evansville Regional Airport and I signed them on the hood of a car."

••••

Cheaney didn't really start playing basketball seriously until high school so it wasn't a matter of him having grown up a lifelong Indiana fan. That was something that came well into his teens.

"I was kind of a late bloomer when it came to playing the game so I wasn't really a big huge dreamer as far as wanting to play basketball at the next level," Cheaney said. "When I did watch the Hoosiers it was more recent than anything from way back. It was watching guys like Jay Edwards play, or Todd Jadlow and those guys.

"I did get an appreciation for Indiana basketball and the Hoosiers' program through watching guys like that play."

Cheaney remembers a basketball clinic he attended in high school that also turned out to be one of his favorite basketball memories growing up. Steve Alford was part of the clinic and Cheaney was afforded a unique opportunity.

"They were having a basketball camp down at Harrison High School and Steve Alford came down and I had a chance to go one-on-one against him for a little bit," Cheaney said. "That was a really a significant moment in my early basketball career. That was a lot of fun.

"Getting a chance to watch Alford in '87 and Keith Smart and Dean Garrett and those guys win a national championship was a lot of fun, too."

Alford smiled when he heard that Cheaney had related that story.

"Well, that's making me feel a little older that's for sure," Alford said."One of the great things about Indiana basketball though is that a lot of players have memories just like that one. We did a lot of clinics and a lot of camps back then and former IU players were often involved."

Cheaney said one of the things that would ultimately make his Indiana experience such a good one was playing for Bob Knight.

"It was great," Cheaney said. "If I had a chance to do it all over again, I'd do the same thing. With coach Knight it wasn't as much about the physical part as the mental part. The mental part you really had to be mentally intune to what he wanted you to do. You had to have a high basketball IQ.

"I always tell people that my mom was worse than coach Knight and that actually, by comparison, he was easy to deal with. I enjoyed it though. Coach was one of the best coaches I've ever been around in my basketball career and he always will be."

Cheaney said he learned a lot of great lessons playing for Knight.

"One thing he taught me when I got there was how to compete and not give up," Cheaney said. "There were times when I first got there that I had all of the tools athletically and skill wise but he taught me to work hard in terms of player development. He taught me that when you're tired you need to practice being tired.

"He always talked about how your opponents are tired as well and that's when we're going to win that battle. He taught me how to compete a lot harder than I ever had when I was in high school. He taught me how to be that great competitor."

Cheaney said he has been blessed to have several outstanding coaches that he has worked with at the college level. He played for the man he considers the best of all-time in Bob Knight and now has coached with Tom Crean at Indiana and currently Jim Crews at the University of Saint Louis.

"I've been lucky to have been around so many great coaches," Cheaney said.

• • • •

Jason Hiner, author of the *Indiana University Basketball Encyclopedia*, had this description of Cheaney in one of the chapters of the book.

"Swingman Calbert Cheaney was the heart of the (1992-93) team," Hiner wrote in the book. "Cheaney came in as one of the lesser-rated prospects of the 1989 group, but it quickly became apparent that he was the hardest-working and most skilled of the seven recruits. He had a smooth left-handed shooting stroke in which he cocked the ball right next to his head, elevated, and followed through with a silky-soft release. He was also a lithe athlete who could put the ball on the floor and drive past defenders, as well as finish inside with a dunk.

"One of his signature moves was a ball and head fake on the wing to draw the defender off his feet, then Cheaney would streak down the baseline for a two-handed dunk. Cheaney was also a good 3-point shooter, but he didn't take ill-advised 3's, because another one of his best qualities was his shot selection. He rarely took a bad shot or one that wasn't in the flow of the offense. Like Hoosier swingmen Scott May and Mike Woodson before him, Cheaney had an excellent mid-range game, and coach Knight's motion offense provided him with lots of opportunities for mid-range jumpers."

Brian Evans, who played with Cheaney his first two years at IU, said there was just something about Calbert that was different than anyone he had ever played with.

"He was so smooth, he would just glide all over the court," Evans said. "He moved in a manner that you didn't see other guys move. It was just silky smooth. Even his run, he didn't look like the other guys."

Dakich remembered that with Cheaney you had a lot of options in terms of how you could play him.

"You could put him on the foul line against a zone, you could put him on a wing or the baseline, you could run him off screens or put him in the post," Dakich said. "Calbert was really one of those players who could do it all."

Dakich said the hardest thing to teach a player in Bob Knight's offense was when you came off a screen to look at the man and not for the ball.

"Everybody wants to come off a screen and look for the ball but Calbert never had a problem with that," Dakich said. "Calbert Cheaney would always read the man. And in my time coaching both at Bowling Green and at IU, 26 years teaching motion offense, nobody ever picked that up quicker. When you do that you can put yourself in pretty good spots and he had a natural touch. He had a natural instinct for playing from 15 feet and in."

Jake Query, the Indianapolis radio talk show host who attended IU while Cheaney was there, said he thought Calbert was the poster child for perfecting the triple-threat position.

"When you learn basketball in Indiana, you learn that when you get the ball that you get in the triple threat position. You're in a position to drive, shoot or pass," Query said. "I think Cheaney had the best shot fake, one step, pull up jump shot in the history of Indiana basketball.

"You could go to the playgrounds or to the HYPER when I was in college and all of sudden in intramurals and everything else you saw every guy carrying the ball and immediately pumping once and then either stepping to either the left or the right and going up," Query said. "Cheaney's first step was unbelievably quick."

Cheaney may have been one of the lesser regarded members of that recruiting class when he signed, but IU coach Bob Knight quickly found that Cheaney was a player who was capable of contributing right away.

Indiana opened the 1989-90 season with Miami of Ohio and Knight opted to start two freshmen. One was Lawrence Funderburke, a McDonald's All-American, but the other was Cheaney.

Cheaney had a memorable debut. He scored a game-high 20 points and hit 9-of-11 shots from the field in IU's 77-66 win over Miami.

So how did Cheaney go from a guy who Bob Knight was unimpressed with when he saw him play in high school to a player that a few months later would start his first collegiate game and score 20 points in the process?

Dakich said it was all about Cheaney's work ethic from the very beginning.

Calbert Cheaney (Indiana University Archives – P0039771)

199

"He just came in and worked," Dakich said. "There were two things about Calbert. Number one he understood how to play in that offense. He was perfect. He could make mid-range shots. And number two he just worked. He was a guy that had terrific athletic ability and could really shoot and he wanted to get better all the time."

Dakich went as far to say that of all the players he coached in 16 years as an IU assistant, Cheaney was the most coachable.

"It wasn't that he was always on time, he was always early," Dakich said. "He always had a great approach. He never bitched, he never moaned, he never questioned, he just went to work. I was there 16 years and he was the easiest and most fun guy I ever coached.

"He would study film. Then he'd be out on the court and he would want to know what he did wrong even when he was All-American. He never changed."

Todd Leary, one of the seven members of the class of '89, said that while no one knew much about Cheaney before he arrived at IU, that changed very quickly. In fact, Leary said that from the very first workout that he attended when the class was first assembled it was clear that Cheaney's game was going to stand out from the others.

"He took over from day one," Leary said. "I think even some of the older guys started to step to the side right away because they could see how good Calbert was going to be. He definitely emerged as like the silent leader because he wasn't a real vocal guy. But as far as our seven guys in the class, I thought he established himself, at least from my viewpoint, as our go-to guy from that very first practice."

Pat Graham said his memory was that it was the third time they played in open gym but the point is basically the same.

"We start playing open gym and we had Mark Robinson who was possibly the greatest open gym player I ever played with," Graham said. "In that street ball, call-your-own-fouls set up, Mark was as good as there ever was. So here is our seven man class coming in and they want us to play open gym. And Mark Robinson and Calbert have to go against each other. The first two open gyms Mark Robinson is the best player there. He didn't play much, so again we're playing street ball, it's open gym and the coaches are there.

"I can remember the third open gym we have, though, Calbert is the best player on the floor."

Needless to say, it was a big surprise to Graham and his vaunted class of 1989 teammates.

"He's the best player on the floor and nobody said anything," Graham said. "You kind of went in the locker room or in the shower or walking down the hallway to your car and no one said 'Did you just see what happened today?' but you felt it. After about a week, I would say I started on level A and now I was at level B in terms of understanding motion and cutting and when the ball goes opposite what you do and all of those things.

"Calbert was like on level F."

Graham said things just happened that quickly for Cheaney. The light bulb went on. He went from a player who was not one of the best high school players in the state as a senior to the best player IU had in a short period of time.

"I try to explain to people and I don't know if it's just that he didn't have confidence or what, but it's hard to explain," Graham said. "It's one of the eight mysteries of the world how Calbert became our best player three days into open gym."

The analogy that Graham likes to use with Cheaney is a comparison to Michael Jordan.

"Jordan was a great player at North Carolina, we all know that," Graham said. "But no one had a clue of what Jordan was going to be in the pros. Calbert was the same way on the high school/college level. We knew he was going to be a nice player but obviously a lot of schools didn't have a clue. It was basically U of E and IU fighting for him and Purdue came in at the end."

Brian Evans said there were certain things you knew coming in with regard to Cheaney and one was his unquestioned work ethic.

"You weren't going to outwork him, you weren't going to get there before he was there and you weren't going to stay later than Calbert," Evans said. "I remember as a freshman and sophomore just going out to the HYPER on random days in the summer thinking I was going to get a little extra work in, and how many times I saw Calbert Cheaney. I might have been randomly showing up to get some shots in but he was always there working on his game.

"And he was already an All American at that time."

Leary said he has spoken at camps over the years and many times has talked about Calbert Cheaney to the young campers. The message was a simple one: Success can come if you're willing to work hard enough.

"The most honest thing I can say about Calbert is that he worked the hardest every day in practice and you're talking about the best player on the team," Leary said. "They say the same thing about Michael Jordan. They say in practice he would just kill guys and he would make it so hard. And they used to say it about Larry Bird, too.

"I don't necessarily know if it's as much of a conscious effort on his part as that it's just a characteristic of a guy that is not only very talented and a leader but he's a winner, too. I think if you asked everybody on our team to name the player who worked the hardest consistently day in and day out, I would debate anyone who didn't say it was Calbert."

Indiana would go on to win the first 10 games of Cheaney's rookie season at IU and have a 10-0 mark heading into Big Ten play.

Actually, IU did have one loss in the non-conference season. But it wasn't a game, but rather a player. That was Funderburke, who quit the team in mid-December and eventually decided to transfer to Ohio State. Before the '89 class had finished its eligibility in college it would also lose Lawson, who would leave after his sophomore season and transfer to Vanderbilt.

"Losing Lawrence and Chris was tough," Cheaney said. "I don't know why Lawrence left but Chris I'm sure left because he wanted more playing time. And I understand that. That's part of it. That's part of college basketball. It would have been nice to have them all the way through. Who knows what we would have done if we had those two all the way through?"

What Cheaney didn't say or wouldn't say if he wanted to was that his emergence made losing Funderburke less of a catastrophic loss for the Hoosiers.

Jake Query, the Indianapolis radio talk show host, said it was actually interesting how it played out.

"So Funderburke goes for like 26 points in his sixth game and then leaves," Query said. "And so here's the promised recruit but it was almost like that was forgotten about within weeks because of Calbert."

As good as Indiana had done in the non-conference season, the Big Ten proved to be much tougher. IU lost a couple of close decisions early and after eight games had slipped to 4-4 in Big Ten play. Four of the next six games would be against ranked opponents, all on the road, and IU dropped them all. The Hoosiers finished 8-10 in the conference. That gave them an 18-10 mark overall and a seventh place Big Ten face.

Based on the fact that IU had beaten some ranked teams though early in the season, the Hoosiers still managed to get an NCAA Tournament berth that year. IU was a No. 8 seed in the East Regional and faced No. 9 California in the first round in Hartford, Conn. IU got knocked out in the first round, 65-63.

Cheaney finished his freshman season having started all 29 games, averaging 17.1 points per game and shooting 57.2 percent from the field.

And that would be his lowest scoring average of his college career.

•••

Cheaney's second season in college was much more successful. The Hoosiers would win the Big Ten with a 15-3 overall record and Cheaney would earn first-team All-Big Ten honors as well as be selected to the All-American team.

Damon Bailey was the Indiana high school storybook legend that arrived on campus that season for his freshman year. He averaged 11.4 points and shot better than 50 percent from the field, earning Big Ten freshman of the year honors.

"During the time I played at IU, I always felt that Damon was the glue for our team," Cheaney said. "If he didn't play well, we probably ended up losing. He was a big time glue guy for us. I enjoyed playing with him. He was a great passer. He was just a winner."

Cheaney, who would end up averaging 21.6 points and shooting 59.6 percent from the field, got off to a good start.

He had 30 points in an 84-73 win at Vanderbilt. He had a big three-point play in an 87-84 win over No. 18 Kentucky. He had 23 points and nine rebounds in that game.

His first 30-point game in college came in the Big Ten opener that year against Illinois when the Hoosiers blew the Illini out 109-74 at Assembly Hall. Cheaney had 30 to lead IU.

Beginning with a 70-67 victory over Notre Dame in late November that season, Indiana had a stretch where it won 14 games in a row and 20 out of 21 overall. That extended all the way through an 18-point win over Purdue at home on Feb. 10. That improved IU's conference record to 10-1 but Ohio State was still the conference leader at 11-1 and IU would travel next to play the Buckeyes. Ohio State had beaten Indiana 93-85 in Assembly Hall earlier in the only IU loss in that 21-game stretch.

Ohio State would win the second game, too, 97-95 in overtime. Cheaney, unfortunately, fouled out with 20 seconds to play in regulation. Ohio State's Treg Lee hit the game-winner with 4 seconds to play to lift the Buckeyes to the win.

Indiana and Ohio State would end up co-Big Ten champions with 15-3 records but the Buckeyes held the tie-breaker with the two wins against the Hoosiers and thus were awarded the NCAA's No. 1 seed in the Midwest Regional. IU was ranked No. 3 in the nation and garnered the No. 2 seed in the Southeast Regional with a first round matchup in Louisville against Coastal Carolina.

IU won the first round matchup by 10 points and then beat Florida State by 22 in a game where Cheaney had a double-double with 24 points and 10 rebounds.

In the Sweet Sixteen though, IU ran into a red-hot Kansas team that had been seeded No. 3. The Jayhawks led by more than 20 at halftime and knocked IU out of the tourney with an 83-65 win.

••••

From a 29-5 mark his sophomore season, Indiana returned
all five starters for the 1991-92
campaign. It would be another
banner season for IU. Indiana
finished 27-7 overall, 14-4 in
conference for second place
and would eventually advance
to the Final Four. The only two
players that IU lost from the
year before were Lyndon Jones
and Chris Lawson. Lawson,
part of the impressive IU recruiting class of 1989,
transferred to Vanderbilt.

*Calbert Cheaney (Indiana
University Archives – P0051655)*

The two additions to that team were 6-9 forward Alan
Henderson, who would go on to become one of the best players in IU history, and 7-foot center Todd Lindeman.

Once again, IU had a big early season win streak. The Hoosiers won 13 in a row including the first six in Big Ten play to
get out of the gate at 15-2 overall. Indiana continued that surge
and was 22-4 overall and 13-2 in the Big Ten with three games
to play. IU also was ranked No. 2 in the nation.

But the regular season ending was a disappointing one for
the Hoosiers. First Michigan, with its Fab Five, beat the Hoosiers 68-60. Then after IU beat Wisconsin, the Hoosiers traveled
to West Lafayette for the Big Ten finale needing a win to clinch
at least a share of the Big Ten title once again with Ohio State.

The first time the teams had played that season, IU had defeated Purdue by 41 points, 106-65 at Assembly Hall. Cheaney
had 23 points to lead IU on 10-of-14 shooting. The Hoosiers
led by 27 at halftime, 51-24.

The second time around IU led by five at the half and by 10
midway through the second half. Then Woody Austin and
Cuonzo Martin and company got hot for the Boilers. Austin
finished with 20 and Martin had 12 including some key shots
down the stretch as Purdue knocked off the No. 4 Hoosiers
61-59. Cheaney led IU with 20.

"If we had won that game we would have clinched the Big Ten title and we probably would have had a No. 1 seed," Cheaney recalled. "But that made us just have work a little bit harder."

Ohio State won the Big Ten by a game over the Hoosiers and once again IU was relegated to a No. 2 seed but this time the Hoosiers were sent out West to Boise, Idaho.

Cheaney said as it turned out the No. 2 seed may have made the Hoosiers just a little bit hungrier.

"It turned out to be a blessing in disguise because as we moved through the tournament we were probably playing the best basketball in the NCAA Tournament," Cheaney said.

IU beat Eastern Illinois by nearly 40 points in the NCAA opener 94-55, hitting 36-of-58 shots from the field, 62 percent. Next up was LSU with big center Shaquille O'Neal. O'Neal was nearly unstoppable against IU. He had 36 points on 12-of-18 shooting from the field and hit all 12 of his foul shots. He also had 12 rebounds.

But IU had an answer with Cheaney. The junior forward scored 30 points in 38 minutes on 10-of-18 from the field and a perfect 9-of-9 from the free throw line. IU advanced to the Sweet Sixteen with an 89-79 victory.

In the regional semifinals, IU beat Florida State 85-74. Greg Graham had 19 and Cheaney had 17 to lead IU. That gave IU a rematch with UCLA, a team that had beaten Indiana in the season opener that year in the Hall of Fame Tipoff Classic in Springfield, Mass. UCLA had won that first game by 17, 87-72. Cheaney was 2-for-9 from the field and limited to eight points.

With a chance to get to the Final Four on the line, IU pummeled the Bruins 106-79. Cheaney had 23 points on 9-of-15 shooting in the rematch. Damon Bailey had 22 on 8-of-11 shooting.

It set up a Final Four national semifinal matchup with defending national champion Duke in Minneapolis.

IU led by 12 in the first half and by five at the break, 42-37.

The second half was a different story. Duke built a 13-point lead as IU's top four scorers – Cheaney, Alan Henderson, Greg

Graham and Damon Bailey – all were in foul trouble. In fact, all four would foul out in a game where IU committed 33 fouls compared to 18 for the Blue Devils.

Duke led by nine with a minute to play when IU guard Todd Leary had a shooting stretch for the ages. He made three consecutive 3-point field goals in a 24-second span to get IU back in the game. Indiana trailed by three and had a chance to tie in the closing seconds. But IU couldn't get the ball to Leary and Jamal Meeks attempted a 3-pointer but it was off and Duke won, 81-78.

Cheaney smiled when he thought about Leary's flurry of 3-pointers. Does he wish that Leary had gotten the ball at the end to have one more shot at a fourth 3 to send the game into overtime?

"Without a doubt," Cheaney said. "But we had all fouled out so we didn't have much of a say in it. But absolutely, we wish he had hit one more shot to force overtime. If you could get to overtime you never know what might have happened. But that was unbelievable. It was an unbelievable individual display of shooting and something you don't see every day."

Looking back, Cheaney said that game and the way it ended it still something he thinks about from time to time.

"For us to go to the Final Four and then have a tough game against Duke it was definitely disappointing," Cheaney said. "It's one of those things where to win a national championship the breaks have to go your way. And the breaks didn't go our way that particular night."

Cheaney finished the season with a 17.6 points per game average, scoring 599 points in 34 games. He earned All-American honors for a second season in a row.

When interviewed for this book in the summer of 2014, Cheaney said that the 1992 team was special.

"That was probably the best team I was on for the entire four years I was there," Cheaney said. "We had a great year my senior year but we were much deeper my junior year. We had so many guys who could come off the bench and do so many things for us."

That led to Cheaney's senior season when IU capped what would turn out to be a magical three-year run of Hoosier hoops in terms of dominance on the court.

• • • •

After going 56-12 overall the previous two years with one co-Big Ten title and a Final Four appearance to show for it, the experts expected IU to contend for a national title in the 1992-93 season.

The Hoosiers opened the year ranked No. 4 in the nation and never slipped any farther than No. 6 the entire season.

Most of the class of 1989 had reached their senior seasons. Two had left the program (Lawrence Funderburke and Chris Lawson) and two others had redshirted along the way. Both Pat Graham and Todd Leary were redshirt juniors in 1992-93.

The seniors that season that came in with Cheaney also included Chris Reynolds and Greg Graham. A fourth senior was Matt Nover, who had redshirted a year of his own.

A highly-touted freshman on that team was Brian Evans, who would go on to have an All-American season of his own in 1996 and would score just over 1,700 points for his career.

IU had a rigorous non-conference season that year but still managed to open up 11-2. The Hoosiers had wins over four top 20 ranked opponents including No. 17 Tulane, No. 7 Florida State, No. 6 Seton Hall and No. 19 Cincinnati. Both of the losses were to teams that were ranked No. 3 at the time, Kansas and Kentucky.

Indiana really got things going in the Big Ten season. IU won the first 13 games of the conference season. The 12th game in that stretch was a 93-72 victory over Illinois as Cheaney scored 29 points and pulled down nine rebounds.

But that's also when Indiana's realistic hopes at a national title slipped away, too.

In practice the day before IU played Purdue, which ultimately would be the 13th win in a row open conference play, Alan Henderson went into the air to catch a long outlet pass and came down awkwardly on his right knee. It turned out Henderson tore his ACL and would require knee surgery when the season was over.

IU was able to beat Purdue without Henderson but then lost on the road at Ohio State, 81-77 in overtime. The Hoosiers rallied to win their final four Big Ten games to finish 17-1 and capture the outright Big Ten title.

One of those final games was a home game against Northwestern where Cheaney scored 35 points and became the Big Ten's all-time leading scorer.

The strong finish gave IU the No. 1 seed in the Midwest Regional of the NCAA Tournament. That was significant because it allowed the Hoosiers to play the first two rounds in Indianapolis in the Hoosier Dome.

Cheaney had 29 points in the NCAA opener in a 43-point win over Wright State. Cheaney led the Hoosiers with 23 points in the second game, a 73-70 win over Xavier.

In the Sweet Sixteen, Cheaney scored 32 points in IU's 82-69 win over Louisville. But the Hoosiers fell in the regional final to Kansas 83-77 to end their season.

Henderson attempted to play in the NCAA Tournament but was ineffective.

Cheaney said in the interview for this book that the most disappointing thing for him was that he left IU without winning a national title.

"You go to Indiana to win national championships and put banners in the rafters," Cheaney said. "We fell short of that goal and the frustrating thing is that I think we had a couple of teams that could have gotten that done."

Cheaney finished having had a spectacular college basketball career. He is one of only three players in Indiana history (Don Schlundt and Kent Benson are the other two) to earn All-American honors three times.

He is still Indiana's all-time leading scorer with 2,613 points. That's a career average of 19.8 points per game. He played in 132 games with 130 starts. His career field goal percentage was a staggering 55.9 percent especially for a player that was shooting a lot of shots from the perimeter.

••••

Pat Graham, who came in with Cheaney as part of the recruiting class of 1989, said whenever any of his friends ask him about his favorite player from his time at IU there's never any hesitation.

"I've always said that Calbert Cheaney was the greatest teammate that I've ever had," Graham said. "Without question. It's not even close. Here's a guy who could score four points or 24 points and did not care. He was the greatest, most unselfish teammate that I've ever been around at any level."

Greg Graham, who was the head basketball coach at Warren Central High School in Indianapolis at the time this book was written, said he was blessed to have had the opportunity to play with Cheaney for four years.

"Coming in, I had heard about Cal but had never really seen him play," Graham said. "All I heard was he was a lefty and that he was pretty much just like me but probably 30 pounds heavier. Having an opportunity to play with him, I was just amazed at how skilled he was and how attuned he was with his jump shot."

Several people who watched Cheaney play used the same adjective to describe him.

"He was just a smooth player," Greg Graham said. "He worked that baseline like a master Zen. It was great having had the opportunity to play with him for four years and see the success that he's had."

IU athletic director Fred Glass had the pleasure of watching Cheaney as a player and then having him on staff as the director of operations and internal and external player development for two seasons under Tom Crean.

"I always felt like Calbert was the quintessential Hoosier," Glass said. "He came in highly regarded but maybe not as heralded as someone who would leave as the all time Big Ten leading scorer."

Glass remembers Knight having to stay on his big forward from Evansville to look for his shot more.

"I remember Knight exhorting Cheaney to shoot more," Glass said. "Usually you don't have to tell your leading scorer to shoot more but he was a team first guy. When he learned that to help his team he needed to shoot and score more, boy did he."

When Cheaney was asked to look back on a favorite memory of his IU playing career, he said it wasn't a single individual accomplishment or team achievement that he would always remember about playing at Indiana. Instead, it was the people he played with.

People like Greg Graham and Alan Henderson and Damon Bailey and Brian Evans. That list went on and on and on.

"The only real thing that stands out for me was the camaraderie I had with my teammates on and off the court," Cheaney said. "The most important thing for me was that I had great teammates, and not only just great teammates but great friends in general that I was lucky enough to play with."

14
Number 1
Don Schlundt

OK, I'll admit it. I never saw Don Schlundt play.

For one, I grew up in Southern California and for the other I was born three years after Schlundt had played his final game at Indiana.

But everything I've heard about the big center out of South Bend, Ind., has convinced me that he should be recognized as the top Indiana University basketball player of all-time from the state of Indiana. You can make arguments for other players but here are a couple of mind-boggling statistics for you to chew on first.

In four seasons at Indiana, Schlundt made 826 of 1,076 free throws. That was a percentage of .768.

Don Schlundt (Indiana University Archives – P0021731)

And what's the significance of that? In the history of Indiana University basketball, those are records that have never been broken – by a long shot.

In terms of free throws made, only two other players have ever made more than 500 in their IU careers. Steve Alford made 535 from 1984-87 and Christian Watford hit 504 from 2010-13.

213

Alford hit those 535 free throws in 125 games. Watford did it in 132 games. Schlundt made nearly 300 more free throws than Alford in just 94 games.

Schlundt's 1,076 free throw attempts are even more of a head-scratching statistic. That means for his career he averaged 11.4 free throw attempts per game.

Alford took 596 for his career. That's 480 fewer free throws than Schlundt attempted.

So that's one pair of statistics that separates Schlundt from the pack.

Another one would be his season scoring averages. As a freshman he averaged 17.1 points per game but he was clearly just getting warmed up. His final three seasons, he averaged 24.3, 25.4 and 26.0 points per game.

Again, looking for the significance of those numbers? They represent three of the top eight single season scoring averages in Indiana history. No other player has ever averaged 24 points or more in three different seasons in IU history. Two have done it twice – Jimmy Rayl and Archie Dees. A total of 19 players in Indiana history have averaged 20 points or more for a single season a total of 26 times.

Finally, here is one more statistic to sink your teeth into. Schlundt holds the Indiana school record for being the quickest in history to score 1,000 points.

He did it in 43 games. Actually, it happened in the Final Four in the '53 national championship season against LSU. Schlundt scored 29 points in that game which moved him past the 1,000 scoring mark.

Second on that IU list is Archie Dees at 47 games, followed by Walt Bellamy in 50 and Calbert Cheaney in 53.

So he scored a ton of points, made and attempted a crazy number of free throws and he was the quickest player in IU history to score 1,000 points. On top of that, he was a three time All-American and he led his team to a national championship.

It adds up to a pretty good resume for the No. 1 player in Indiana University basketball history to hail from the state of Indiana.

Don Schlundt was a Hoosier Through and Through.

Those statistics are meant to give you a taste of Schlundt. He still ranks third in Indiana school history in total points scored at 2,192. He only trails Calbert Cheaney and Steve Alford. But the asterisks should indicate that his points came before there was a 3-point line (Cheaney had 148 career 3's and Alford had 107 as he only played one season with the 3-pointer) and should also indicate the number of games played to reach those point totals.

Cheaney, IU's all-time leading scorer with 2,613 points, accomplished that feat in 132 games. That's a 19.8 career scoring average. Alford, second all time with 2,438 career points, needed 125 games. His career scoring average was 19.5

Schlundt, the No. 3 player on the scoring list, scored his 2,192 points in 94 games. That's a career average of 23.3. The only career average in IU history that is higher is George McGinnis at 29.9 points but he only played one season.

And Schlundt's Indiana career scoring mark lasted 32 years before Alford eventually broke it and later Cheaney.

So who was Don Schlundt? With most of the players I have chronicled in this book, I had either seen them play or in the case of Jimmy Rayl, I had the good fortune of driving up to Kokomo one day and spending a few hours with Jimmy and his wife Nancy to revisit the past.

Schlundt, however, is the only member of my all-time IU top 10 that is deceased. Schlundt died Oct. 10, 1985 of stomach cancer. He was 52.

There were a couple of ways to accurately tell the Don Schlundt story. One was reading past accounts of his accomplishments. As I've done with many of the profiles here, the *IU Basketball Encyclopedia* written first by Jason Hiner and then updated by myself in 2013 was a big help. Also the book, *Branch*, by Bill Murphy added some color to Schlundt's accomplishments as well.

I then attempted to contact the five living members of that '53 national championship team that would have played with Schlundt. Because Bill Murphy knew them all and had talked with them in the past, he graciously agreed to reach out to them again for this project. Many of the quotes on the pages to follow about Schlundt came from Murphy's interviews. Some also came from an interview conducted with Bobby 'Slick' Leonard by my colleague, Justin Albers. Hopefully through those interviews and other book accounts, a picture of just who Don Schlundt was will begin to emerge.

•••

Generally, freshmen were not allowed to participate in college basketball until the early 1970's. The NCAA passed legislation on Jan. 8, 1972 that permitted freshmen to play varsity basketball beginning with the 1972-73 season. Prior to that, college freshmen could play on Frosh or Frosh/Soph teams only.

But Don Schlundt was able to take advantage of a special ruling that enabled him to play right away.

When Schlundt came to Indiana for the 1951-52 season, he was eligible to play immediately because of the Korean War Waiver. According to the IU Basketball Encyclopedia, the waiver allowed freshmen to compete in varsity athletics because the U.S. Draft had depleted the number of young men on college campuses. The waiver only existed for one season and Schlundt was the only player on the 17-man IU roster that was a freshman.

"The Korean War provided an exemption to players so that freshmen were eligible at that particular time," said Bill Murphy, author and IU basketball historian. "For Indiana that was big though because it meant that Schlundt got a third year to play with (Bobby) Leonard who was a year older than him."

It was also huge for Indiana because it meant that Schlundt, a 6-9 freshman from Washington Clay High School in South Bend, Ind., could get in the mix right away. That gave IU two big men in the middle as 6-10 sophomore Lou Scott from Chicago was also a post player for the Hoosiers.

Jim Schooley played at Indiana from 1951-53 and is actually partly responsible for Schlundt attending IU. When Schooley was a sophomore in 1951, he played behind legendary IU center Bill Garrett. He only played a half of one game though and was hopeful that the following year he would get a chance to play.

The arrival of Schlundt would ultimately put an end to that dream. Schooley remembers IU coach Branch McCracken coming to him during Schooley's sophomore year and asking him if could host a recruit.

That recruit was Don Schlundt.

Schooley remembered that recruiting visit despite the fact it occurred more than 60 years before.

"Don was a very happy and nice individual who was very much in love with a girl he knew back home named Gloria," Schooley recalled. "Don wanted to be in the fraternity that I was in (Theta Pi Beta) so it worked out well for me to host him.

"We did our duty and set him up for a date and he did his duty and went out on the date but his heart was not in it because of Gloria."

Schooley said later they met with McCracken and then returned to the fraternity where they shot some baskets in the back.

"Somehow he twisted his ankle and we took him in to have it checked out," Schooley said. "I remember he had a pair of crutches and when he left to go back to South Bend, unbeknownst to me, he put the crutches under the covers of my bed. Well I was worn out from showing Don around and I flopped on my bed only to hit my head on the crutches. That's what I remember from the end of the visit any way."

Shortly thereafter, McCracken called Schooley over one day and told him that Schlundt had told the IU coach he would come to Indiana with one condition – that he could room with Schooley.

"And so that was that," Schooley said.

After he saw Schlundt play, Schooley realized that the 6-9 recruit was so good that it would mean he would no longer find his way into the lineup. But he said the important thing was that the team be successful.

•••

Schooley, who as of the summer of 2014 was living in Middletown, Md., remembered his first impressions of Schlundt as a player were that he could handle the basketball well for a player his size. In fact, Schooley thought he was as comfortable as a guard as he was in the post.

"Don was a natural 6-10 guard," Schooley said. "He could run the court extremely well and got a lot of his points on the break. He could shoot from midrange and was a very smooth player. He would run the court and tip in any missed shots by his teammates."

Murphy, the author of *Branch*, had his own first hand memories of Schlundt. He said he was a young boy at the time and remembers vividly watching Schlundt play. He guessed that he probably saw Schlundt play in person 10 times.

"His size was the most overwhelming thing to me because he was so tall," Murphy said. "But as a little kid I loved his sweeping hook shot and the way he moved around the basket. He seemed to gobble up every rebound that was available. And he was just so smooth when it came to playing on the court.

"They were the Hurryin' Hoosiers and so they would go really quick and that was extremely entertaining to a young person."

If you're a more modern day Indiana basketball fan, the thought of Cody Zeller getting out and racing down the floor on a break is something that is likely etched in your memory. That was a similar memory that Murphy had of Schlundt.

"He would get out and run, too," Murphy said. "He was incredibly graceful to watch. And he could really shoot, too. Back then it was amazing to see a guy of his size hit free throws as accurately as he did. Usually your big guys were the ones you wanted to foul because they weren't very good free throw shooters but Schlundt was completely the opposite of that. He was someone you didn't want to foul because he would bury the free throw every time."

In each of his final three seasons at IU, Schlundt made at least 77 percent of his foul shots. That was a significant edge for a player who averaged 13 free throws per game for the final three seasons of his career.

Because of his ability at the free throw line, Murphy described his range as being solid from 15-feet and in.

"It was kind of amazing that IU went from (Bill) Garrett to Schlundt to (Archie) Dees and they were all really good shooters," Murphy said. "Now of course Garrett was much smaller than the other two but all of those guys could really shoot."

Dr. Marvin Christie, who played for Branch McCracken as a sophomore on the 1950 team but then left the program to focus on medicine, echoed the views of others about what Schlundt was able to do in the open floor.

"Schlundt was a big boy but he could handle himself like a big guard which was very unusual back then," Christie said. "Don could feed his teammates and set them up for a pass when they would go for the bucket. Don was very quick with his feet and he would sidestep his defender when going to the basket to avoid a charging foul."

Most of all, he loved to get out on the break and play up tempo Hoosier basketball, a staple of Branch McCracken's teams.

"He could play McCracken basketball which is to say he could run the floor as well as any of the little guys that could play Hurryin' Hoosier ball," Christie said. "McCracken and all of Schlundt's teammates would never see Don get tired. He was in great shape. He had a motor that would just keep going all game long."

Clarence Doninger, who would go on to be IU's athletic director from 1991-2001, was a sophomore when Schlundt was a senior. Doninger played his high school ball at Evansville (Ind.) Central and his senior year in high school was the year IU won the national title in 1953.

One Friday night, Doninger's high school team had a game in Bloomington and his coach took the whole team the next evening to see Indiana face defending Big Ten champion Illinois. It would be Doninger's first time seeing the Hoosiers in person and he came home hooked on IU basketball.

He would see Schlundt play many more times over the next two years but the big IU center left a lasting impression on him.

"He was one of the first really big men," Doninger said. "Now you see 6-10, 6-11, and 7-foot players all over but back then there weren't that many players that tall in the country.

And the nice thing about Don is that he could really shoot. He wasn't as athletic as you see some of the big guys today but he was athletic enough and smooth enough that he just fit in perfectly with that team."

Doninger remembers the hook shot that Schlundt seemed to perfect early in his IU career. And he was also impressed with how well Schlundt could shoot free throws.

"He had a really nice hook shot and a smooth free throw shooting touch," Doninger said. "I've always said you can tell if someone can shoot by just watching them shoot free throws. And he was very good at shooting free throws and that was something that really helped his game, too."

Schlundt's free throw shooting was continually a topic repeated in nearly every interview conducted for this book. It was clear the free throw line was a huge weapon in Schlundt's arsenal. But the question that begged to be answered was this: Was it simply that Schlundt was unstoppable and that was the only way to slow him down or was there something else that contributed to the IU center getting to the line that many times?

Dr. Marvin Christie explained it this way.

"Don would get fouled a lot because of who he was and the way he played the game," Christie said. "He could go to his right or to his left, either way with the same ability which kept the defender guessing and allowed Don to get by his man many times."

Christie said Schlundt was also different from many big men of his time in that he would not pull up for a short jumper when trying to avoid a charge.

"Instead, he would use his foot quickness to go around his defender and straight to the basket and score," Christie said. "Sometimes he would draw a foul as well and sometimes just getting hammered at the basket because that seemed to many opponents to be the only way to stop him.

"Of course, Schlundt was an excellent free throw shooter so that (strategy) didn't work very well."

Schooley said that because Schlundt ran the floor so well and was active around the basket, he wound up getting fouled a lot.

"With his ability to score and rebound around the basket and with his pure size, he was able to draw so many fouls by other teams trying to keep him from scoring," Schooley said. "And he was really quicker than his opponent so he was able to draw more fouls back of his quick first step to the basket.

"I just remember he was more of a natural 6-10 guard and so the other big men were more prone to foul him."

Doninger said Schlundt had two things going for him – he could shoot free throws at a

Don Schlundt (Indiana University Archives – P0028885)

high percentage and he found himself constantly at the foul line.

"He was just so good shooting free throws and the opposing teams really couldn't stop him," Doninger said. "There was only one guy in the Big Ten at that time that was really his size and that was Red Kerr. But most of the teams we played really had their hands full trying to guard Don Schlundt."

Tom and Dick Van Arsdale were just 10 years old and living in Indianapolis when Schlundt and the Hoosiers won the '53 national championship. But they were enamored with that team and followed it closely.

"The '53 team was the team that caused Dick and I to really think about playing at IU," said Tom Van Arsdale. "Despite being a superstar Don Schlundt played as a team with the other players. They were amazing how they played so well together as a team. We kept score of every game they played that year."

What Tom Van Arsdale remembered about Schlundt most of all was that he was the ultimate go-to guy.

"Schlundt was the player you would get the ball to when you needed a score," Tom Van Arsdale said. "He was fouled so much because it was the only way the other team had to keep him from scoring. That wasn't all that effective though, because he shot free throws so well."

Archie Dees, an IU basketball legend himself and two-time Indiana All American, was a freshman at IU when Schlundt was a senior. He didn't remember the part as well about Schlundt running the floor but he did say he was nearly unstoppable when he got the ball inside.

"He was just a really good post player and he could make some good moves around the basket to get himself free and score pretty much at will," Dees said. "I remember trying to guard him in pickup games and stuff and he was really a handful."

●●●●

Schlundt's first game in an IU uniform was not an indication of things to come. In a 68-59 win over Valparaiso, Schlundt managed to hit just 1-of-5 shots from the field. In his second game, also at home against Xavier, Schlundt led the Hoosiers in scoring with 16 points in a 92-69 win.

His first big scoring game came in the fifth game when he had 28 points in an overtime victory over Kansas State. He bettered that on the road at Purdue in Big Ten play when he hit 12-of-18 shots from the field and scored 29 points in IU's 82-77.

The second time IU played Purdue that season, Schlundt set the single game IU scoring record with 35 points in a 93-70 win. Eventually, Schlundt would set an IU single season scoring record with 376 points in 22 games, an average of 17.1 points per game.

Schlundt's first breakout season came in 1953, the year the Hoosiers finished 23-3 overall, 17-1 in the Big Ten and won the national championship. Schlundt averaged 25.4 points and 10 rebounds per game. He attempted 310 free throws that season and hit 249 to shoot a cool 80.3 percent.

In 1953, the Big Ten experimented with a full round robin schedule. That meant instead of playing 14 conference games as they had previously, the Hoosiers would play 18. But that also meant that the Big Ten season would start in December and that the non-conference slate would only include three games.

Throughout the season, Schlundt routinely put up big numbers. On a trip north to play Michigan and Michigan State, Schlundt scored 39 against Michigan and 33 against Michigan State.

IU had a home game against Butler in early February where the Hoosiers broke the century mark in scoring for the first time in history, beating the Bulldogs 105-70. Schlundt had 33 points and 10 rebounds in that game. Later, on the day that IU clinched its first outright Big Ten title with a win over Illinois, Schlundt had 33.

Indiana entered postseason play with the No. 1 ranking in the nation. After a first round bye, IU beat DePaul 82-80 as Schlundt scored 23 and Bobby Leonard chipped in 22. In the regional final against Notre Dame, Schlundt was unstoppable down low and scored 41 points in IU's 79-66 win over the Irish.

This put the Hoosiers into the Final Four. Schlundt had 29 in an 80-67 victory over LSU who was led by All-American center Bob Pettit. In the title game, he had 30 points and 10 rebounds to lead the Hoosiers to a 69-68 victory over Kansas.

When Branch McCracken was called up to present the regional championship MVP award to Schlundt in that tournament, he had this to say about his sophomore center.

"If Don here, a sophomore, continues to improve and if he works hard, he may turn out to be a pretty fair country ballplayer before he's finished," McCracken said.

In the book, *Branch*, by Bill Murphy, the author quoted Schlundt talking about his coach in an interview that took place in 1970.

"You take five individuals as smart aleck as probably we were back then, and well, you have to have a certain type of coach," Schlundt was quoted as saying. "I don't think there were any other coaches in the country that could have handled five young underclassmen as well as McCracken did."

Schlundt said that McCracken just had a way with his IU teams.

"McCracken had a way of uniting the team, exploding when he had to, knocking our ears back when he had to, which we certainly needed back then, and then just to be a father off the court for us and give us advice," Schlundt said.

• • • •

His junior season, Schlundt and the other four players in the starting five off the national championship team tried to repeat. They won the Big Ten with a 12-2 record but lost to Notre Dame 65-64 in the NCAA Tourament.

Schlundt had another All-American season that year. He averaged 24.3 points in 24 games.

He had 25 points in an early win over Kansas State and then scored 34 points in a win over Oregon State. In the Big Ten opener at Michigan, Schlundt scored 30 in a game that was decided on a 25-foot shot at the buzzer by Leonard. IU won 62-60. In IU's next game, Schlundt had 29 in a narrow win over Wisconsin. He followed that up with 30 against Purdue and 33 against Wisconsin in Madison. That was four games of 29 or more in the first five games of conference play.

Schlundt then erupted for a new Big Ten scoring record of 47 points against Ohio State. The IU big man was clearly on a roll.

Things continued on a high pace heading into the NCAA Tournament but that's when IU's luck ran out. Notre Dame double-teamed Schlundt with a strategy of forcing someone else to beat them. Unfortunately, IU's other players had a cold shooting night. Notre Dame won 65-64 to end Schlundt's junior season.

In Schlundt's senior season, the Hoosiers didn't fare nearly as well on the court. Bob Leonard, Dick Farley and Charley Kraak had all graduated. Schlundt still averaged 26 points that season and would earn his third All-American honor but the Hoosiers finished 8-14 overall and 5-9 in the conference for sixth place.

"It's kind of interesting because Schlundt's career really parallels Kent Benson's," said author and IU basketball historian Bill Murphy. "Their senior years they were both players that were All-Americans, great, great players but all of their highly-touted teammates had pretty much gone at that time.

"And so their senior year neither of their teams really had a good year but both their sophomore and junior years were considered absolutely great seasons. Each of them won an NCAA championship and each of them lost an absolutely heart-breaking game in the NCAA Tournament when they were probably the best teams in the country."

Schlundt's most memorable game from that season was the final one, an 84-66 victory over Ohio State. With 10 minutes to play, Ohio State led by one at 61-60. But the Hoosiers closed the game on a 24-5 run that included 17 points by Schlundt.

The season before Schlundt had set a Big Ten single game scoring record with 47 points against Ohio State. On this day, he tied his own conference record with 47 more against the Buckeyes.

That performance moved him from third place in the Big Ten in scoring to first. It also allowed him to become the first player in Big Ten history to lead the conference in scoring three seasons in a row.

He also finished the season as the all-time leading career scorer in Big Ten history.

After his Indiana career was over, Schlundt was selected in the second round of the 1955 NBA Draft by Syracuse. But he never played professional basketball. He chose to go into the insurance business instead.

"Don didn't go into the NBA but he very well could have played professionally," said teammate Bobby Leonard. "He had an insurance business. At that time the NBA didn't really pay anything and he was making a lot more in the insurance business."

Schlundt first started in the insurance business in Bloomington and later had an office in Indianapolis. He teamed up with another former IU basketball player, Archie Dees, to sell insurance after their college careers were over.

Dees was a freshman at IU when Schlundt was a senior. He said the first time he ever met Schlundt was on one of his three recruiting visits when he was a senior in high school. He said on one of those visits, Schlundt was shooting baskets in the Fieldhouse and they took him over there to meet him.

Don Schlundt, left, and Bobby Leonard, right. (Indiana University Archives – P0043445)

"He was a really nice and very friendly," Dees said. "He was someone who was easy to root for because he was so good natured. At the same time he was a very private person but he and I were always very good friends."

Dees remembered a game that his freshman team played against the varsity of which Schlundt was a senior captain. In those days, the freshmen did very little. They would practice during the week and then often times scrimmage against themselves in a game right before the varsity would play.

One time, Branch McCracken decided to try something different and he let the freshmen team scrimmage the varsity. Dees' freshmen group though was a pretty formidable bunch. Players on that team included Indiana All-Stars Jerry Thompson, Ray Ball and Pete Obremsky, as well as a couple of pretty solid players from Chicago in Paxton Lumpkin and Charlie Brown who had played on a state championship team in Illinois.

Well, not only did the freshmen give the varsity a game, they were actually leading with just a minute or so to play before as Dees put it, McCracken said 'enough was enough.'

"We should have beat them but Branch said that was the last time we would do that," Dees said. "He subbed someone in for me and two or three of other good scorers out there and the varsity was able to come back and beat us. There was no way that Branch was going to allow the varsity to lose that game."

Most of what Dees remembers about Schlundt, however, came later when Dees got out of school and went into the insurance business with the former IU three-time All-American. Dees said that when Schlundt was drafted by Syracuse in the NBA Draft, they weren't paying that much in those days to play. Dees said Schlundt was offered $6,500 a season.

"He just ran out of places to play," Dees said. "Leaving (Indiana University) was probably the worst thing that happened to him as far as if he wanted to play ball because it just wasn't something you could do back then and try to make a comfortable living."

Knowing he could do much better in the insurance business, Schlundt opted to do that instead. When Dees graduated, he joined him, and they started an insurance business together called 'The Tallest Insurance in Town.' With Schlundt at 6-9 and Dees at 6-8, the name certainly fit.

"We catered a lot to kids at the universities," Dees said. "Most of that business was Indiana University but we branched out to a few other places, too. I met Bobby Plump and he took me up to Franklin College one day and we had a guy set up some interviews for us. We wrote $250,000 in business in a single day. That was crazy."

Dees said they stayed in business together for three or four years before Schlundt moved to Indianapolis and went to work for an insurance company there.

Dees said the two kind of drifted apart after Schlundt moved to Indianapolis. They would see each other from time to time because Schlundt was a regular at IU basketball home games right up until he died in 1985.

Dees said when he heard that Schlundt has passed he just couldn't believe it. Most people didn't realize he was sick and Schlundt, being a private person, didn't let on about it.

"I remember reading about it in the paper and I just couldn't believe it was true," Dees said. "What a shame. He left us way too early. I'll always remember him as being one of the nicest guys around."

••••

Leonard was asked to describe just how good Schlundt was when he played at Indiana. He said there was one example in particular that could illustrate his point.

Leonard said one of Indiana's biggest rivals was Illinois at the time. He said the top four schools in any given season were Minnesota, Iowa, Indiana and Illinois. When the Hoosiers faced the Illini, Schlundt was matched up with Johnny Kerr.

Kerr played 13 seasons in the NBA, mostly for the Syracuse Nationals. In 1954 he was the sixth player selected overall in the NBA Draft by Syracuse. He would go on to be a three-time NBA All-Star and scored more than 12,000 points and pulled down more than 10,000 rebounds in his career. In his NBA career, he averaged a double-double with 13.8 points and 11.2 rebounds.

This is all significant, according to Leonard, because there was one thing that Kerr couldn't do as a collegiate player. He couldn't stop Don Schlundt. When Schlundt was a sophomore in '53, the IU center scored 22 points and pulled down 11 rebounds against Kerr and the Illini the first time. The second time he scored 33 in a game that gave IU its first ever undisputed Big Ten basketball title.

And Schlundt gave Kerr fits. The first time in particular, Kerr was 6-of-30 from the field against the Hoosiers and his counterpart, Schlundt.

"Don had to match up with Johnny Kerr of Illinois," Leonard said. "And Johnny Kerr is a dear friend of mine who passed away a couple of years ago. He played almost 15 years in the NBA and he could not handle Schlundt.

"That should give you an idea of the type of player Schlundt was."

15
Lists

In putting this book together I gathered lists from 10 people that I thought had a good feel for Indiana basketball history.

I asked them to rank the top 50 Indiana players of all time. All of them had a top 25 but some just listed players they thought should be in the 26-50 range.

After the fact, I interviewed many of them to tell me how they decided upon their top five.

Here's a sampling of those interviews, and the top 10 lists provided by the 10 experts.

DON FISCHER: The voice of Indiana University football and basketball

1. Don Schlundt

2. Calbert Cheaney

3. Kent Benson

4. Steve Alford

5. Mike Woodson

6. Alan Henderson

7. Randy Wittman

8. Brian Evans

9. Jimmy Rayl

10. George McGinnis

Five of the people who gave me lists had Don Schlundt No. 1. Four of the other five had him in the top three. Don Fischer was one of those who had the three-time IU All-American in the top slot.

"I thought Don Schlundt affected the program with his physical size and the numbers that he put up as much as anyone in that era of college basketball," Fischer said. "And the statistic that really jumps out at me and ever since I heard it I can't get it out of my head is the number of free throws he attempted and made. No one else even comes close to those numbers. That means that two or three guys were hanging on him all the time because he was such a physical presence on the basketball floor.

"In my mind, he changed the game for Indiana and I just thought his numbers and the way he affected the game and his school were the reason he's my No. 1 player."

•••

JEREMY GRAY: IU Associate Athletic Director for Strategic Communications and Fan Experience

1. Don Schlundt
2. Calbert Cheaney
3. George McGinnis
4. Steve Alford
5. Mike Woodson
6. Kent Benson
7. Randy Wittman
8. Bobby Leonard
9. Jay Edwards
10. Alan Henderson

Jeremy Gray is another one who had Schlundt in the top spot. The problem with putting Schlundt No. 1 is that most of the people compiling these lists weren't old enough to have seen him play. And yet people are going on blind faith because of the accomplishments he garnered in his time at Indiana.

"There were a couple of things that really pushed Schlundt into my No. 1 position," Gray said. "First, prior to Schlundt no one in Big Ten history had ever scored 1,000 points in their career. When he graduated he had 2,192. So he almost tripled the career scoring mark for Big Ten basketball. It's kind of like what Babe Ruth did with home runs. I think the number was 158 before Ruth, and Ruth had 714.

"He also was our best player on one of our two or three best teams, an NCAA championship team. He won multiple Big Ten titles and was a three-time All-American. And what really stands out is that probably the best big man pre-Bill Russell and Wilt Chamberlin in the NBA was Bob Pettit. Schlundt played Pettit in the '53 NCAA Tournament and dropped 29 points on him.

"He ended up going into the insurance business because it was more lucrative than the NBA but I think there's a better than even chance that he would have been considered one of the best players in the history of the NBA had he gone to play NBA basketball. For those reasons, I think Don Schlundt is the best basketball player in Indiana history."

• • • •

KIT KLINGELHOFFER: Former associate athletic director at IU and Sports Information director

1. Don Schlundt

2. Calbert Cheaney

3. George McGinnis

4. Steve Alford

5. Mike Woodson

6. Jimmy Rayl

7. Kent Benson

8. Damon Bailey

9. Alan Henderson

10. Bill Garrett

Klingelhoffer said in his mind there was little doubt as to who would be the No. 1 player from the state of Indiana to play at IU. In fact, he said it's more than that.

"For me it's more than Schlundt being the best player from the state of Indiana, I think he's the best basketball player in

Indiana history, period," Klingelhoffer said. "For me it comes down to one simple thing. The fact that he shot nearly 400 more free throws in his career than any other player in Indiana history tells me that he was absolutely unstoppable. And when you take into account that he did that while playing 30 or 40 games less than most of those other players, I just think that's remarkable.

"When you look at box scores when he played against really good big men, it didn't matter who they were, no one ever stopped him from scoring. The only way to stop Don Schlundt was to foul him and they found out pretty quickly that wouldn't work either because of what a great free throw shooter he was."

•• ••

MIKE PEGRAM: Publisher, Peegs.com

1. Calbert Cheaney

2. George McGinnis

3. Don Schlundt

4. Jimmy Rayl

5. Mike Woodson

6. Steve Alford

7. Kent Benson

8. Steve Downing

9. Randy Wittman

10. Bobby Leonard

Pegram was one of two people who had Calbert Cheaney as their No. 1 player. Seven of the 10, though, had Cheaney listed in the top two. I asked Mike what stood out about Cheaney to have him as the No. 1 player on his list.

"He was good from the start and he fit the motion offense of Bob Knight better than any player that I watched since I followed Indiana basketball," Pegram said. "His personality was perfect for Indiana basketball and he proved his worth by being the all-time leading scorer at Indiana.

"The one thing that might be held against him by others is that he didn't have a national championship but if Alan Henderson doesn't get hurt maybe he does. I think he was the victim of a little bad luck there."

• • • •

JAKE QUERY: Radio Talk Show Host, WNDE 1260-AM, Indianapolis

1. Steve Alford

2. Don Schlundt

3. Calbert Cheaney

4. Kent Benson

5. Randy Wittman

6. Alan Henderson

7. Mike Woodson

8. Everett Dean

9. Bobby Wilkerson

10. Bobby Leonard

I asked Jake what it was about Alford that stood out to where he believed Alford should be No. 1 all time.

"If this is a list in terms of their contributions at IU after having been players in the state of Indiana, I think Steve Alford more embodied being from the state of Indiana than any other player on the list," Query said. "He represented the state in the Olympics while playing for Bob Knight. He was a Mr. Basketball that came in with this incredible expectation."

Query said he believed Alford should be No. 1 because he was the one player on the list that Indiana kids growing up felt gave them a chance.

"Not every kid was 6-foot-6, not every kid had an unbelievable first step or a 70-inch wingspan," Query said. "But every kid if they work on it long enough can learn how to shoot 90 percent from the free throw line or hit an open shot by getting themselves open and understanding an offense. Now I'm very biased but it's hard for me to discount the fact that I was Steve

Alford in the driveway. I couldn't be Calbert Cheaney and I couldn't be Kent Benson. Kent Benson was 6-foot-10 and I was never going to be 6-foot-10.

"I could be 6-foot-3, though, and shoot from the outside and work on my shot."

●●●●

CHRONIC HOOSIER: IU Super Fan, lives in Bloomington, Indiana.

1. Calbert Cheaney

2. Steve Alford

3. Don Schlundt

4. George McGinnis

5. Kent Benson

6. Mike Woodson

7. Jimmy Rayl

8. Randy Wittman

9. Alan Henderson

10. Bobby Leonard

Chronic Hoosier, who prefers to go by his message board name than reveal his actual identity, was one of two experts to put Cheaney No. 1. I asked him what it was about Cheaney that elevated him to that lofty status.

"It was such a tough list to compile, especially when you're just narrowing it to the list from the players from Indiana but I tried to strike a balance between individual accomplishments, team contributions and their impact on the game in the state of Indiana," Chronic said. "I kind of looked at his overall legacy to the game of basketball in the state of Indiana. I know Calbert didn't have the individual accolades that a lot of those players had racked up in their careers such as Mr. Basketball but there is one accomplishment that stands out for me. To be the leading scorer in conference history at the time that he played, which was possibly the pinnacle of competitiveness in the Big Ten, is difficult to top.

"And I have to admit my bias, too. It was right in the wheel-house of my youth, living in Indiana and growing up an arm's reach from the program. He was a key player."

Chronic Hoosier said it was difficult putting Cheaney ahead of Alford, too. That was the other one that he strongly considered as No. 1.

"In my mind, Steve was the guy," Chronic said. "When I went to get a haircut , I said 'I want the Steve Alford' which didn't work so hot for a guy with a side cowlick. But we tried awful hard.

"But at the end of the day it was really difficult for me to put someone on top of Calbert on that list."

••••

SCOTT DOLSON: IU Deputy Athletic Director and former IU basketball manager

1. Don Schlundt

2. Steve Alford

3. Calbert Cheaney

4. Mike Woodson

5. George McGinnis

6. Kent Benson

7. Jay Edwards

8. Cody Zeller

9. Ray Tolbert

10. Eric Gordon

Dolson has not only worked in the IU athletic department for more than 20 years but when he was in college he was a manager for Bob Knight from 1984-88. Still, he said it was difficult to have anyone but Don Schlundt be No. 1 on his list.

"For as long as I can remember I've heard what a great player Don Schlundt was and when I made this list it seemed that he was the natural player to be No. 1 of all time," Dolson said. "I was a manager at IU when Steve Alford played, including the 1987 national championship team, and having watched him up close and seeing how hard he worked every day, it was easy for me to put him at number two."

•••

DANNY BRIDGES: Avid Indiana University Fan from Indianapolis, Indiana.

1. George McGinnis

2. Don Schlundt

3. Tom Van Arsdale

4. Dick Van Arsdale

5. Bill Garrett

6. Calbert Cheaney

7. Mike Woodson

8. Alan Henderson

9. Kent Benson

10. Steve Downing

When I did my top 50 players of all-time regardless of state affiliation in 2012, Danny Bridges was convinced that George McGinnis deserved to be No. 1. It became an ongoing debate for us.

When I decided to write this book I definitely wanted to get a list from Danny, even though I knew who his No. 1 player of all time was going to be.

One of the things I was looking forward to was interviewing him for this chapter so he could make his case for George McGinnis one more time. Here was what he said when I asked him why he thought McGinnis deserved the top spot in IU history.

"I don't know who your other panelists are and how old they are and I'm not asking but I just remember as a 10-year-old kid my dad taking me to Hinkle to see him play in the Semistate," Bridges said. "And I remember my dad talking about how he had never seen a guy that big, that athletic, that quick who could do everything with all that size.

"I just think what he did in one year down there was remarkable. He just obliterated the whole Big Ten. It wasn't a great team that he was on but he carried that team on his shoulders. As I got older and watched him, I've just never seen a guy who was that quick, strong, athletic and gifted all in one package."

Bridges said he simply never was able to get beyond that in his own mind.

"I know there have been a lot of great players at Indiana but I just have never seen a guy who could do the things that George McGinnis did," Bridges said. "So for me, it was a relatively easy decision that McGinnis should be the No. 1 Indiana player of all time."

● ● ● ●

BILL MURPHY: IU historian and author of book, *Branch* about the life of Branch McCracken.

1. Don Schlundt

2. Calbert Cheaney

3. George McGinnis

4. Steve Alford

5. Kent Benson

6. Mike Woodson

7. Bobby Leonard

8. Jimmy Rayl

9. Steve Downing

10. Damon Bailey

Murphy's list pretty much mirrored the top five that I ended up with except he flip-flopped George McGinnis and Steve Alford. He had McGinnis third and Alford fourth.

I asked him about what made him put McGinnis ahead of Alford.

"I could have gone either way to tell you the truth," Murphy said. "As far as contributions to IU throughout an entire career I would have to put Alford ahead of McGinnis. But when you look at the single body of work by George and the reason I put him third was that no IU player in the history of Indiana basketball ever has had a statistical season like George did.

"George McGinnis was a man among boys. He averaged more points in a single season than anyone else in history. He led both IU and the Big Ten in both points and rebounds which is a pretty special thing. I've said this before about him but the only person who was ever going to stop George McGinnis was George McGinnis."

•••

BRIAN EVANS: Former IU All-American in 1995

1. Steve Alford

2. Calbert Cheaney

3. Kent Benson

4. Alan Henderson

5. Mike Woodson

6. George McGinnis

7. Don Schlundt

8. Randy Wittman

9. Jared Jeffries

10. Jay Edwards

Evans had a list that was weighted heavily toward players of the more modern era. He had Don Schlundt in the No. 7 spot for example. So I asked him his thought process there.

"The difficult thing for me was the older guys because I never saw them play," Evans said. "I just guess I'm too young and don't appreciate the old guys enough. As for Schlundt, I never saw the guy play and I don't respect the 5-foot-10 players he played against. Plus, my idols growing up were guys like Alford, Cal (Cheaney), Wittman and players like that."

16
Roll Call

There are 587 Indiana University basketball players in history who hailed from the state of Indiana. They are all Hoosiers Through and Through. And each of them deserves to be mentioned in the pages of this book. The following is an alphabetical list of every IU player from the state of Indiana, the years they played at IU and their Indiana hometown.

Now, I'm certain we have forgotten some people. The odds are certainly against us having them all. The sources for this information were the Indiana Basketball Encyclopedia as well as the Indiana University basketball media guide. If you know of someone I missed drop me an email at *Terry_Hutchens@yahoo.com* and we will add any names if we do other editions of the book.

Hopefully a few of the names on the following list will jog your memory and take you back to a different time and place and the memories that live on through this list of former IU players.

A

Lymon Abbot	1936-1938	Martinsville
Jasper Abel	1909-1910	Tampico
Tom Abernethy	1972-1976	South Bend
Adam Ahlfeld	2004-2008	Indianapolis
Steve Ahlfeld	1972-1975	Wabash
Lee Aldridge	1956-1959	Switz City
Relle Aldridge	1920-1923	Lyons
Steve Alford	1983-1987	New Castle
Frank Allen	1914-1915	Logansport
Lawrence Alleyne	1941-1942	Bloomington

Bill Altman	1959-1962	Mooresville
Ken Alward	1922-1925	South Bend
Ernie Andres	1936-1939	Jeffersonville
Harold Anderson	1926-1927	Lapel
William Anderson	1935-1936	Marion
Bob Armstrong	1946-1949	Fort Wayne
Curly Armstrong	1938-1941	Fort Wayne
Freeland Armstrong	1944-1946	Paoli
Lucian Ashby	1928-1931	Evansville
Rick Atkinson	1967-1970	Evansville
Harry Ayers	1901-1903	Hartford City

B

Wilfred Bahr	1921-1923	Evansville
Damon Bailey	1990-1994	Heltonville
William Baise	1934-1935	Seymour
Dee Baker	1945-1946	Indianapolis
Tommy Baker	1977-1979	Jeffersonville
Bill Balch	1956-1959	Crawfordsville
Ray Ball	1955-1958	Elkhart
Jim Barley	1953-1956	Marion
Kory Barnett	2008-2012	Rochester
Dean Barnhart	1908-1911	Rochester
Hugh Barnhart	1912-1913	Rochester
Jerry Bass	1959-1962	Morristown
Kevin Bass	1968-1969	Morristown
Armon Bassett	2006-2008	Terre Haute
Dick Baumgartner	1952-1955	LaPorte
Art Beckner	1924-1928	Muncie
Mike Bedree	1966-1967	Fort Wayne
Zygmund Belsowski	1944-1945	LaPorte
Kent Benson	1973-1977	New Castle
Charles Benzel	1924-1928	Bedford
Arthur Berndt	1908-1911	Indianapolis

Daniel Bernoski	1923-1924	Michigan City
James Birr	1935-1938	Indianapolis
Bill Blagrave	1929-1932	Washington
Joe Blumenthal	1947-1948	Rochester
Louis Boink	1934-1935	Evansville
Tom Bolyard	1960-1963	Fort Wayne
Karl Bordner	1923-1925	Brookston
Walt Bossert	1906-1907	Brookville
Steve Bouchie	1979-1983	Washington
David Bowman	1937-1938	Veedersburg
Philip Bowser	1943-1944	Goshen
Phillip Bowser	1915-1918	Syracuse
Cecil Boyle	1906-1908	Shoals
George Braman	1934-1935	South Bend
Ray Brandenburg	1943-1945	Corydon
Jacob Bretz	1929-1931	Huntingburg
Carlos Brooks	1935-1936	Mays
Delray Brooks	1984-1986	Michigan City
Jack Brown	1947-1951	Bloomington
Hallie Bryant	1954-1957	Indianapolis
Phil Buck	1948-1951	Rossville
Joy Buckner	1919-1922	Bluffton
Lawrence Busby	1919-1922	Lapel
Severin Buschmann	1914-1917	Indianapolis
Glenn Butte	1958-1960	Milan
Phil Byers	1952-1955	Evansville
Arlo Byrum	1917-1920	Anderson

C

Cam Cameron	1981-1983	Terre Haute
Charles Campbell	1935-1936	Shelbyville
Jack Campbell	1963-1964	East Gary
Jay Campbell	1929-1932	Shelbyville
Keith Campbell	1932-1934	Logansport

Guy Cantwell	1900-1903	Spencer
Charles Carr	1903-1905	Anderson
Gilbert Carter	1932-1934	Indianapolis
Clarence Cartwright	1907-1908	New Harmony
Otto Case	1950-1951	Jeffersonville
Stephen Chaleff	1945-1946	Indianapolis
Goethe Chambers	1952-1953	Union City
Harry Champ	1922-1924	Rochester
Clyde Chattin	1909-1912	Shoals
Calbert Cheaney	1989-1993	Evansville
George Cherry	1944-1945	Greensburg
Stuart Chestnut	1947-1949	Terre Haute
Marvin Christie	1949-1950	Indianapolis
Zora Clevenger	1902-1903	Muncie
James Clifton	1939-1940	Bentonville
Russell Clifton	1939-1940	Bentonville
Cline Clouse	1911-1913	Hope
George Coffey	1921-1924	Bloomington
Edmund Cook	1906-1908	Indianapolis
Thomas Cookson	1903-1905	Anderson
Donald Cooper	1927-1930	North Vernon
James Copeland	1944-1946	Elwood
William Cordell	1931-1933	Bloomington
Robert Correll	1925-1929	Bloomington
William Coulter	1932-1935	Paoli
Willis Coval	1901-1902	Indianapolis
Tom Coverdale	1999-2003	Noblesville
Bob Cowan	1942-1943	
	1946-1947	Fort Wayne
Don Cox	1978-1979	Indianapolis
Frank Cox	1920-1921	Indianapolis
John Cox	1923-1924	Richmond
Lawrence Crane	1922-1923	Indianapolis
John Crouch	1943-1944	Evansville

William Crowe	1921-1923	Bedford
Harold Curdy	1966-1967	Marion

D

Dan Dakich	1981-1985	Merrillville
Rex Dale	1914-1915	Lebanon
Dean Daniels	1944-1945	South Bend
Phelps Darby	1900-1902	Evansville
Ray Dauer	1931-1933	Gary
Victor Dauer	1929-1933	Gary
Devin Davis	2013-present	Indianapolis
Merrill Davis	1909-1912	Marion
Mike Davis Jr.	2005-2006	Bloomington
Jim DeaKyne	1951-1954	Fortville
Ed DeHority	1920-1921	Elwood
Everett Dean	1918-1921	Salem
Gene Demaree	1962-1963	New Marion
Ed Denton	1940-1943	Jeffersonville
Harold Derr	1925-1927	Huntington
Don Dewer	1945-1946	Aurora
Bernard Dickey	1930-1933	Fort Wayne
George Ditrich	1935-1936	Bloomington
William Dobbins	1918-1921	Bloomington
Bob Dobson	1950-1952	Bloomington
Clarence Doninger	1956-1957	Evansville
Harry Donovan	1919-1921	South Bend
Steve Downing	1970-1973	Indianapolis
Clyde Dreisbach	1901-1902	Fort Wayne
Hal Driver	1940-1942	Aurora
Bob Dro	1938-1941	Berne
Emory Druckamiller	1923-1925	Syracuse
Devan Dumes	2008-2010	Indianapolis

E

Don Earnhart	1943-1944	Marion

Millard Easton	1924-1926	Sanborn
William Easton	1917-1919	Bloomington
Carl Eber	1929-1930	Plymouth
Elder Eberhardt	1921-1923	Evansville
Louis Edmonds	1945-1946	Frankfort
Jay Edwards	1987-1989	Marion
Scott Edwards	1911-1913	Greenfield
Edmund Elfers	1901-1902	Rising Sun
Derek Elston	2009-2013	Tipton
Ralph Esarey	1919-1920	Bloomington
Dave Etchison	1944-1945	Alexandria
Austin Etherington	2011-2014	Cicero
Bob Etnire	1934-1937	Logansport
Brian Evans	1992-1996	Terre Haute

F

Joe Fagan	2013-2014	Indianapolis
Dick Farley	1951-1954	Winslow
Ed Farmer	1925-1927	Bloomington
Gene Farris	1945-1948	Campbellsburg
James Fausch	1937-1938	Michigan City
Fred Fechtman	1933-1937	Indianapolis
William Ferguson	1913-1914	Gaston
Kevin "Yogi" Ferrell	2012-present	Indianapolis
James Fields	1952-1953	Andrews
Marion Fine	1944-1945	Indianapolis
Brett Finkelmeier	2008-2010	Carmel
Warren Fisher	1953-1956	Fort Wayne
Floyd Fleming	1911-1913	New Albany
Gene Flowers	1956-1959	Muncie
John Flowers	1981-1983	Fort Wayne
Rick Ford	1969-1972	Cloverdale
Cliff Forsyth	1940-1941	Terre Haute
Tracy Foster	1982-1984	Fort Wayne

Chet Francis	1938-1941	Avon
Chuck Franz	1979-1984	Clarksville
Haynes Freeland	1910-1913	Indianapolis
Bill Frey	1939-1942	Kokomo
James Frenzel	1913-1916	Indianapolis
Neil Funk	1941-1943	LaPorte

G

Leroy Gamble	1958-1959	Gary
Steven Gambles	2008-2010	Indianapolis
Joe Gansinger	1932-1934	East Chicago
Bill Garrett	1948-1951	Shelbyville
Sam Gee	1955-1958	Washington
Dale Gentil	1937-1939	Mount Vernon
Carl Gerber	1932-1933	Decatur
Joe Gerich	1947-1948	Francesville
Tom Geyer	1997-2000	Indianapolis
Ward Gilbert	1913-1914	Russiaville
James Gill	1926-1930	Washington
Larry Gipson	1968-1971	Michigan City
Eric Gordon	2007-2008	Indianapolis
Evan Gordon	2013-2014	Indianapolis
Greg Graham	1989-1993	Indianapolis
Pat Graham	1989-1994	Floyds Knobs
Peter Grant	1937-1938	Indianapolis
Phil Graves	1909-1912	Orleans
Steve Green	1972-1975	Sellersburg
Jim Gridley	1938-1941	Vevay
Gary Grieger	1963-1966	Evansville
Russell Grieger	1934-1935	Wanatah
Raymond Guard	1936-1937	Chalmers
Louis Guedel	1906-1907	Evansville
Ken Gunning	1934-1937	Shelbyville

Robert Gwin	1941-1942	Shoals

H

Ross Hales	1993-1994	Elkhart
Charley Hall	1959-1962	Terre Haute
Ralph Hamilton	1941-1943	
	1946-1947	Fort Wayne
Al Harden	1962-1965	Covington
James Hardy	2004-2005	Fort Wayne
Chester Harmeson	1902-1906	Anderson
Elton Harrison	1923-1925	Lebanon
Thomas Harrison	1901-1902	Evansville
Steve Hart	1993-1995	Terre Haute
Collin Hartman	2013-present	Indianapolis
Stephen Harvey	1922-1923	Zionsville
Max Hasler	1939-1941	Elnora
Russell Hauss	1919-1922	Sellersburg
Jack Heavenridge	1932-1933	Washington
Ordine Heine	1940-1941	New Haven
Steve Heiniger	1971-1973	Fort Wayne
Alan Henderson	1991-1995	Indianapolis
Dick Hendricks	1952-1953	Auburn
Don Henry	1952-1953	Evansville
Floyd Henry	1932-1935	Kendalville
Al Herman	1946-1947	Bloomington
Norbert Hermann	1944-1948	Brownstown
Jack Herron	1943-1946	Logansport
Byard Hey	1947-1949	Fort Wayne
Cassius Hiatt	1904-1906	Kirklin
John Hickey	1969-1970	Indianapolis
Stan Hill	1957-1959	Seymour
Tony Hill	1949-1952	Seymour
Morris Himmelstein	1932-1933	Fort Wayne
Bob Hines	1941-1943	Fort Wayne

Jim Hinds	1956-1958	Muncie
William Hipskind	1908-1911	Wabash
John Hobson	1935-1936	Indianapolis
Charlie Hodson	1954-1957	Muncie
Glendon Hodson	1930-1933	Amo
Taylor Hoffar	1930-1933	Seymour
Everett Hoffman	1939-1942	Evansville
Dave Holland	1961-1962	Toledo
Charlie Hollers	1932-1933	Switz City
Jeremy Hollowell	2012-2014	Indianapolis
Maurice Hooper	1942-1943	Anderson
Ron Horn	1958-1959	Gas City
Willis Hosler	1934-1937	Huntington
Jim Houlihan	1966-1967	Bluffton
Samuel Houston	1921-1922	Salem
Jeff Howard	2010-2014	Westfield
Jessie Hubble	1903-1904	Francesville
Don Huckleberry	1939-1940	Salem
Marv Huffman	1937-1940	New Castle
Vern Huffman	1934-1937	New Castle
Jordan Hulls	2009-2013	Bloomington
John Hunter	1972-1973	Danville

I

James Ingles	1917-1918	Indianapolis
Erv Inniger	1964-1967	Berne
John Isenbarger	1967-1968	Muncie
Phil Isenbarger	1977-1981	Muncie

J

Paul Jasper	1928-1931	Fort Wayne
Jared Jeffries	2000-2002	Bloomington
Urban Jeffries	1917-1920	Rockville
Lou Jensen	1946-1948	New Albany
Gene Johnson	1944-1945	Hartford City

Glen Johnson	1920-1921	Huntington
Jack Johnson	1964-1967	Greenfield
Ken Johnson	1967-1970	Anderson
Leroy Johnson	1958-1960	Mishawaka
William Johnson	1936-1939	Jeffersonville
Edward Jones	1925-1926	Oolitic
Lyndon Jones	1987-1991	Marion
Butch Joyner	1965-1968	New Castle

K

John Kamstra	1972-1975	Frankfort
Ted Kaufman	1948-1949	Brownsville
Willard Kehrt	1932-1935	Shelbyville
Edgar Kempf	1905-1906	Jasper
Bobby Kent	1967-1968	Unionville
James Kessler	1907-1908	Portland
Roy Kilby	1941-1943	
	1945-1946	Muncie
Dick Kirkpatrick	1954-1955	Terre Haute
Russell Kirkpatrick	1913-1916	Rushville
Ted Kitchel	1978-1983	Galveston
Kenneth Kizer	1903-1904	Poneto
Sean Kline	2002-2006	Huntington
Pat Knight	1990-1995	Bloomington
Earl Knoy	1922-1924	Martinsville
Al Kravolansky	1944-1947	East Chicago
Julius Krueger	1924-1927	Bloomington
Ray Krupa	1946-1947	East Chicago
John Kyle	1919-1920	Gary

L

Mike LaFave	1980-1981	Indianapolis
John Laskowski	1972-1975	South Bend
Chris Lawson	1989-1991	Bloomington
Irvin Leary	1943-1944	Greenfield

Todd Leary	1989-1994	Indianapolis
Herbie Lee	1958-1960	South Bend
Charles Leedke	1944-1945	Connersville
Art Lehman	1943-1944	Cedar Lake
Kevin Lemme	1995-1996	Granger
Bobby Leonard	1951-1954	Terre Haute
John Leonard	1926-1928	Rochester
Jim Lettellier	1938-1939	Bloomington
Broderick Lewis	2008-2009	West Lafayette
Michael Lewis	1996-2000	Jasper
Warren Lewis	1941-1943	New Castle
Phil Liehr	1935-1936	Indianapolis
Byron Lingeman	1913-1914	Brownsburg
Harlan Logan	1923-1925	Bloomington
John Logan	1940-1943	Richmond
Joseph Lohrei	1918-1919	Goshen
Bob Lollar	1946-1948	Indianapolis
Gary Long	1958-1961	Shelbyville
Max Lorber	1923-1925	Columbia City
Bob Lukemeyer	1948-1949	Jasper

M

Bill Maetschke	1954-1955	New Albany
Emil Mangel	1909-1910	Huntingburg
Leroy Mangin	1942-1943	Washington
Edgar Mansfield	1938-1939	LaPorte
Sherrill Marginet	1953-1954	Fort Branch
Jonny Marlin	2012-2014	Greenwood
Robert Martin	1905-1908	Dana
Robert Marxson	1920-1921	Bloomington
Maurice Massy	1929-1931	Indianapolis
Bob Masters	1949-1952	Lafayette
Allen Maxwell	1913-1916	Indianapolis
Leslie Maxwell	1905-1906	Indianapolis

Wyatt May	1921-1922	Bloomington
Scott May Jr.	2001-2002	Bloomington
Kermit Maynard	1920-1921	Columbus
Ralph McClintock	1925-1926	Bloomington
Harlan McCoy	1905-1908	Chrisney
Branch McCracken	1927-1930	Monrovia
Jay McCreary	1937-1938	
	1939-1941	Frankfort
Everett McCullough	1911-1913	Brazil
Jack McDermond	1950-1951	Attica
Richard McGaughey	1938-1939	Crawfordsville
Billy McGinnis	1942-1943	Eminence
George McGinnis	1970-1971	Indianapolis
Jon McGlocklin	1962-1965	Franklin
Robert McKinnis	1947-1948	Evansville
Gordon McLaughlin	1938-1939	Terre Haute
Ron McMains	1964-1965	Frankfort
Robert Mehl	1945-1947	Indianapolis
Jerry Memering	1970-1973	Vincennes
Charles Mendel	1936-1937	Bourbon
Murray Mendenhall	1946-1948	Fort Wayne
James Menefee	1936-1937	Fort Wayne
Robert Menke	1938-1941	Huntingburg
William Menke	1938-1941	Huntingburg
Jack Mercer	1943-1945	Brazil
Charley Meyer	1946-1950	Jeffersonville
George Milan	1944-1945	East Chicago
Bernard Miller	1928-1931	Waldron
Henry Miller	1915-1917	Bloomington
Leonard Miller	1929-1930	Waldron
Mike Miller	1972-1973	Bloomington
Milton Mink	1944-1945	Rochester
Daniel Moore	2008-2012	Carmel

Ken Morgan	1968-1971	Indianapolis
Winston Morgan	1981-1986	Anderson
Tom Motter	1938-1941	Fort Wayne
DeWitt Mullett	1914-1917	Columbia City
Glen Munkelt	1910-1913	Salem

N

Stout NA	1912-1913	Thorntown
Cleon Nafe	1914-1915	
	1916-1917	Rochester
W. Penn Nash	1916-1917	Brazil
William Nash	1914-1916	Brazil
Dick Neal	1954-1957	Reelsville
Gordon Neff	1948-1949	Terre Haute
Ed Newby	1939-1940	Indianapolis
Wade Nichols	1912-1913	Danville
Robert Nicholson	1924-1925	Bloomington
Ben Niles	1968-1970	Warsaw
Mike Niles	1967-1970	Warsaw
Ralph Noel	1904-1905	Star City
Mike Noland	1967-1969	Indianapolis
Joseph Normington	1945-1946	Greenwood
Matt Nover	1989-1993	Chesterton
Michael Nyikos	1922-1924	South Bend

O

Frank O'Bannon	1949-1950	Corydon
Pete Obremskey	1955-1958	Jeffersonville
Jarrad Odle	1998-2002	Swayzee
Jeff Oliphant	1986-1990	Lyons
Jim Ooley	1937-1940	Spencer
Andre Owens	2000-2001	Indianapolis

P

Ed Page	1937-1938	Shelbyville
Paul Parker	1922-1925	Kokomo

James Partheimer	1941-1942	Huntingburg
Ray Pavy	1960-1961	New Castle
Vern Payne	1965-1968	Michigan City
Ron Pease	1962-1964	Muncie
Richard Peed	1943-1944	Richmond
Kim Pemberton	1970-1972	Osgood
Albert Penn	1903-1904	Camden
Vern Pfaff	1963-1967	Ellettsville
Ardith Phillips	1917-1920	Amo
Jim Phipps	1953-1956	Kokomo
Joe Pitake	1947-1948	Hammond
Pete Pithos	1943-1944	Fort Wayne
Joseph Platt	1935-1938	Young America
Paul Poff	1952-1955	New Albany
George Poolitson	1942-1943	Bloomington
Dave Porter	1960-1963	Noblesville
John Porter	1914-1916	Lebanon
Robert Porter	1932-1935	Logansport
Jim Powers	1945-1946	South Bend
Clinton Prather	1913-1916	Wheatland
Dan Prickett	1960-1961	Wolf Lake
Frank Pruitt	1913-1914	Coatesville

Q

Claudius Quinn	1905-1907	Cutler

R

Charles Radcliffe	1944-1946	Paoli
Wayne Radford	1974-1978	Indianapolis
Frank Radovich	1957-1960	Hammond
Franklin Rainbolt	1930-1931	Salem
A.J. Ratliff	2004-2008	Indianapolis
Roger Ratliff	1935-1938	Mooresville
Les Ray	1943-1944	Sullivan
Jimmy Rayl	1960-1963	Kokomo

Luke Recker	1997-1999	Auburn
Steve Redenbaugh	1962-1965	Paoli
George Reed	1916-1917	Bloomington
George Reed	1931-1932	Kokomo
Bob Reinhart	1958-1960	Dale
Steve Reish	1978-1979	Union City
H.N. Replogle	1924-1925	Muncie
Claude Retherford, Jr.	1943-1944	French Lick
Gilbert Rhea	1919-1920	Clayton
Greg Ricke	1937-1938	Shelbyville
Lindley Ricketts	1923-1924	Lynville
Gene Ring	1948-1951	South Bend
Elliott Risley	1917-1918	Bloomington
Steve Risley	1977-1981	Indianapolis
Don Ritter	1946-1949	Aurora
John Ritter	1970-1973	Goshen
Robert Ritter	1947-1948	Anderson
Godfred Ritterskamp	1904-1906	Freelandsville
Gale Robinson	1925-1926	Connersville
Stew Robinson	1982-1986	Anderson
Tyrie Robbins	1948-1951	Gary
Arthur Rogers	1907-1909	Washington
Bob Rogers	1916-1917	Bloomington
John Rosenberry	1923-1924	Anderson
Charley Roush	1960-1962	Columbus
Bob Rowland	1943-1944	Martinsville
Rick Rowray	1981-1982	Muncie
William Royer	1941-1942	Terre Haute
Alvah Rucker	1900-1902	Evansville
Bill Russell	1964-1967	Columbus

S

James Sanders	1904-1907	Jasonville
Harold Sanford	1921-1924	Lebanon

Michael Santa	2005-2009	Huntington
Tom Satter	1950-1951	Franklin
Herm Schaefer	1938-1941	Fort Wayne
Carl Scheid	1926-1929	Vincennes
Anthony Scheidler	1940-1941	Muncie
Ed Schienbein	1942-1945	Southport
Al Schlegelmilch	1957-1960	Monticello
Don Schlundt	1951-1955	South Bend
Dick Schnieder	1944-1945	LaPorte
Earl Schneider	1966-1969	Evansville
Jerry Schofield	1956-1957	Columbus
Jim Schooley	1950-1953	Auburn
Herm Schuler	1918-1921	Elkhart
Kipp Schutz	2008-2009	Evansville
Tom Schwartz	1945-1950	Kokomo
Burke Scott	1952-1955	Tell City
Charles Scott	1933-1936	Jeffersonville
John Scott	1949-1950	Madison
Sterling Scott	1942-1943	Hammond
Adolph Seidensticke	1923-1924	Indianapolis
Roy Shackleton	1901-1903	Chatterton
Bill Shephard	1945-1946	Hope
Dave Shepherd	1971-1972	Carmel
Paul Shields	1943-1944	Monrovia
Errek Suhr	2003-2007	Bloomington
Frank Sibley	1924-1927	Gary
Ed Sidwell	1943-1944	New Castle
Robert Sinks	1923-1924	Lafayette
Byard Smith	1918-1919	Decatur
James Smith	1942-1943	Shelbyville
Kreigh Smith	1984-1988	Tipton
Raphael Smith	2011-2013	South Bend
Trent Smock	1974-1977	Richmond

Dick Sparks	1960-1962	Bloomington
Palmer Sponsler	1923-1926	Bloomington
WIlliam Squier	1936-1937	Richmond
Williard Stahr	1917-1918	Hagerstown
Maurice Starr	1926-1928	Anderson
Chester Stayton	1910-1912	Mooresville
Frank Stemle	1953-1955	New Albany
Jim Stepler	1945-1946	Greentown
Jack Stevenson	1937-1940	Indianapolis
Jason Stewart	2002-2004	Edwardsport
Maurice Stohler	1942-1943	Anderson
William Stone	1901-1903	Spencer
Roscoe Stotter	1909-1911	Forest
Lester Stout	1933-1936	Winimac
William Stout	1934-1935	Bloomington
Ernest Strange	1900-1901	Arcana
James Strickland	1927-1930	Owensville
Harlan Sturgeon	1948-1949	Indianapolis
Ed Stuteville	1947-1948	Attica
Jerry Stuteville	1946-1950	Attica
Arnold Suddith	1931-1932	Martinsville
Jim Sutton	1961-1964	Anderson
Dick Swan	1951-1952	Gary
Wayne Swango	1921-1922	Oolitic
Irv Swanson	1940-1943	LaPorte

T

Earl Taber	1903-1905	Marion
Kyle Taber	2005-2009	Evansville
Ryan Tapak	2001-2005	Indianapolis
Louis Teats	1944-1945	Aurora
George Teter	1904-1905	Sheridan
Eugene Thomas	1920-1923	Fortville
Frank Thompson	1906-1909	Winchester

Jerry Thompson	1955-1958	South Bend
Bill Tipmore	1938-1939	Elkhart
George Tipton	1943-1944	Terre Haute
Gary Tofil	1964-1965	Indianapolis
Ray Tolbert	1977-1981	Anderson
Herod Toon	1943-1944	Indianapolis
John Torphy	1939-1940	Bedford
William Torphy	1939-1942	Bedford
George Trimble	1905-1909	Evansville
Bill Tosheff	1948-1951	Gary
Warren Tucker	1931-1933	Salem
Gene Turner	1944-1946	Kokomo
Landon Turner	1978-1981	Indianapolis
Sheldon Turner	1949-1950	Albany
Larry Turpen	1963-1967	Shawswick

U

Charles Unnewehr	1900-1902	Batesville

V

Robert Vaden	2004-2006	Indianapolis
Rich Valavicius	1975-1977	Hammond
Dick VanArsdale	1961-1965	Indianapolis
Tom VanArsdale	1961-1965	Indianapolis
Charles Vaughn	1949-1950	Lafayette
Claron Veller	1928-1931	Linton
Dale Vieau	1949-1952	Hammond
Lloyd Vogel	1947-1948	Fort Wayne
Edward Von Tress	1919-1921	Vincennes

W

Markham Wakefield	1918-1920	Worthington
Dave Walker	1945-1947	Loogootee
Earl Walker	1900-1901	Huntington
Wendel Walker	1933-1936	Vincennes
John Wallace	1945-1948	Richmond

Marvin Wallace	1901-1904	Milton
Lou Watson	1946-1950	Jeffersonville
Taylor Wayer	2010-2014	Indianapolis
Woodrow Weir	1931-1934	Scottsburgh
Guy Wellman	1940-1941	Valparaiso
WIlliam Wellman	1908-1090	Indianapolis
Dale Wells	1926-1929	LaPorte
Richard Westlake	1945-1946	New Palestine
Frank Whitaker	1913-1916	South Bend
Bootsie White	1970-1973	Hammond
Dick White	1952-1955	Terre Haute
Evan White	2008-2009	Fort Wayne
Richard White	1936-1937	Lebanon
Claude Whitney	1909-1911	Muncie
Cliff Wiethoff	1939-1941	Seymour
Bob Wilkinson	1957-1960	LaPorte
Bobby Wilkerson	1973-1976	Anderson
Sherron Wilkerson	1993-1996	Jeffersonville
Heber Williams	1918-1920	Kokomo
Randy Williams	1958-1959	Gary
Ward Williams	1942-1943	
	1946-1948	Colfax
Cliff Williamson	1953-1956	Kokomo
Frank Wilson	1970-1973	Bluffton
Jack Winston	1924-1927	Washington
Al Wise	1941-1942	Brookville
Courtney Witte	1983-1986	Vincennes
Norbert Witte	1957-1960	Decatur
Dick Wittenbraker	1943-1946	New Castle
Randy Wittman	1978-1983	Indianapolis
John Wood	1953-1955	Morristown
Mike Woodson	1976-1980	Indianapolis
Richard Woodward	1922-1923	Lapel

Clifford Woody	1907-1908	Thorntown
Clifford Woody	1903-1906	Thorntown
Jack Wright	1952-1953	New Castle
Swift Wunker	1941-1942	Lawrenceburg

Y

Harry Yoars	1922-1923	Amboy
Sam Young	1942-1944	Rushville
Ernest Youngblood	1931-1932	Veedersburg

Z

William Zellar	1916-1920	Brazil
Cody Zeller	2011-2013	Washington
Joseph Zeller	1929-1932	East Chicago
Andy Zimmer	1939-1942	Goodland

Did you enjoy this book?

For more of Terry Hutchens on Indiana University Basketball, be sure to visit ALLHOOSIERS.COM.